FLY FISHING EVOLUTION

FLY FISHING EVOLUTION

Advanced Strategies for Dry Fly, Nymph, and Streamer Fishing

GEORGE DANIEL

STACKPOLE
BOOKS
Essex, Connecticut
Blue Ridge Summit, Pennsylvania

STACKPOLE BOOKS
An imprint of The Globe Pequot Publishing Group, Inc.
64 South Main Street
Essex, CT 06426
www.globepequot.com

Distributed by NATIONAL BOOK NETWORK

All photographs by the author unless otherwise noted
Fly pattern photographs by Jay Nichols
Illustrations by Amidea Daniel

British Library Cataloguing in Publication Information available

Library of Congress Cataloging-in-Publication Data

Names: Daniel, George, author.
Title: Fly fishing evolution : advanced strategies for dry fly, nymph, and streamer fishing / George Daniel.
Description: Essex, Connecticut : Stackpole Books, [2023] | Includes index.
Identifiers: LCCN 2023010555 (print) | LCCN 2023010556 (ebook) | ISBN 9780811738767 (cloth) | ISBN 9780811774734 (epub)
Subjects: LCSH: Fly fishing.
Classification: LCC SH456 .D235 2023 (print) | LCC SH456 (ebook) | DDC 799.12/4—dc23/eng/20230515
LC record available at https://lccn.loc.gov/2023010555
LC ebook record available at https://lccn.loc.gov/2023010556

Printed in India

Contents

Acknowledgments

A fly fisher is a sum of their total experience and the people they've come in contact with (in person and online). I've had too many wonderful influences in my life to list them individually. From my countless mentors, fly-fishing professional peers, to all my students, I want to say thank you for making me a better angler and fly-fishing instructor.

Introduction

This is not a book for a complete beginner. I like to think about my audience when teaching and writing any fly-fishing advice. Beginners likely have little experience and knowledge, so they need structure with a few concrete step-by-step processes to build their fly-fishing foundation. This means more rigidity and less flexibility, which may be necessary when you're starting out. However, once you develop the basic fly casting, presentation, and fly-tying skills, I feel you need to take control of the steering wheel and decide how you're going to get to your final destination. In other words, don't follow the dogmatic fly-fishing path once you've honed the fundamental fly-fishing and fly-casting skills.

With that being said, you will find that I often break down many of the tactics discussed into very simple/rudimentary steps. I believe fundamentals form the foundation of any advanced fly-fishing approach or cast, so I attempt to discuss tactics in a very simple and straightforward tone—just as I do when teaching or coaching anglers streamside.

I've organized this book into three major parts: nymphing, dry fly, and streamer tactics. I'll discuss everything from basic equipment, favorite fly patterns, proven rigs, casting approach, and common troubleshooting scenarios, along with my best tips for each of the three categories. The information below is a culmination of personal fishing experience, learning from other excellent anglers and guides, and the countless hours I've conducted lessons and clinics. The benefit of being a full-time fly-fishing instructor and guide is understanding common issues every angler has when learning any fly-fishing skill. As a result, I've organized

Mike Komara (former US Youth Fly Fishing Team member) conducts an onstream clinic for aspiring US Youth Fly Fishing Team members. Fly fishing is a lifetime activity, and keeping a beginner's mindset will allow you to not only continue to improve your tactics over the years but more importantly continue to enjoy this wonderful activity.

much of this book around the most common questions and trouble areas I've witnessed over the last 20 years of instruction.

The only rule in fly fishing is there are no rules, only suggestions. What I love about fly fishing is the endless ways to fly-cast, present a fly, or design a pattern for your next outing. As long as you keep this mindset, fly fishing will never get old or feel stagnant. I feel the best fly-fishing books (i.e., books for intermediate to advanced anglers) most often provide suggestions rather than absolutes. I believe the best fly-fishing information teaches you how to think rather than telling you what to do.

The purpose of this book is to share the best tips, tactics, and concepts I've learned through my fly-fishing evolution. The best experience is evaluated experience, and over the last 20 years I've painstakingly looked at every aspect of my fly-fishing game, hoping to find any improvement. Basically, I've become a micromanager—looking at every small detail. What you will find within these pages is a shift to simplifying all equipment, rigs, and patterns but with a greater focus on tactics. Having the right tools is important, but too often anglers spend excessive time and energy thinking about patterns and rigs rather than learning presentation skills. As the saying goes, "it's all in the details," and I hope the information I share with you will help you achieve your fly-fishing goals. I want to wish you the best during your fly-fishing journey!

If nothing else, I hope this book helps you develop situational awareness and create a specific plan to approach the water. Remember, the approach or fly pattern you had success with yesterday doesn't mean it will yield the same results today. Think before you cast. Study the water. Understand the mood and average behavior of the trout within these waters before making a cast. Talk with local anglers or fly shops to better understand what tactics and patterns are currently working. Recall past successful and even non-successful experiences on similar waters to sketch out a working plan of attack. If it works, then I'll consider this book to be a success.

Wishing you nothing but the best as you continue your fly-fishing journey.

PART I

Nymphing

The Pareto principle states that 80 percent of consequences come from 20 percent of causes. I have to admit this ratio transfers over to my fly-fishing success rate, as I feel 80 percent of the fish I catch come from one specific method—namely euro nymphing. Nymphing is more efficient than any other tactic. Trout spend most of their time feeding on drifting insects below the surface, so if you want to increase the chances of catching fish, fish patterns that drift below the surface. It's as simple as that.

While any form of nymphing is a more efficient means of presenting a fly, it still offers several issues to contend with since we usually cannot see the nymph during the presentation—for example, knowing if your presentation is drifting naturally and at the correct depth. Seeing a dry fly drag on the surface is straightforward, but it takes a closer look to understand how a nymph is drifting below the surface. Another issue is knowing when a fish has taken your fly. Despite popular belief, you don't always feel a nymphing strike, as many strikes are detected through sight rather than just feel, and this is where ultra focus is needed when fishing below the surface. So, nymphing is more effective but only if you're able to read the drift, know if your fly is drifting at the correct depth, and have the ability to register the take when a strike occurs. The focus of this section is to help you better understand how to tackle these main issues, along with patterns selection and rigging for conditions for both euro and suspension tactics.

Nymphing offers you the best chance to consistently catch trout throughout the season. Tailwaters like the South Holsten in Tennessee become challenging during low flow and bright sun. When dry fly and streamer tactics failed to produce a fish, Amidea Daniel caught this and several other trout using a dry-dropper setup.

Amidea Daniel revives a central Pennsylvania brown trout, taken during a chilly May morning. Nymphing was our best option with little to no action on the surface.

CHAPTER 1

Nymphing Tools

Within the last five years, I've gone from carrying a large number of specialized tools to only a few essential tools that can cover a wide arc of scenarios. The former approach was the result of my earlier competition days where carrying specialized tools for every conceivable situation may have meant the difference in catching just one additional fish during a session, which can translate into victory versus defeat. This specialized approach required carrying excessive gear and far more time organizing, which was the cost I was willing to take in order to achieve greater results during fly-fishing competitions. However, I've found this specialization became a burden when fishing in my post-competition days. I have no interest in carrying two or three rods streamside if it means catching several more fish at the end of the day. I would rather pack light, carry less gear, and enjoy my experience more, even if it means catching fewer fish.

Don't get me wrong: I use specialized tools. But I pick tools that may be specific for a certain tactic (e.g., the tactic I plan to use the most) but still capable of producing with other approaches. For example, my main trout

Nymphing isn't a new concept but modern tools have revolutionized the way we approach drifting nymphs below the surface. Although I discuss various nymphing methods, my focus is on modern European nymphing tactics. Pictured is the author euro nymphing while drifting an eastern tailwater. PHOTO BY CHRIS DANIEL

rod for my home waters is a beefed-up 11-foot 3-weight euro rod. This rod may not be as sensitive as other euro rods, but it also allows me to fish dry flies, indicator rigs, and even light streamer work. If you find yourself carrying too much gear and fly patterns, the following information may provide some guidance, but I strongly suggest you spend time developing a tool kit that best fits your approach.

Rods

The concept of "thin for the win" has been trending with fly fishing, especially nymphing tactics. By thin, I mean lighter lines, leader, tippet, and flies—basically a lighter system. Lighter nymphing systems spook fewer fish and drift more naturally than traditional nymphing tactics. Plus thin means greater sensitivity, which helps in easily recognizing strikes. Traditional action rods (e.g., the popular 9-foot 5-weight) are still excellent rods, but those rods have stouter tips designed to cast actual fly lines (e.g., weight forward or double tapers), which is what the euro nympher tries to avoid due to the mass of the fly line sagging.

Basically, the goal is to thin out the line and leader to provide a natural drift without excessive drag caused by the fly line sag. Now we need a fly rod that is designed to cast/flex with thinner systems. While traditional action rods can be used for modern nymphing systems like euro nymphing, it will require more power and energy from the angler while casting. Remember, traditional fly rods are designed to cast traditional fly lines, and attempting to cast a long, thin euro leader on one of these rods often ends in frustration due to how forceful the cast needs to be to load the rod. On the other hand, modern nymphing rods (also known as euro-style rods) will make casting these lighter systems easier and also allow you to detect strikes. After my first nymphing book was published in 2010, the most common question I got was in relation to anglers having trouble casting longer leaders. The biggest issue anglers faced was trying to cast the long leaders I wrote about on traditional action rods. I believe the majority of the problem was not with the anglers themselves but with the type of rod they were using. The long leaders lacked the mass to properly load these traditional action rods. The result was a poor cast and immediate frustration.

Again, I want to point out that you can euro nymph with any rod, but if you choose to euro nymph with long leaders while using a traditional action rod, you will need excessive force to effectively cast the lighter system. Today's modern nymphing rods make casting light systems a pleasure and also reduce casting fatigue.

My preference is for a long rod (10–11 feet) that has a soft tip for casting light- to medium-weight rigs with a strong butt section for playing larger trout. Just about every rod manufacturer these days makes excellent

Notice the low rod tip angle as I play a fish. This applies greater force when playing fish and keeps the fish's head under the water during the fight while using the rod's "strongest muscle." PHOTO BY JUSTIN IDE

Use as long a rod as you're comfortable fishing with. Longer rods allow greater line and leader control, along with the ability to reach over more currents. The author's favorite rod for central Pennsylvania is a 10-foot 3- or 4-weight. Knowing how to control the height and shape of the loop of leader coming off the rod tip, you'll quickly realize how you can fish long rods on smaller bodies of water. PHOTO BY JUSTIN IDE

Modern nymphing rods have light tips and powerful butt sections, giving you the ability to cast light euro rigs but still have the power to play bigger fish. These rods are sensitive, fun to fish, and easy to cast, which are all reasons why my children learned to fly-fish with these longer rods. Pictured is 8-year-old Logan Daniel working a mono rig on his father's favorite trout stream.

Notice the finger on top of the grip. This is a grip I like to use when I need pinpoint accuracy at short distances, while I use the thumb on top when needing power during the cast. PHOTO BY JUSTIN IDE

euro nymphing rods. Although classified as a euro rod, these rods also are excellent for short-range suspension nymphing, general dry fly presentations, and even small streamer tactics. What I like about these rod tapers (soft tip and stouter mid/butt section) is how little casting movement with the hand is needed to make a short-range trout cast. Basically, nothing more than a short tap of the wrist is needed to make casts of up to 35 feet with light rigs. For example, some euro rods are designed to actually cast level lines or all mono rigs. As I discuss in the dry fly chapter, I've actually used these rods in combination with an all-mono rig to cast smaller to medium-sized dry flies. In fact, this style of rod has quickly become my go-to rod for most trout fishing scenarios.

Much of nymphing involves highly repetitive casting. Drifts are short and the number of casts are many in a day's outing. If you're having to work hard to load the rod during each cast, you'll soon fatigue after a full day of nymphing. Fishing a rod that loads easily and with little movement will make a full day of fishing that much more enjoyable and pain-free.

Although the tips are soft, the butt sections are powerful and can handle larger fish on larger waters, so don't be concerned that you can't play big fish on these lighter nymphing rods. These rods offer two levers: a soft tip for casting light rigs and playing fish on light tippets and a lower butt section to apply maximum power. I've used these lighter nymphing rods to hook and play big fish on many larger western waters with no issues. You can land good fish on modern euro rods. Keep a lower rod tip angle when applying force to the fish, as you'll be playing the fish with the lower/thick mid- or butt section of the rod, which is the beefier and more powerful section of the rod.

TENKARA RODS

Today's tenkara rods are a modernized version of a long-standing Japanese fly-fishing approach. Think of them as an old fixed-line cane pole that has been modernized. Tenkara rods are fixed-line (meaning no reel or guides) telescoping rods reaching lengths of 14 feet or more but can easily fit into most backpacks when broken down. I believe tenkara rods make excellent light euro rods given their length and soft tips, providing excellent strike detection along with ease of casting light nymphs and long leaders. Due to their compact size, I often carry one just as a backup if my regular euro rod breaks.

Although not originally intended for euro nymphing, the action of tenkara rods possesses similarities with that of modern nymphing rods. Tenkara can be used for light suspender/indicator tactics as well. My only suggestion is not fishing too heavy of a rig as the softer tenkara rod tips lack the power to accurate/efficiently cast heavier payloads.

Amidea Daniel euro nymphing with a tenkara rod on Idaho's Big Wood River. The action on most tenkara rods are perfect for casting and fishing euro rigs. I usually carry a tenkara rod as a backup when fishing far from my vehicle.

One downside to nymphing with tenkara is getting stuck on stream bottom. Usually, you can tug the rod tip upstream/above the hang-up to free the fly. Basically, you're positioning the rod upstream to slingshot the hung fly in the opposite direction from which it was pulled into the hang-up. However, given the very soft nature of tenkara rod tips, there's rarely enough spring in the rod to pull the fly. The result is having to wade into the water to free the fly (if it can be done safely) or just break off the fly.

Tenkara is also a great tool for beginning euro anglers who are having difficulty casting light euro rigs, as the light tips make casting long euro leaders an ease. Due to the significant flex in the rod tip, a short, wristy method works best during the casting stroke. And by wristy, I mean a soft flick of the wrist—very little power. These rods are not designed for powerful casting strokes. A speedy but mildly powered application is all that is needed to make a good nymphing cast, making these rods excellent choices for rank beginners and children who lack the power needed to cast faster-action rods. Tenkara rods do not respond well to powerful casting movement. In my experience, tenkara rods will falter if too much power is used during the casting stroke.

The ease of casting tenkara rods also makes it great for anyone with injuries to their casting hand or shoulder. For example, I've developed a bad case of tennis elbow several times in the last 5 years. The power needed to cast regular fly rods was literally painful, so I would switch to a tenkara-style rod when attempting to mend my injury.

Leaders for tenkara fishing are straightforward. Since only the rod tip (not the line hand) is used to manage slack during the presentation, my preference is for a total leader length no more than 1½X rod length. For example, I use a maximum length of an 18-foot leader for my 12-foot tenkara rod. If you're just starting out, I recommend using a leader length approximately the same length as the rod (e.g., 12-foot leader for a 12-foot tenkara rod).

Remember, a longer leader forces you to hold the rod tip too high in the air, making it difficult to fish on streams with overhanging limbs. It also puts you in a tactical disadvantage when trying to set the hook, and gives wind (if occurring) a larger surface area to blow around in, so take that into consideration when choosing the correct leader length.

Staying with the "thin to win" concept when fishing a 12-foot tenkara rod, my tenkara euro leader is 12 feet of 3X sighter material followed by 3 to 6 feet of level 4X–6X tippet. The sighter material acts as both leader and sighter. No taper is needed as these soft action rods do a beautiful job casting level leader and light nymph rigs. A tippet ring between sighter and tippet material is

Logan Daniel euro nymphing a run with tenkara while his mom watches. The ability to hold leader off the water is a must with nymphing tactics. Children start out at a disadvantage given their height and arm reach, so I feel the worst thing you can do is give them a short rod to start off with. However, give that same child a 13-foot tenkara rod with a light tip and the scales tip back to their favor.

I've simplified my leader formulas to the point of using nothing but level mono systems for the majority of my nymphing leaders. This means no tapers or various lengths. However, other anglers, such as Guy Murray, use a tapered leader to euro nymph, along with dry fly and indicator tactics. I've tried using his leader system several times with limited success but it works great for him. Use what leader system you're most comfortable with.

an option, but normally I just connect tippet to sighter with a two- or three-turn surgeon's knot. Two rubber twist ties, positioned at either end of the cork handle, store the leader when not in use. A storage device like the Orvis dropper rig or Loon's dropper rig is another option when a rod is collapsed. I like the rubber twist ties positioned approximately 1 foot apart, so one full wrap around both twist ties equals 2 feet of leader being stored. So it only takes eight full wraps to secure a 16-foot tenkara leader.

Lines, Leaders, and Tippet

My 3-weight trout system is simple: I have a 3-weight double-tapered line mounted on my reel, even when euro nymphing with mono. I simply add my mono rig to the 3-weight fly line to use when euro nymphing. If I decide to use the actual fly line for another tactic, I'll pull the entire mono rig off the reel and store it in my pack. Also, I keep the loop on my fly line for two purposes: The larger tip adds buoyancy and floatability to the fly line tip and allows multiple leader/rig changes without having to cut back on the fly line taper. If the loop eventually breaks after several seasons of fishing, then I'll add a heavy nylon butt section using a nail knot or Whitlock splice and form a tiny perfection loop for a connection point. I'll attach (loop to loop) a powerful tapered leader when suspension nymphing or when fishing longer distances. If I decide to euro nymph, I'll take off the tapered leader and add a 40-foot euro mono system using a clinic to attach mono directly to the line loop. When not in use, I'll store the leaders and mono rig on a Orvis dropper rig, empty tippet spool, or a Loon dropper rig device.

MONO SYSTEMS

I rarely use euro lines given the fact I can use all mono when nymphing. Mono weighs less and is far more sensitive than the best euro line on the market, plus it's far less expensive. As a result, my simple system allows me to have a traditional line spooled on the reel when needed, along with the ability to quickly add a long mono system when I plan to euro nymph. If all mono rigs were allowed with international fly-fishing competitions, you would hear far less (if anything) about competition/euro fly lines. The one downfall with mono is the small and sleek makeup, which may be difficult for some anglers to grab on to while implementing a strip or hand-'n-twist retrieve.

Find and use what works for you. Although thin mono rigs are currently the rage in euro tactics, I know several excellent nymph fishers who prefer the feel and performance of a thin fly line, especially during the colder months when hands function at half capacity. Although these lines are basically level, there's still enough mass within the line to cast lightweight rigs. So if you feel your mono rig lacks the power to cast a lightweight nymph rig, it may be beneficial to try a euro/competition fly line. Pictured is a small brown taken while using an Orvis Tactical Nymph Line on a cold March morning.

The mono system I use contains a long and knotless section of level mono that acts as my line and leader. The key is using a long-enough section of mono so the attached fly line (if you decide to store your mono rig on top of a fly line within the reel) never comes off the reel when euro nymphing. My typical mono system is a minimum of 33 feet when nymphing with an 11-foot fly rod. Rarely do I fish more than two rod lengths of leader outside the rod tip, so I want to make sure if I do need to euro nymph longer distances away, I have enough length to ensure that I don't pull any of the attached fly line off the reel and into the guides. Remember, any fly line (even just a few feet) hanging within the guides will sag, which not only causes slack but also lifts the nymphs off the bottom and pulls them toward the surface. The fly line should never come off the reel, except when a large hooked trout makes a long run.

Let me break down the typical setup I use with my 11-foot 3-weight, starting with the backing:

- 75 to 100 yards of 20-pound backing
- 3-weight double taper line attached to backing (keeping the loop attached to front end)
- Attach my mono rig (typically 40 feet in total length) to fly line loop using a simple five-turn clinch knot

If I decide to switch to using the fly line, I unwind the 40-foot mono system onto an Orvis dry dropper rig cartridge and clip the clinch knot connection off. Then I connect a tapered leader using a loop-to-loop connection. Another option is simply carrying two separate reels, one loaded with a 3-weight line and the other with a full mono system, but I prefer to reduce the amount of gear I carry.

A variety of monofilament types, colors, and diameters can be used for euro nymphing. The options are endless, and your biggest obstacle is allowing yourself to get overwhelmed. I would suggest experimenting with several before you come to your own conclusions. Most monofilaments are not expensive, so little is lost if you decide if one type doesn't work for your needs.

I will vary the diameters/breaking strength based on the size of the fish I target and more importantly the weight of the flies I'm using. The smaller and lighter-weight nymphs I use, the smaller the diameter used to reduce sag in the system. For example, when fishing low water and lightweight nymphs during the summer months, my mono system may consist of a 4-to-6-pound base followed by a thin sighter and 6X–7X tippet. Smaller-diameter nylons weigh less than thicker-diameter mono, which is essential when fishing smaller and lighter-weight nymphs. If you use a section of mono that is too heavy/thick when nymphing lightweight nymphs, the sag caused by the mono mass will lift your nymphs off the bottom and force you to either use a heavier fly or add split shot to keep the nymphs riding deeper.

With the growing popularity of mono rigs, it's helpful to use full-frame reels. The construction of these reels prevents thin euro lines or mono from slipping between the spool and frame. A number of manufacturers today are making these full-frame "euro reels" to prevent thin euro line or mono rigs from slipping between the frame and spool.

The two mono types I use are Maxima Chameleon and Fluorescent Chartreuse Maxima in the 6-to-15-pound range. Maxima chameleon is darker and sometimes difficult to see, but I'm not concerned with that since a bright-colored sighter is built into the leader. If you need the entire mono system (except for the tippet) to be bright-colored, then you may want to look at other options. However, Maxima Chameleon's stiffness is the reason for it being my favorite mono. Since I spend the majority of my time fishing lightweight nymphs, I feel the stiffness aids in casting these lighter rigs. Also, the stiffer Maxima Chameleon is excellent when I want to cast smaller dry flies without having to change. Contrary to popular belief, you can cast smaller dry flies with an all-mono rig, as long as you have a stiffer and heavier mono to aid with the turnover. I'm not saying you can't cast smaller dry flies with soft/limp mono, but I find it incredibly challenging given this material lacks the stiffness and power to cast wind-resistant dry flies.

I like the stiffness of Maxima Chameleon for most mono rigs, but it is difficult for some anglers to see, so experiment and find a material and color you enjoy nymphing with. Pictured is Jason Piccola using a mono rig constructed from an entire spool of 3X sighter material for added visibility.

Another reason I prefer the stiffer Maxima Chameleon is because of its lack of stretch when setting the hook. Softer mono tends to stretch more, which absorbs a great deal of the force when setting the hook. In other words, you're losing power in your hook set when any part of your leader stretches. For example, most sighter material is softer and has a good deal of stretch, but I find this to be negligible given that most sighter lengths are short, causing a minimal amount of stretch. However, if your entire mono rig is made of soft mono, you'll see a lot of stretch when applying force during the hook set of playing fish. Given that most of the euro rods I use already have a great deal of flex, I feel the last thing I need is a leader that also has a great deal of flex for most situations I encounter.

The softer mono option may be best for the waters you fish. For example, maybe you fish ultra-clear spring creeks and use 7X–8X tippet when nymphing, the softer mono rig will help you protect those lighter tippets. Also, maybe you're prone to overpower the rod tip during the hook set and often break off when setting the hook. In this case, a softer mono rig may be perfect for you. And this is when I may opt for the fluorescent-colored maxima. Although the name on the packaging is the same, the physical makeup of the two nylons differs drastically, as the fluorescent is easier to see but has significantly more stretch. As a fishing instructor, I've worked with countless anglers who are easily excitable and tend to overpower the hook set, causing countless breakoffs during the hook set. Switching to a softer mono is an excellent remedy for those heavy-handed hook sets.

Although my preference is for thinner mono, it provides greater challenges when using the line hand to manage slack and playing fish, so my suggestion is to start out heavier/thicker at first (15–20 lbs.). Begin to thin out (i.e., use thinner mono) your mono system as you become more comfortable casting and fishing with all mono. The most important thing to consider is to make sure you use one long continuous piece of mono. Avoid placing any knots within part of the mono rig that is likely to move through the guides when casting, implementing line control, and playing fish.

Let the tippet diameter you plan to fish also help determine the size and breaking strength of the mono you fish. The mono system should be larger in diameter or stronger than the tippet used. I nymph mostly 5X (approximately 5.5-pound breaking strength) down to 7X, so I can use a thin 6-pound mono system, given my tippet is weaker than my mono line. If you nymph with heavier tippet (e.g., steelhead fishing with 2X), then you'll want to use a heavier-diameter mono system.

A smaller-diameter tippet may be less visible, but I feel the smaller diameter has less surface area, which allows your nymph to drop faster into the depths and causes less drag during the drift. It's no secret that larger-diameter tippets will increase drag on any pattern so I stick with the smallest diameter I can get away with. PHOTO BY AMIDEA DANIEL

In the past I likely complicated leader formulas. Today, I keep my mono rigs and leaders simple. Here's a simple template I use for euro mono rigs. Remember, the smaller and lighter the nymph, the smaller-diameter mono needed. I'll use 4-to-6-pound for my mono base when fishing small- to medium-weighted nymphs. Substitute whatever material you like to fish with—there is no wrong or right material for these setups.

Listed below is my current mono system:

- 35–40-foot level 4–15-pound Maxima Chameleon connected to 3-weight fly line loop using a five-turn clinch knot. This is a single-strand piece of mono with no knots.
- 20–24-inch 0X–4X Scientific Anglers Sighter Material connected
- Tippet : 4X–7X Fluorocarbon Tippet. Tippet is often 1 foot longer than the average water depth being fished.

Note: I'm a sponsored Scientific Anglers ambassador as of this writing but like the color and brightness of their sighter material. It's a three-tone sighter material that isn't too bright but just bright enough for me to see. I think there's such a thing as having a sighter that is too bright, especially when fishing low and clear water conditions.

One tip that I'd like to pass on is to reduce any potential hang-ups when fishing mono rigs. Compared to fly lines, mono is thinner and more likely to catch any item hanging off your waders or pack. As a result, I've switched to a backpack or any waist/sling pack I can position behind me to create a clean and tangle-free working space near my chest or waist area. I'll even attach duct tape to the hanging flap on my waders or pack to reduce the possibility of the mono hanging up. Lastly, I won't walk a long distance through brush with a fly rod setup with an all-mono rig. As mentioned before, mono is thinner than fly line and will catch/grab any possible hang-up. If you've ever walked through brush with a rod rigged with an all-mono system, you know the struggle of the mono grabbing every tree branch and piece of brush. This is why I'll keep my four-piece rods in the rod sock or case (with no reel attached) while walking through thick brush. I'll assemble the rod once I'm

A clean working area is essential for reducing (not eliminating) snags between mono rigs and your packs. Think about where you place your hands while stripping or retrieving fly line and do everything you can to clear that area of any possible snag.

in the clear. While this is a good practice for traditional fly line rigs, it is most helpful with mono rigs. While I can navigate most walks through brush with a rod strung up with fly line, I'm always hanging up on brush with a thin mono system. Just a suggestion if you need to walk through a long section of tight brush to the stream.

TIPPET

The softer-tipped euro rods protect lighter tippet, and I like to use as thin a diameter tippet as possible. I mostly use 5X–7X fluorocarbon for nymphing medium-sized streams with small to medium-sized trout near my home waters in central Pennsylvania. If you fish larger rivers for bigger trout, then I suggest using heavier systems. The smaller-diameter tippet drifts in the water with less drag and allows the nymphs to drift more naturally. Plus, smaller-diameter tippets like 6X and 7X allow flies to sink faster so I can fish smaller-weighted nymphs without the need for additional weight.

Another recent development for me is to forgo using a tippet ring to connect the tippet to the sighter with the ultra-thin mono systems due to sag. Tippet ring sag is not an issue with heavier rigs as the mass in the flies/supplemental weight pulling downward will not allow a lightweight rig to form any sag in the system but will likely cause sag when fishing ultra-light nymphs.

EURO LINE LEADER

My preference is using an all-mono rig, but if you find yourself enjoying the qualities of a euro line more than mono, here's a simple leader formula I use. First, the leader is short—usually no more than 1½ times the length of the rod. This means using a leader 15 feet or shorter when using a 10-foot rod. This ensures the euro line tip stays outside the rod tip to prevent the line from falling back through the guides when nymphing with light rigs. Euro are thin but still contain mass. If part of the fly line tip is positioned somewhere within the guides, during the presentation the light mass of the line will still pull downward and lift light nymph rigs off the bottom. If this does happen, you'll need to fish heavier flies or add supplemental weight to the rig. In short, the greater the mass you have within your line and/or leader, the more weight you'll need within your flies or supplemental weight to keep the presentation drifting deeper.

Anglers are switching to all-mono systems as the reduction in line mass not only adds strike detection sensitivity but allows them to use little weight to achieve deeper presentations. For example, a size #16 perdigon with a. 2.5-mm tungsten bead is all the weight I need to fish many of my central Pennsylvania waters, while used in tandem with a level 6-pound mono system. If using a euro line system mentioned above, I would need to go a bead size heavier or add supplemental weight to counter the sag created by the mass of the euro line. If using a traditional double taper or weight-forward line, the weight needed would be significantly more. This is why traditional high sticking practitioners advocated the use of lots of split shot and heavy nymphs to counter the mass of traditional fly lines. The thinner the line or mono system you use, the less weight needed to achieve a deeper/natural drift.

When using any line with euro tactics, use a shorter leader to keep fly line tip outside the rod during presentation. I've simplified all my leaders, so all I do is shorten my mono rig setup to be 15 feet or less.

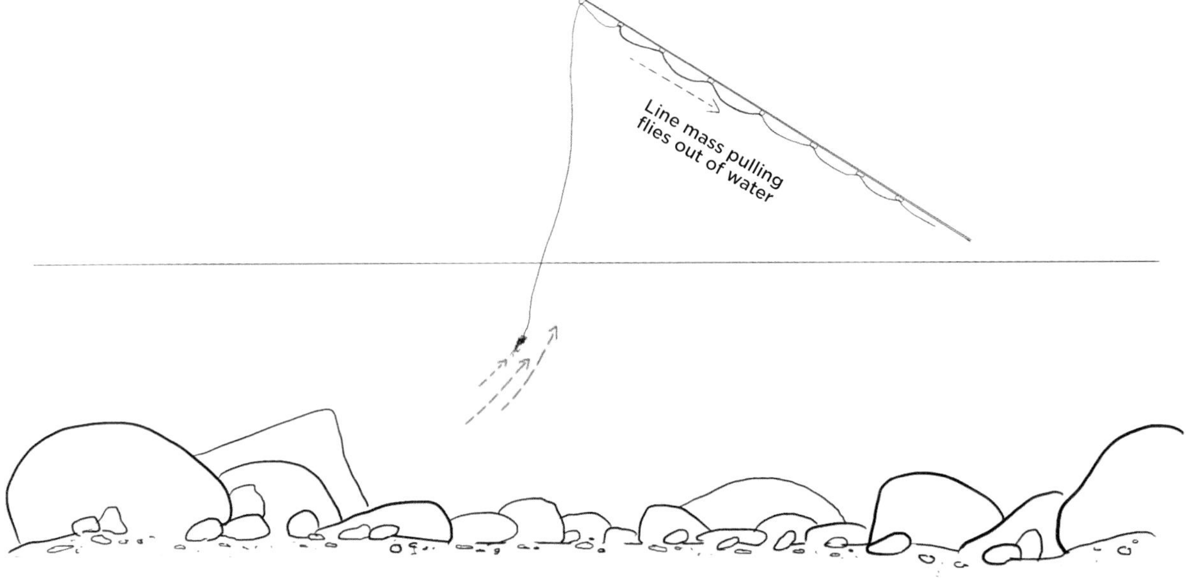

This is what happens if only a portion of the fly line is positioned within the guides while drifting a euro rig. The mass of the fly line hanging in the guides creates sag and creates a counterweight with drifting nymphs, causing them to get pulled toward the surface.

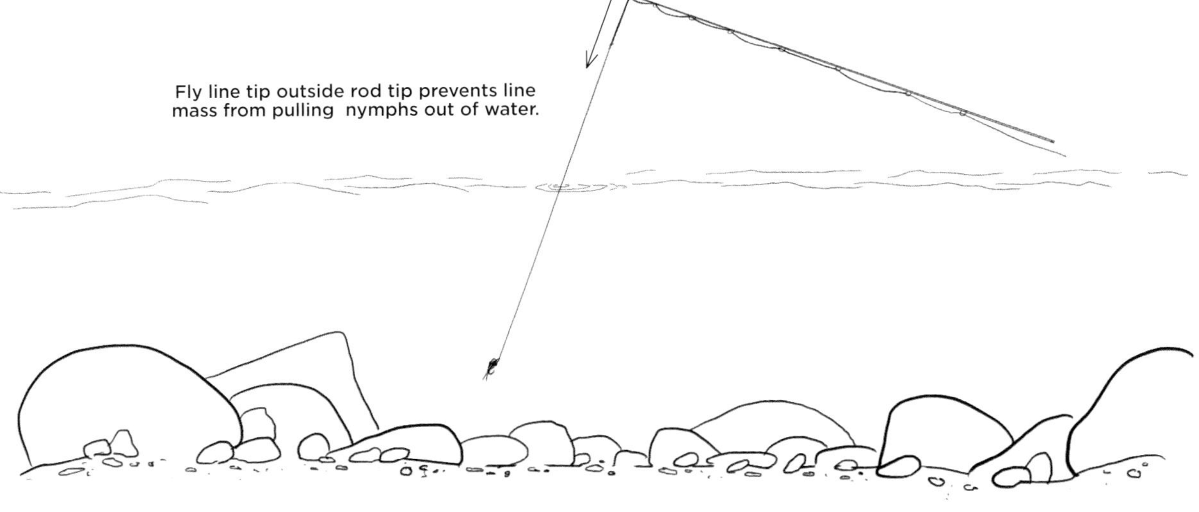

This is where traditional weight-forward fly line or euro line (if used) needs to be positioned during the drift. Having 2 to 3 feet of fly line outside the rod tip creates enough mass to prevent the line from sliding back down the guides and pulling the nymphs out of the water. If your fly line slides back down through the guides, you will need to shorten the leader and allow more fly line outside the rod tip to prevent this pullback effect.

Supplemental Weight

Casting and fishing with only weighted flies has several benefits including better strike detection and reduction in tangles. Sometimes the weight within the fly isn't enough to get into the strike zone, so I carry both split shot and tungsten putty for the few times additional weight is needed. Another time I use shot and putty is when using a drop shot/ bottom-bouncing approach, which we'll discuss later in this chapter.

For supplemental weight, I often use a combination of split shot and tungsten putty. I use the minimum amount of split shot to achieve a desired drift in shallower water and will add tungsten putty onto the split shot when moving to faster/deeper water. The shot is my constant and acts as a foundation to add tungsten putty to. Without the shot, putty has a tendency to slide and fall off the leader. The benefit of using putty is the ease of putting on and taking off the tippet, allowing weight adjustments to be made with ease. Instead of having to pry off split shot for fishing shallower waters, all you need to do is pinch the putty off the shot. ■

TOP: As much as I enjoy using nothing but the weight of the fly while nymphing (euro or suspension), sometimes you need a little weight. Instead of having to use a larger and heavier fly (likely reducing the chance of catching fish for some situations), just add a single split and/or putty to help sink your nymph to the correct depth. If I do need to add shot, I try to keep the shot 6–8 inches above the fly. The distance appears to reduce tangles while reducing any hinge effect between weight and fly.

BOTTOM: Pictured is the constant (a.k.a. split shot) and the variable (a.k.a. tungsten putty). Use only a minimal amount of shot, while adjusting the putty allows you to easily adjust weight without having to take split shot on and off the leader. That is, if you need to use supplemental weight. Find a high-quality putty that doesn't melt during warm temps or become rock-hard in colder water. JP's Nymphing Mud is some of the best soft tungsten I've ever used.

Sighter Material

Just about every manufacturer makes good sighter material. First, make sure you use material you can see, because some sighter materials are not as bright or opaque as others. My preference is for Scientific Anglers Absolute Sighter material because it's visible to my eye in most conditions but not overly bright. I feel too bright of a sighter may spook fish during challenging water conditions, which is why I use mostly SA. If you have poor to OK vision, then you may want to look at another manufacturer's sighter like Cortland, which is a usually brighter and more opaque than Scientific Anglers'.

I like a multicolored sighter because each transition of color creates additional points for my eye to focus on and detect strikes. Also, some colors show up better than others in certain lighting/background conditions. For example, chartreuse or yellow is great when looking toward bright-green vegetations. White shows up great when fishing darker/dirty water. This is why I may cover several spools of different colors or purchase one sighter material that has multicolor strands.

Previously I used the larger 0X diameters, but now I often use 3X–4X sighter diameter for most current nymphing scenarios, especially when I'm fishing small and/or lightweight patterns. Smaller-diameter sighter material is usually softer and provides better strike detection.

I will use 0X sighter material when floating the sighter, a technique where the angler greases the sighter with floatant and uses it as a suspension device. Or I may use 0X when using heavier tippets. Remember, you want the sighter to have a stronger breaking strength than the tippet, so when you break off, the tippet (not the sighter) breaks off. However, the majority of the time I use smaller 3X and 4X diameters when nymphing with 5X–7X tippet material.

Remember to let the sighter diameter be determined by the diameter mono rig and tippet diameter you use. For example, when fishing heavy euro flies on 3X or 4X tippet, I'll use an 0X sighter diameter. I'll downsize to a 4X sighter material when tippet diameter is 6X or smaller.

Just one of countless possibilities for your sighter. If you have trouble seeing the sighter, I suggest placing several tags in your sighter using a blood knot or any knot that creates perpendicular tag ends. It helps with visibility, but they do increase the chance of tangling with your nymph after a poor cast. Usually 1 to 3 inches for each tag or ear seems to be the norm. Plus the knotted sections or tags can be used as a depth gauge—a reference point on how high the sighter is drifting over the surface, which affects how deep the nymphs are drifting. Adjusting the height and angle of the sighter is common practice every day on the stream, and having a reference point helps with those tweaks.

Tags left from blood knot

Today most tippet and leader manufacturers are making excellent sighter material, so spend time finding the best sighter material that works for your eyes and the conditions you fish. For example, this Scientific Anglers material has three colors, providing good visuals in a variety of lighting conditions.

Amidea Daniel holds the sighter off the water while drifting a slow pool. She prefers the larger 0X diameters for better visibility. The sighter is your lifeline to your nymphs. If you can't see the material, you can't see strikes. Build sighters with different colors or experiment with different colors and diameters until you find one that works for you.

I prefer a sighter made of several colors, which provides greater contrast in varying light conditions. Most manufacturers are making sighter material made of multiple colors. The colors are spaced 6 to 10 inches apart, and I may snip the sighter at each transition and reconnect using a blood knot with a short tag remaining at each knot, which I refer to as ears. As previously mentioned, I like the Scientific Anglers sighter material because it has just enough brightness for me to see strikes, but it's not so bright that it may spook fish while fishing low and clear water conditions.

The ears provide better visibility and also act as a depth gauge. For example, if you're euro nymphing and your fly gets stuck on the bottom, don't immediately attempt to free your fly. Instead, hold the sighter off the water and notice to how far the first ear is off the water's surface, then attempt to free your pattern. The next time you drift your nymph through the same run, simply hold that first knot 6 inches higher off the water surface to avoid getting stuck on stream bottom. The same is true when you feel your nymphs are not drifting deep enough in the water column—allow the sighter to drop several inches deeper in the water column until you feel you're in the strike zone. Getting a deeper drift isn't always about using heavier rigs—sometimes all that is needed is holding the sighter lower to the water surface to allow a deep ride.

SIGHTER WAX

Although not as visible as an opaque nylon sighter, sighter wax is useful for quickly adding a strike aid onto

You may not need a sighter if your mono rig is constructed of a hi-vis mono, such as this mono rig made of 8-pound fluorescent chartreuse Amnesia. A section of 5X tippet was connected directly to the high vis Amnesia, which acted as both leader and sighter.

any leader. For example, you're using a tapered leader to throw dry flies but have the urge to switch over to a nymph, but don't want to change leaders. Replace the dry fly with a weighted nymph, add this sighter wax onto the leader, and you have a functional setup within a minute.

Although you can add a sighter to any leader, here's an example of a simple thinned-out euro leader and sighter wax. This mono rig is ultra-thin and the ability to quickly adjust the sighter position is nice, but visibility is not as good as when using actual sighter material. As always, experiment until you find the best system for your needs.

Use 30 feet of 4X nylon leader for the main mono section. No need to use fluorocarbon, because this nylon will likely be kept off the water. Use a tippet-to-leader knot (e.g., surgeon's) to connect the 4X nylon to your tippet (5X–7X). Tippet length is approximately the same depth as the water. Now place the sighter wax on the 4X nylon in a manner that keeps the sighter close to the water surface during the presentation. If you move to another location with a different depth, use the cloth to wipe off the wax and reapply on the leader. Keeping the sighter closer to water's surface allows focus on both drift

Instead of adding a sighter mono, you can add Skafers Neon Sighter Wax onto a clear leader to act as an "emergency" sighter.

I prefer fluorocarbon tippet when fishing anything subsurface, especially when it comes to euro nymphing. The main reason is the tippet's ability to resist abrasion when coming in contact with structure below the surface, including boulders and wood. I like to ride my nymphs tight to structure so there's an excellent chance of my tippet coming in contact during the presentation, which will likely cause some degree of abrasion within the material.

and watching for strikes. If the sighter is too far off the water, your eyes often bounce back and forth between watching the drift and looking for strikes. Therefore I feel keeping the sighter closer to water's surface is helpful, and it's one reason I carry sighter wax for quick changes. For example, if you're nymphing deep water with a fixed sighter and long tippet and then decide to move to another location containing shallow water, keep the sighter as is and use the sighter wax to create another visual aid closer to your nymphs. You can use a cloth to easily remove the sighter wax.

Suspenders/Indicators

Picking the right tools for the job is part of a successful outing, and suspenders will play an important role in your nymphing game, even if it's only a fraction of the time you are fly fishing. I believe one important consideration is picking a suspender that can attach to a thin tippet section without slipping.

Pinch-on indicators, airlocks, and New Zealand Wool–style indicators are just several examples of indicators that can be attached and hold onto thin tippet material. Yes, there's a chance you will sometimes lose your indicator when hanging up, but the benefits of a straight-line connection and enhanced strike detection are worth it.

Another consideration for choosing a suspender is the weight of your nymphing rig. The idea is to use an indicator that can suspend/hold your rig but will register a strike the moment a fish takes the nymph. The suspender may barely move if it's too buoyant for a lighter-weight rig. The suspender will continually sink if too small for the nymphing rig. Use a suspender that will suspend the rig but also register a clear strike. When I started

in the slower current while the surface currents drag the suspension device. The bobbing or rocking-chair movement is caused by the nymph pulling back on the suspension device. While this pullback occurs with all suspension devices (when the rig is correctly set), the visual really shows with the longer tufts of wool.

Another advantage of the longer tufts of wool is using them to show the direction of the nymph(s) in relation to the device. For example, if the wool is standing straight up, then the nymphs are directly below. If the tuft is angled backward, the nymphs are angled upstream, and vice versa. Usually, I'm looking for the wool to be straight up when drifting over my targeted location, with the troll's head bobbing from side to side.

What makes this suspension device so sensitive is the wedge shape of the NZ Wool's base. This wedge has little surface area (hence the reason only light rigs can be used) and immediately shoots under the water the moment the fly comes in contact with any subsurface item (stream bottom or trout). This sensitive strike detection is helpful in slower water or any situation where the strikes are slow and soft.

I cannot help but continue to mention the importance of fishing your nymphs at the correct depth. If you find yourself hanging up too frequently, slide the indicator closer to the nymph, which shortens the distance between the two to keep the nymph riding higher in the water column. Vice versa for periods when you are not occasionally meeting bottom or when you feel you need your nymphs to ride a little deeper.

The high and wide profile provides excellent visibility, while the narrow wedge on the bottom shoots under the water anytime resistance sets in, making the New Zealand Wool suspender ultra-sensitive.

nymphing with indicators, my mistake was using too big an indicator, and I missed many strikes because the trout take barely moved the suspender. If you spend a little time dialing in the suspender size to the rig you use, you'll notice more strikes. Plan to carry a small variety of suspender sizes to match varying nymphing rigs.

NEW ZEALAND WOOL INDICATORS

New Zealand Wool indicators are by far my favorite suspension device for nymphing light rigs. They ride high above the surface, offer incredible strike detection, and allow you to make quick depth adjustments.

I like to leave longer strands sticking out of the plastic tube. Although this increased height creates additional wind resistance, the increased height allows better strike detection, especially when fishing from longer distances. The tall taper looks like a troll's head bobbing in the current. I look to see the top of the troll's head bobbing back and forth (like a rocking chair) during the presentation. The tapping indicates my nymph is positioned

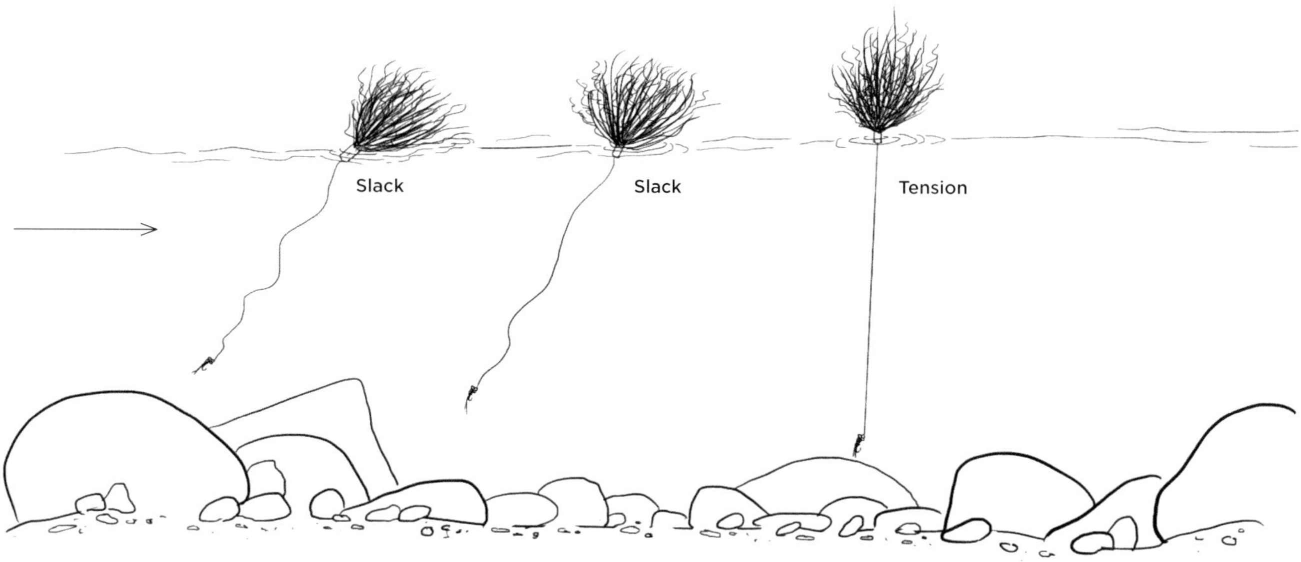

NZ Wool indicator also provides immediate feedback on whether there's slack or tension within your rig. Slack occurs when the tool is leaning on the side. Tension and control is had anytime the NZ system is standing straight up. So if you're drifting over a likely spot and not seeing the wool stand vertical, you may need to add weight or adjust the distance between wool and nymph.

The depth of the nymph(s) drift is easily changed by sliding the suspension device up and down the tippet, allowing for hassle-free adjustments. The key to quick and easy adjustment here is having just wool stuffed within the tube to create enough tension to hold the tippet loop from sliding, but not packed too tight to allow the angler to simply grab the base of the tube to slide up and down the tippet for adjustment.

The one downside to this system is tippets will twist and coil if placed under too much tension. Simply stretch the tippet (do not use leader straightener) when coiling occurs. It's a small inconvenience but worth the extra work to have a delicately landing suspender with excellent strike detection.

Another downside to this tool is the wind resistance, which requires a tapered leader to aid in turning over. In the past I would try switching from an all-mono system for euro nymphing and just add the wool system onto the level mono and attempt to cast the wind-resistant tool. While this isn't out of the realm of possibilities, I do know my tangling percentage greatly increased while attempting to cast a wind-resistant suspender on a mono rig, especially during windy days. I strongly suggest using a shorter tapered leader to help turn over the cast. A taper in the leader is helpful when you need a little extra power casting wool indicator systems. Casting errors will immediately create a tangle, so I only recommend these tools to fly fishers with adequate casting skills. A hard-sided plastic or cork bobber is a better choice for beginning anglers as the mass within the tool aids in casting.

A third issue is the maintenance required to keep floating high and sensitive. At a minimum, I try to pretreat the wool with a gel/liquid a few minutes prior to fishing. Usually, I have the rod equipped the night before and try to pretreat the wool (or dry fly if dry dropper fishing) with a dunking solution like Loon's Fly Dip to provide time for the floatant to dry and bake into the suspender. Eventually, the indicator will become waterlogged after time so I use several false casts to wick most moisture out, squeeze with a paper towel, then re-treat with liquid floatant when needed. Also, after time the wool fibers will become matted, so use a comb to separate and help fluff out the matted wool fibers. While it does require more maintenance than most suspenders, it makes up for it with excellent strike detection.

AIRLOCK SUSPENDER

I use the airlock style for fishing medium to heavy rigs and for casting in the wind. The hard-sided walls aid when casting into windy conditions. I rarely use this style indicator when fishing my home central Pennsylvania waters but do find it useful while fishing western waters. The wider surface area allows this tool to suspend heavier rigs and is my first choice when using rigs such as the drop shot/bottom-bouncing rig. Try to avoid using this style on calm waters as it tends to land heavier on the water.

This screw-on style indicator allows easy adjustment when necessary, unlike the original Thingamabobber, which has a small loop. Simply lay the tippet within a narrow plastic thread (extending out from the round suspender), then place a plastic thread washer over the thread and begin twisting down. Eventually this washer will sandwich the tippet between the bobber and plastic washer, keeping the suspender locked in one place on the tippet. If you need to adjust the depth of your

The airlock suspender style is an excellent choice for fishing heavy rigs given its buoyancy. The heavy nature of this indicator style is also helpful when casting during strong winds.

presentation, unscrew the plastic washer just enough to relax the tension, allowing you to slide the suspender up or down the leader. Then tighten back down on the plastic screw washer once the desired position is achieved.

PINCH-ON

Although only a single-use suspender, pinch-on styles are easily positioned on the tippet by pinching the two adhesive sides together and sandwiching the tippet between the pieces of foam. They cast well, are high floating, and are very sensitive. They come in at least three different sizes to handle medium to ultra-light nymphing rigs. Or you can buy the larger sizes and cut them to size yourself.

One issue with these suspenders is you are unable to adjust the position of the suspender once pinched on the leader. You will need to peel the old suspender off the leader and attach a new one (at a different location) to make your adjustment. For this reason, I use this suspender type when I don't plan to make constant adjustments with my suspender.

Placing two suspenders on the leader or tippet can help you understand where your nymph is positioned in relation to the suspender. If the top suspender (i.e., the one closest to fly) begins pulling to the side, either a fish has taken your nymph and has begun swimming away to the side or it may indicate your fly is drifting in a separate current seam. If you opt to use a dual suspender system, my suggestion is to use two different-colored suspenders to provide a better reference, so you know which color should be closest to the fly, and vice versa.

Amidea Daniel is shown holding a dual pinch on suspender rig while using a two-handed rod. Two-handed rods not only provide additional length but also make roll casting and mending suspension rigs easy. For example, if I'm traveling to fish for steelhead and plan to do nothing but fishing suspension rigs, I usually opt for a two-handed rod as these rods (when paired with the right line) make casting and mending them a joy.

Any dry fly can be used as a suspension tool, but make sure the pattern has enough buoyancy to suspend the nymph. This is why I carry a small range of dry fly sizes, so I can match the weight of the nymph I intend to use. For example, I may use a small #16 hi-vis foam ant to suspend a #20 bead head zebra midge or use a #8 chubby Chernobyl with a heavy #12 tungsten bead head.

DRY FLIES

Lastly, any high-floating dry fly can be turned into a suspension device. When using a dry fly as a suspender, try to imitate a food source the trout is likely to take during the time period you fish. Terrestrials, mayflies, caddis, stoneflies, and even midge patterns can be bulked up to suspend a nymphing rig. I only use dry flies as suspenders when I feel there's a chance of a trout taking the dry fly on the surface. Otherwise, I'll use manufactured suspenders as they usually require less maintenance and offer better strike detection.

Also make sure to carry not only a variety of sizes but also colors to allow visibility for most conditions. For example, I'll use chubby Chernobyl patterns with a white or some fluorescent-color wing for visibility in most conditions, but will also tie a few with a black wing for better visibility when glare occurs on the water. Basically, I use some version of a chubby for most of my dry dropper patterns but tie them in a few sizes and vary the color of the wing. I'll tie and fish this pattern as small as a #16 when fishing a light nymph or tie them as large as a #6 when fishing heavy nymph patterns on large western waters.

A large foam ant with a chubby Chernobyl feel is a favorite when fishing a sunken ant. It covers two levels simultaneously and is visible with its high poly wing post. Use a colored wing that suits your eyes and the fishing conditions best.

CHAPTER 2

Nymph Patterns

Pattern selection is the most discussed subject but not the most important consideration. Yes, having the right pattern is a must, but I feel too much emphasis is placed on fly selection and not enough on presentation. In other words, don't blame the pattern when your results are less than ideal. There's only a handful of times in my angling career where I felt poor fly selection was the reason for my failed efforts. Poor execution and technique on my part, not the fly, was the true reason for not catching fish.

In my former life, I coached/captained both US Youth and Adult Fly Fishing teams. I learned much by observing great anglers during five World Fly Fishing Championships. I witnessed so many great anglers fishing in close proximity, so I would walk along the bank and observe everything from tactics, riggings, and pattern selection. During my limited tenure, I never observed all competitive anglers fishing with identical patterns. Instead, pattern selection varied greatly, yet almost all these anglers were catching lots of trout with drastically different patterns.

Anytime I see an angler doing well on a stream, I'll observe them for a while and usually approach them to see how they're catching fish. I may do this with a

I try to organize all the patterns I intend to fish in a working box. For me, I love Cliffs Day's Worth boxes as they're durable, and I enjoy the open space to drop a handful of patterns into. PHOTO BY JUSTIN IDE

My working box is always evolving. The time of year or location I'm fishing are two variables I consider when choosing flies to fish. I took this picture on a cold January morning while preparing for a short trip to a local spring creek. Eggs, midges, and a few other simple nymphs are all I use during a time like this. However, this box will become more complicated as springtime hatches occur. Most important, I take patterns out of the box if I have no plans to fish them within the immediate future. This daily fly box housecleaning keeps this small box organized.

handful of anglers within a short time period. While it's fun looking through the fly boxes of great anglers, I'm more interested in seeing how the pattern is fished rather than the pattern design itself. I don't downplay the importance of choosing the right pattern as I have spent years thinking about carrying the best possible nymph selection. However, I spend more time working on tactics and presentation, which I feel is time better spent. As the saying goes, the more you know, the less you need. Today, I'm slowly becoming more confident in my tactics and that is the reason I carry far fewer patterns with me on the water.

Within the last few years, I've thinned out and simplified many of my favorite nymph patterns. I do this for two reasons: First, thinner profile patterns sink faster. In the past I was taught all nymph patterns need to look shaggy and buggy. This thought process of building lots of movement into nymph patterns is adopted by some of the best fly fishers I've known, and without a doubt, it works.

The second reason is I feel a thinner-diameter fly is more true to the shape/form of many of the natural insects in the water. I feel many popular nymph patterns are way bulkier than the naturals they imitate. Within recent years, patterns like the perdigon have gotten fly

Fly boxes represent an investment in both time and money. This box contains close to 800 tungsten nymphs and has taken an entire season to tie. So I put my name and contact info on every fly box I own in the event I accidentally lose the box while fishing. Over the years I've found some valuable fly-fishing gear lost streamside without any contact information, so my suggestion is to plan for the worst but hope for the best. Put your contact information on some of your most valuable fly-fishing accessories in the event they become lost. There are still honest people out there, and many of them are fly fishers.

I've bought into the "thin for win" concept with fly designs. I'm still not sure if it helps or hurts with the overall look of the pattern, but I do know I need far less weight when fishing these thinned-out flies. I still love the look of buggy-looking nymphs but always seem to need a little additional weight to help sink the nymph. PHOTO JUSTIN IDE

tyers thinking about thinning out their patterns to not only sink faster but appear more natural during the drift. The one issue with buggy patterns is you need additional weight (e.g., split shot) to sink the pattern, and I only use shot as a last resort due to the increase in casting tangles and loss of connection.

As a result, I've thinned out many of my favorite nymph patterns by reducing bulk and eliminating unnecessary steps and materials. For instance, I've turned Higa's SOS into a Perdigon-style nymph with no dubbed thorax, just a small bump of thread. I still use dubbing but use far less than with past nymph patterns. If I do use lead wire, it's only five to seven wraps I can slide under a bead. I may only use three or four fibers when tying a pheasant tail nymph. A tungsten bead, a few wraps of wire, and a thinned-out body is often all that is needed to sink the fly into the trout's feeding zone.

When I first saw perdigon-style patterns and simple pheasant tail (no thorax or wing case), I thought there was no way these sickly-looking patterns would catch fish. I was wrong. Not only did they catch just as many trout as my shaggier-style patterns, but I believe the increased sink rate of these thinned-out patterns caught more fish. It takes a conscious effort to thin out your patterns. Using smaller-diameter tying thread, reducing

I like to carry a smaller variety of patterns but tie them in a variety of weights. The depth and speed the nymphs travel is more important than fly selection. I no longer weigh them on a scale but instead organize them according to bead size. I've realized over the years that the more I fish, the fewer patterns I carry. Years ago I carried thousands of patterns. Today I carry hundreds. Hopefully I'll continue to reduce that number so I can spend more time focusing on techniques.

I break nymph patterns into three categories: imitative, suggestive, and junk. It's just a simple way for me to categorize patterns in my box, but I strongly suggest you find a system that meshes well with your approach.

thread wrap, and eliminating any unnecessary material takes practice. Thinning out your patterns will reduce the need for split shot or other types of weight, which provides greater strike detection and reduces the chance of tangles. This thinning process will also reduce your tying time if you tie your own patterns.

Though it takes time on the water, it's important to find a handful of patterns/styles/colors you have confidence in. If you don't have confidence in the patterns you fish, success will be limited. I'm introduced to new patterns all the time when fishing with guides or friends on new waters. I respect the opinion on the guide's fly choice, but I must admit that it's hard for me to fish the pattern with utmost confidence if the pattern's look is not what's normal for me. For example, I have confidence in using silver, black, and copper bead euro-style nymphs and lack confidence using gold beads. I know gold beads catch fish, but I have so much confidence in using silver, copper, and black beads. My confidence levels drops anytime I put on a gold bead when fishing my home waters. If my confidence is lacking, my technique and attention to detail quickly wane just as fast during the presentation. No matter how effective the pattern is, the results are less than satisfactory due to my poor technique. The pattern is only as good as the angler fishing them.

Lastly, it's still important to keep learning and trying new patterns from time to time, so don't get stuck in a rut with your nymph selection. Try to incorporate a new confidence pattern into your box every season. And don't forget to weed out patterns you no longer use. If I haven't fished a pattern in over a season, I discard it into a container that I donate to anyone in need of fly patterns or cut the bead off the hook with wire cutters and reuse it.

Imitative Patterns

This pattern category attempts to closely imitate the natural. Some tyers will fuss over the exact color shade, the number of tails, and so on. I feel there are only a few situations where you need to closely imitate an insect. Insects unique in shape, color, and behavior are candidates for imitative patterns. For example, look at the giant Hex mayfly nymph. This mayfly is classified as a burrier and has a long, extended body with prominent gills. The Hex not only looks significantly different than most common mayflies, but also wiggles in the water as it begins to emerge. As a result, my Hex patterns look and move like the natural, often tying them with a long marabou tail or with an articulation. This is one example of where I feel being imitative provides a better return on your investment. Also, you'll find situations where trout key in on a specific insect. For example, our sulphur hatch occurs for over 4 weeks in central Pennsylvania, and our trout will key in on this nymph during emergence. This is when I feel a more imitative pattern like sunburst sulphur does an excellent job imitating emerging sulphur nymphs. I carry imitative patterns during specific time periods when trout are keyed in on unique insects.

I keep my nymph boxes simple as I carry the following flies in a variety of sizes and colors. The idea is to have a small variety of light, dark, flashy, and bright-colored patterns. I may tie some with varying amounts of weight to deal with current speed. I no longer feel the need to carry dozens of boxes (holding dozens of varying nymph designs) streamside as I feel confident approaching any stream with the patterns I've listed below.

I tie most nymphs with a tungsten bead head. I've heard so many arguments regarding the unnatural appearance of a bead placed on a nymph. While maybe no aquatic insects appear to have a large bulb attached to their head, there's some attraction a trout has toward a bead head nymph. Also, emerging insects develop gas bubbles to lift them toward the surface during emergence. Granted, there are times I felt a gold or silver bead spooked fish. If that's the case, then I switch over to a copper, black, or another darker/natural-colored bead. I currently use more silver beads since I feel it reflects light and may stand out better, especially in darker or more turbulent water.

I organize my nymph box according to weight via bead size. The waters you fish should reflect how you weight your patterns. For my home central Pennsylvania waters, I most often use 7/64 (3.0 mm) or a 3/32 (2.5 mm) slotted tungsten bead. I'll also slide three or four wraps of lead wire under the bead for additional weight and to help lock the bead in place. When learning to euro nymph, I began using heavier bead head patterns, dredging and dragging them along stream bottom. Over time I've learned how to drift (not drag) nymphs for a more natural presentation. If you're constantly hanging up on stream bottom or needing to pull the rod tip fast downstream to prevent the fly grabbing bottom, you likely have too much weight.

I feel the key to a good presentation is having just enough weight built into the fly so it drops fast enough into the strike zone but still light enough for it to drift naturally downstream with little assistance from the angler. This is called a natural drift and is the same concept as you would apply when drifting a dry fly on the surface. I only use the heavier beads when I must dredge bottom or when dealing with turbulent waters, which is not often on my home waters. If I lived out west rather than central Pennsylvania, my average bead size would

Amidea Daniel works a cut with a single 3/32 tungsten bead nymph. Rarely do I need bead sizes greater than 7/64 or 3.0 mm when fishing such waters. It's surprising how fast a small/dense nymph, paired with good technique, will plummet into the depths.

likely increase. Let the conditions and streams you fish dictate the amount of weight used.

Even if I'm not using a jig hook, I prefer slotted beads as less tungsten metal is bored from these beads during production and they weigh more than traditional beads. If I do use lead wire, I use only three or four wraps to snug up under the bead to add weight and to prevent the bead from sliding down. Again, my desire is to keep the body as thin as possible, and I can hide these three or four lead wire wraps within the bead's bore hole without adding bulk to the body. Adding lead wire to the entire hook shank will add weight, but it will also bulk up the pattern, which is sometimes a desired result. Bulk is fine for some patterns like a rubber leg stone, where stoneflies are naturally large and bulky. However, I feel bulkier bodies are overkill for the majority of small aquatic insects trout feed on.

Though I still will use traditional nymph hooks, I enjoy the look and performance of barbless competitive-style jig hooks, especially for patterns designed to drift close to stream bottom. The hook point will usually invert, reducing the chance of snagging bottom. The ultra-sharp barbless point is excellent for fly tyers who forget to de-barb hooks (speaking about myself) while providing excellent hook sets. In the past many of these needlepoint competition hooks would become fragile or bend out when hanging up or playing larger fish, but many of these issues have been fixed with updated manufacturing processes.

ARTICULATED GREEN DRAKE NYMPH

For many, the Eastern (not Western) green drake hatch is the season's highlight, and it is a hatch where I will fish imitative patterns. I've seen and fished so many good-looking green drake nymph patterns, but my favorite is from local tyer Karl Gebhart. Although not much to look at in the vise, this pattern is deadly when it swims in the water. By swimming, I mean swinging the pattern while wiggling the rod tip. This simple articulated pattern brilliantly represents the erratic wiggling movement made by the emerging green drake nymph. So while this pattern is good during a drifting presentation, I feel this pattern is most effective while slowly swinging down and across. This same concept can be applied to other wiggle-style mayfly nymphs.

CRESS BUG

Cress bugs live within tailwaters and spring creeks and provide a year-round food source for trout of all sizes. Although I'm fond of fishing thin and densely tied nymph bodies, cress bug patterns are an exception. These wide-bodied aquatic insects are poor swimmers, rocking side to side when becoming dislodged. This is where I prefer to fish unweighted/lightweighted patterns with split shot, preferably a drop shot rig. The shot rolls and bounces along stream bottom while the lighter and larger profile of the cress bug rocks back and forth with the currents. Fishing a cress bug on a drop shot is like flying a kite in the wind—the shot holds the rigs closer to stream bottom while the currents push on the cress bug's wider profile.

Ray Charles, Hump's Cress Bug, and UV Cress Bug

Feathered Hook Green Drake

Rear hook: #10 2X-long nymph hook
Tail: tan ostrich herl
Body: tan ostrich herl
Connection: 15-lb mono
Front hook: #10 1X-long nymph hook
Body: ginger dubbing with rubber legs mix
Wing case: brown thin skin
Bead: ⅛" gold bead

Hump's Cress Bug

Hook: 1X-long nymph hook #14
Thread: tan 140 UTC thread
Lead wire: 10 wraps of .020 flattened with plier
Body: Joe Ackourey Hare's Ear Blend
Top Coat: thick UV resin

Ant Perdigon

Hook: 1X nymph hook #14
Thread: black 8/0 uni thread
Rear body: Black Hare's Ear Dub
Legs: Mirco black sili legs
Front body: black thread tapered behind bead
Bead: 7⁄64 black tungsten
Coating: thin UV resin

I fish three different patterns: a modified Ray Charles cress bug for smaller patterns, a variation of Joe Humphreys's cress bug, and the UV cress bug. Hump's Cress Bug has a wider profile and holds its shape when drifting while the currents help rock the pattern from side to side during the drift while split shot keeps the rig anchored closer to stream bottom. The UV cress bug is a flashier version I use when dealing with turbid water or anytime I feel I need additional flash within my pattern.

SUNKEN ANT

Ants are a trout favorite from spring to fall. While most ant patterns focus on surface presentations, sunken patterns are deadly. I first heard about sunken ant patterns while fishing during the 2006 World Fly Fishing Championships, when our guide Jorge Pisco stressed the importance of fishing wet ants during rain events. I've been using wet ant patterns ever since and recently I've been using a perdigon-style sunken ant. Although you can tie any size ant pattern, I prefer #14 and #16. I often use this pattern with a dry dropper presentation.

SUNKEN SPINNER

Just as with ants, spinners are a popular surface food item that eventually begins sinking below the surface. For central Pennsylvania waters, I only focus on the sunken sulphur and Trico spinners, but any mayfly spinner can be turned into a sunken pattern. My sunken patterns are a cross between a thread body perdigon

A northern Michigan trout stream in July after a rainstorm—the perfect time to fish a sunken ant as many terrestrials are washed into surrounding bodies of water. I think "sunken ants" the moment I see water droplets on lush green vegetation.

and George Harvey krystal flash Trico. The nail polish-coated thread body along with krystal flash wings will ride partially submerged—just as the partially submerged spent spinners ride in the water column. I may add a brass (not tungsten) bead to partially submerge the pattern. Normally I fish this pattern a short distance off the bend of a high-floating dry fly. I feel the best presentation for a sunken spinner is just under the surface. Hence, the reason for a lightweight pattern fished only 10 to 20 inches under a dry fly.

Rusty Spinner Perdigon

Hook: #14 1X nymph hook
Thread: 6/0 rusty brown UTC
Tail: medium Coq De Leon
Body: thread
Wing: Pearl Flashabout
Coating: UV resin

Suggestive Patterns

When it comes to nymphing, I believe presentation depth and good technique are more important than closely imitating aquatic insects. Close enough is generally good enough to catch trout on nymphs as long as your presentation is solid. To reduce carrying excessive patterns, I carry only a handful of suggestive patterns that I hope will roughly match the bulk of aquatic insects in the waters I fish. Size, shape, and color are considerations, but I feel it doesn't have to be exact. Size and color variations with classic patterns like hare's ears and pheasant tails can cover most major mayfly and smaller stonefly patterns. Also, perdigon-style patterns can be tied in a variety of sizes and colors to match most aquatic trout food. You can tie either of these patterns without tails and you have caddis, crane fly, or midge larva imitations.

Below are several of my favorite suggestive patterns. Size and color and/or hot spot variations will occur depending on the streams and the time of year. My goal is carrying one box of nymphs to fish any trout water in the country and beyond. For years, I've carried multiple boxes to closely match every hatch and season. Today, I've streamlined my selection and haven't noticed a decrease in my productivity.

SOS PERDiGON

Higa's SOS has been a favorite for years, but last year I thinned out the original and turned it into a perdigon style. Although the original color scheme is still my favorite, I also tie them to better imitate other mayflies including the sulphur/PMD and olive. I'll tie this pattern as large as a size #10 to imitate slate drake all the way down to size #18.

THREAD SULPHUR PERDIGON

The split back–style nymphs imitate the mayfly as it begins to break free of the nymphal shuck. The idea is that trout will key in on this helpless transition stage, and the split back concept can be applied to any mayfly

SOS Perdigon

Hook: #14 jig hook
Thread: black 70 UTC
Bead: 7/64 slotted tungsten
Tail: medium Coq De Leon
Rib: small silver wire
Wingcase: medium red holographic tinsel
Wings: Black Flashabou
Coating: UV resin

Thread Sulphur Perdigon

Hook: #14 jig hook
Thread: Camel 6/0 UTC
Bead: 7/64 slotted tungsten
Tail: medium Coq De Leon
Rib: small copper wire
Wingcase: medium yellow holographic tinsel
Coating: UV resin

Quill Perdigon

Hook: #18 jig
Thread: 8/0 olive uni thread
Bead: 3/32 slotted tungsten
Tail: medium Coq De Leon
Body: polish quill
Coating: UV resin

species. I find the original split back design too time-consuming and complicated, so I wanted to simplify the process. By adding a yellow holographic flashback to a basic pheasant tail or brownish perdigon, I feel it accomplishes the same results with a fraction of the tying time. Also, to imitate the emerging adult breaking free of the nymphal shuck, you can leave a short tab of yellow tinsel sticking upward. You can add this flap to any nymph to achieve similar results.

QUILL PERDIGONS

Although a wired ribbed thread body perdigon is a great pattern, I love the look of the polished quill perdigon. Again, changing size and color can match almost any mayfly. I'll sometimes add a thread hot spot (not dubbing), but most quill perdigons I fish consist of a Coq de Leon tail, quill body, and nail polish finish. I prefer using Sally Hansen nail polish to coat all my nymph bodies. Although nail polish takes time to dry, it's significantly

Quill perdigons look great, are easy to tie, and drop like a rock. Pictured is a simplified version using Coq de Leon for the tail, olive quill for the body, and the silver bead for the weight to add some additional flash.

cheaper, possibly less harmful to breathe in, and doesn't darken the color of the fly as much as many of the UV products on the market today.

FLASH PERDIGONS

This flashy attractor is tied with a thin perdigon-style body for rapid descent. The gasolinia color flash material looks like spilled gasoline, and it works! I prefer flashback or flash body patterns like the gasoline when fishing pocket water, where a trout's visibility is decreased due to broken currents. I feel flashier-style patterns provide an easier visual for trout to find your fly in such conditions. Color schemes are unlimited as I've used blue, purple, and black. Lance Egan's rainbow warrior was a favorite attractor of mine, and now I tie this pattern as a perdigon style (i.e., I no longer tie in a dubbed thorax).

WALT'S WORM VARIATIONS

The Walt's Worm is without a doubt one of the simplest yet effective flies ever created, hence the reason it has become a common pattern among both competitive and recreational fly fishers. Just about any insect larva (e.g., caddis, crane fly, or midge) can be imitated by varying the size and color. The sexy Walt's Worm variation is an excellent choice when flash is needed, and it is a perfect example of how the simplest patterns will catch fish.

SAWYER PHEASANT TAIL

If I only had one nymph to carry with me, it would be a pheasant tail like the original tied by Frank Sawyer. The original was thin and minimalist-looking—maybe due to the lack of materials when Mr. Sawyer developed the pattern? Less is more when it come to a nymph's profile. For years my pheasant tails were too bulky. Through competitive fly fishing I learned how many of the world's best anglers fished with the simplest pheasant tail variations, including the Frenchie. Only several pheasant tail fibers made up both tail and body—just enough to cover the hook shank. No thick wing case and no legs tied in on the side like the American pheasant tail version. A thin tail, thin pheasant tail body, and ribbing is all you need to imitate most mayflies. Natural, dark brown, and olive are three favorite pheasant colors.

Gasolinia Perdigon

Hook: #14 jig
Thread: Fl red 140 UTC
Bead: 7/64 slotted tungsten
Body: 233 hends perdigon body
Coating: UV resin

Simple Pheasant Tail

Hook: #14 jig
Thread: dark olive 70 UTC
Tail: medium Coq de Leon
Body: 4 pheasant tail fibers
Rib: small copper wire

CHEWY CATNIP

Still one of my favorite larger caddis larva anchor patterns for faster/turbulent water, I tie this pattern in sizes #8 to #10. I've simplified this pattern over the years to reduce tying time and increase sink rate. Olive and chartreuse are my two favorite color schemes. I tie in a thin collar of dark dubbing to imitate legs. Epoxy or a flexible UV resin layer is placed on top to add durability and increase sink rate. When tying larger #8 and #10 patterns, this is one nymph for which I'll wrap the entire hook shank with thin lead wire to add additional weight.

One interesting thing that I have observed is that sometimes fishing larger patterns during the winter is better than matching the hatch. Though midges can be abundant at this time of year, overall, less food availability equals more willingness to eat whatever food is available. This doesn't work on every stream, but I've had excellent results fishing large Czech/Polish-style caddis larva on several local limestone streams during the coldest February days. I don't fully understand this phenomena, but I've witnessed it enough times to know larger #6–#10 nymph patterns can produce excellent results during the coldest winter months.

Partridge or CDC Soft Hackles

As mentioned earlier, trout are masters of efficiency and will position themselves where food is most abundant. This often means higher in the water column during a major emergence. I look at soft hackle patterns as emerging patterns that can be fished dead drift or on the swing. I'll add a soft hackle to a dropper(s) when trout are feeding higher in the water column or immediately below the surface on emerging insects. CDC and partridge are two of my favorite soft hackle materials, as these materials add liveness to imitate an array of emerging insects. I may add a brass bead along with a pearl tinsel to provide some flash, but the concept is the same as the original soft hackle patterns. I use soft hackles especially when I plan to swing out or dab the patterns at the end of the presentation. I don't want much weight as I want the soft hackle fibers to come alive and dance in the currents. Just as with other patterns, I modify the size and color to match current hatch activity.

Chewy Catnip

Hook: #8 scud hook
Thread: black 70 UTC
Bead: 5⁄32 tungsten
Body: UV Olive Midge Polar Chenille
Collar: Black Hare's Ear Dubbing
Coating: UV resin

Bird of Prey

Hook: #16 scud
Thread: camel 8/0 uni thread
Tail: Partridge
Body: Natural Hare's Ear Dubbing
Rib: Pearl Sukly Tinsel
Collar: Partridge

The use of a soft tackle while drifting or swinging is a great choice during any significant insect emergence. I'll usually fish the soft hackle higher on a dropper and it is useful for both the drift and the swung presentations. Simply modify size and color of the bird of prey to match current hatches. Pictured is a clump of freshly hatched grannoms on a central Pennsylvania freestone stream.

BIRD OF PREY CADDIS

This modified soft hackle is a favorite deeper-riding caddis pupa imitation. I'll fish this pattern on the point (end of tippet) for a deeper drifting presentation. A CDC or partridge feather is used for the collar, but at times I'll add an ostrich collar (behind the CDC or partridge feather) to give the fly a fuller look. I learned about using ostrich herl for a secondary collar from the late Nick Nicklas, a legendary guide and fly tyer from West Yellowstone. I'm not sure if the ostrich is more effective, but I love the look and have more confidence fishing it. I will often substitute the partridge collar with CDC, especially when I want the pattern to fish deeper in the water column. I find partridge creates more surface area, causing the pattern to ride a bit higher in the water column, which is an excellent choice when wanting your pattern to ride higher during the presentation.

ZEBRA MIDGES

Midges are everywhere. From rancid ditches to beautiful spring creeks, midges provide a small but plentiful food source for trout. During the winter months, midges may provide one of only several readily available food

Big fish do eat small flies. Although I did discuss earlier the idea of using larger flies in the winter, I would say smaller zebra midges are one of my favorite patterns to use during the coldest winter months. I suggest carrying a variety of sizes and colors of zebra midges if you plan to fish throughout the winter.

Zebra Midge

Hook: #20 scud hook
Thread and body: olive dun 8/0 uni thread
Bead: 5⁄64 tungsten
Rib: small wire
Coating: UV resin

sources to trout. I tie the bead head zebra midge in black, olive, red, and cream in sizes #20 to #24. Coating the body with either UV resin or nail polish will add durability and density to the patterns. When it comes to fishing midges below the surface, I feel the simpler the pattern, the better it will fish.

Junk Flies

Like it or not, junk flies simply work, and with amazing results. Some junk flies represent absolutely nothing while others represent natural forage. Eggs and worms occur naturally within the aquatic world just as mayflies, stoneflies, midges, and caddis do. In these situations, you are matching the "hatch" given current events. For example, one of the best "hatches" in central Pennsylvania during the spring is when suckers spawn. I've seen trout stacked on top of each other competing hard to feed below pods of spawning suckers. This event offers some of the season's best fishing but only if you choose to fish a small egg pattern. A pattern like a golden yellow mop doesn't represent anything natural but works great in both stocked and wild trout waters. Here are several of my favorite junk flies for waters near and far.

SQUIRMY WORMY/SAN JUAN

I still bounce back and forth between old- and new-school worm patterns. As much as I like the look and fish-catching capabilities of the squirmy wormy, I feel the pattern lacks durability compared to the traditional San Juan worm. I'll stock up on San Juan worms if I plan on going for a long road trip without my fly-tying kit as I know their patterns will hold up longer. I'll stick to squirmy wormy patterns when I have my fly-tying kit nearby. I carry worms small, medium, and large in a variety of colors to deal with any condition. Larger #8–#10 worms are used for blown-out water conditions with low visibility. Medium-sized #12 to #14 are great for just regular flows and clarity. Smaller #16 worms are only used for extreme conditions where trout are keyed on smaller earthworm presentations. Red, earthworm brown, pink, purple, and black are my favorite colors. Black is also an excellent small leech pattern.

Squirmy Wormy

Hook: #14 1X long nymph hook
Thread: Fl. fire red 140 UTC
Bead: 7⁄64 tungsten
Body: squirmy worm material

Pictured is the squirmy wormy, which is glued directly to the hook rather than being tied onto the hook. Basically products like Krazy Glue and Super Glues melt the rubber onto the hook, creating a stronger and longer-lasting bond. This was a great tip my friend Bret Bishop shared with me on a recent fishing trip in Idaho.

Try fishing larger patterns during the coldest winter months. While I do have good success fishing midge patterns during the colder seasons, I find more success catching larger fish during the cold season with larger patterns. It's worth a shot, and these patterns are so much easier to tie on rather than midge patterns during the bitter cold season.

EGGS

I would choose an egg if I was only allowed to fish one junk fly. Eggs are a natural part of a trout's diet but also work when natural eggs are not available to trout. Either by eating the eggs of other spawning trout, baitfish, or even suckers, eggs provide a tasty source of protein to trout. After trout are done spawning on my local waters, my favorite pattern is a #14 or #16 light-orange egg, and it remains a favorite pattern of mine throughout the winter. The only time I use larger eggs, #10 and #12, is when fishing for steelhead or migratory brown trout during high- and off-color water conditions. A slim #14 egg has been a fall/wintertime staple of mine for over 14 years. Shades of oranges and pinks are my two favorite colors. I used eggstacy material for size #14 and a slim Y2K egg for size #16. I would tie smaller eggs with eggstacy if a smaller-diameter material is available.

MOPS

While many consider the mop a junk fly, I believe tan or light-brown mop patterns do an excellent job imitating crane-fly larva. Some river systems, including the Wind River, are famous for large trout routinely feeding on large crane-fly larva. The gaudy chartreuse and orange colors look nothing like anything I've seen in nature, but both wild and stocked trout will eat these patterns with reckless abandon. While these patterns will catch fish in any conditions, I would say they've been the most effective when dirty water exists. A large golden-orange pattern has been my number-one high-water pattern. I usually tie this on a large #8–#10 jig hook with a heavy tungsten bead to help sink the large pattern.

Eggstacy Egg

Hook: #14 scud
Thread: Fl. fire red 140 UTC
Bead: 7/64 tungsten
Body: Eggstacy egg material

Mop

Hook: #8 jig hook
Thread: yellow 140 UTC
Bead: 5/32 slotted tungsten
Body: yellow mop

CHAPTER 3

Nymphing Tactics: Key Concepts

Before we discuss the specific tactics for tightline (a.k.a. euro) and suspension nymphing, let's talk about some of the concepts that apply to both approaches. I've developed these over the years through thousands of hours of experience fishing and instructing streamside. While these concepts are the result of my own personal experience, I feel it's important for all anglers to begin developing their own set of guiding principles. If you're just starting out fly fishing, then it may be helpful to draw from the concepts listed below (along with other experienced anglers) until you've compiled enough experience to build your own. They create a roadmap to follow when faced with difficult fishing.

Depth and speed are the two most important variables. As far as I know, trout are unreasonable creatures that rarely succumb to your wishful thinking. Trout survive by using a keen eye and being efficient with all movements. If food is moving too fast or too far above them, they won't budge no matter how many times you recast your fly or change flies. For a couple of years, I was on a realistic-fly-tying binge. I believed if my fly looked just like the natural, success would follow.

You can still get a decent enough drift if forced to cast across stream, but it will be shorter. When fishing across the stream, strive to keep a lower/level rod tip angle as you see pictured. This places less force on the flies, allowing the nymphs to drift rather than drag when presenting directly across stream. Drag will occur if you elevate the rod tip when presenting across stream, as the rod tip angle will pull the nymphs back to you (i.e., across stream).

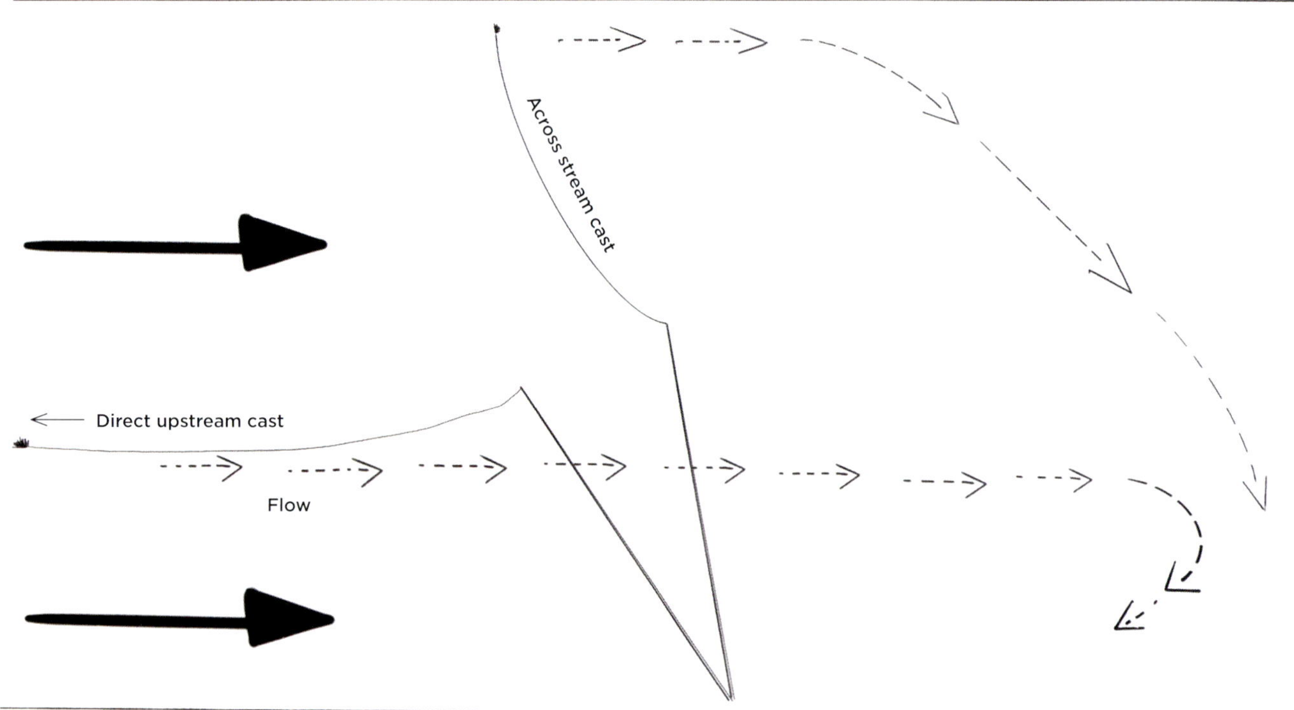

The length of a natural drift depends on the casting angle. Usually, a longer drift occurs when casting directly upstream before drag sets in. The drift length lessens the more you angle across stream. If you're looking for a long drift with no drag, cast more upstream. If you want to drift and swing out your presentations, cast more up and across.

Amidea Daniel works an upstream presentation during the cold season, when trout are less likely to chase smaller food items toward the surface during a swinging presentation. Casting angles are everything when it comes to achieving depth. Always strive for an upstream presentation when seeking a deeper and more natural drift.

Even brook trout will become less active after a cold snap during prime fishing season. Compared to brown trout, brook trout tend to be more aggressive feeders, willing to move longer distances when feeding. If you're not catching brook trout in waters you know hold good populations, it's most likely your presentation (not your fly). Sometimes a more direct upstream presentation will allow a longer and deeper presentation.

This realistic-fly phase resulted in a fly box of beautiful tied flies and a drastic reduction in the number of fish I caught. Too much focus on beautifully tied flies and less on techniques. If you enjoy tying realistic patterns, great! But be warned that no matter how nice the pattern looks, trout are not going to jump out of the woodwork to eat the fly if the fly doesn't drift at both the correct speed and level.

The angle at which you present your nymph(s) on the water determines the speed and height the pattern takes during the presentation. I would say that the bulk of my presentations are casting directly upstream or parallel with the flow of water. Why? Trout spend most of their lives near stream bottom feeding on drifting (not swinging) insects. Casting in-line with the current places less tension on the rig and allows the pattern to drop faster in the water column and drift at a slower rate. Think of the concept "go with the flow" when looking to present flies with a deeper and slower presentation. Drag will likely occur anytime you cast across current giving your pattern little time to drop to the correct depth before tension swings the pattern upward. Unless you're fishing a sterile stream with little to no trout food, trout are less likely to chase down a fast-moving nymph. Trout in fertile streams understand food will drift to them, if positioned near a current transporting drifting insects. So there's no urgency to chase down a single random pattern that is drifting too high in the water column and at an unnatural speed. You must give trout what they want. They will not compromise or meet you "halfway."

The relationship between trout and angler is a one-way street, with trout dictating the terms. If trout are looking for a slower-drifting nymph, try presenting line, leader, and fly parallel to the flow. If trout are lifting for emerging insects, cast more up and across stream to let the fly drop toward stream bottom before drag sets in and lifts the fly upward. Success in fly fishing doesn't involve supernatural powers. Success occurs when the angler develops situational awareness of the aquatic environment and takes an educated guess when developing an approach. Good guesses come with time on the water, and there is no substitute for time on the water.

Drift Speed

The dynamic nature of moving water is what makes nymphing so exciting and involved. Being aware of the speed and depth of the water along with the trout's feeding level are some of the most important variables to consider when approaching the water. A question I still ask myself is, "at what speed should my nymphs drift?" You hear about how nymphs should travel slower than the surface currents. Yes, this is a good general statement, but how much slower?

No book can depict every conceivable nymphing situation. Below I'm providing a short list of situations I've recently encountered both near and far from my home waters. The goal here isn't to tell you how to fish but instead hoping to make you *think* about how you approach the waters you fish.

Situation 1: Fish taking emergers below the surface. It's worth a trout's effort to fight surface currents to feed on emerging insects. This is the perfect situation for fishing a shallow dry dropper rig, where the nymph drifts several inches below the surface. Water speed between surface and several inches below doesn't greatly differ so I'm looking for my dry fly suspender to drift about the same speed as the current. The partially submerged nymph may cause a little pullback, slowing the dry fly down, but it shouldn't be much. So remember if you're drifting an emerger immediately below the surface, the suspender should move about the same speed as the surface currents.

Situation 2: Fast shallow riffle with small substrate. The substrate size on stream bottom has a great effect on current speed. Larger substrate (e.g., boulders) creates larger hydraulic cushions fish can hold in. These hydraulic cushions drastically reduce the current speed immediately in front of and behind the substrate. On the other hand, smaller substrate (e.g., pebbles or gravel)

I spotted this brown and some of its friends taking emergers several inches below the surface along a western riverbank. In these situations, I'll drift a shallow nymph just below the surface. I look for my sighter or suspender to move about the same speed as the surface current due to how high the nymph is drifting. You don't always want your fly to drift slower than the current.

This beautiful Madison River rainbow was fooled by a shallow dry dropper rig. A lightweight shop vac pattern was dropped 10 inches off a #14 X Caddis. If you fish too heavy or too deep during active feeding, you may be fishing below the trout. During prime feeding time trout are more willing to lift, so my approach is usually fishing higher in the water column during these times. I will eventually begin working deeper in the water column if action slows down or is nonexistent.

This Pennsylvania spring creek is known for shallow water with small substrate. Although the top and bottom water speed differ, they may not differ as much as you think. In this case, my ideal drift is for the sighter to drift just a little slower than the surface currents. PHOTO BY JUSTIN IDE

has less surface area, creating smaller cushions and less impact on slowing down the current. For example, Spring Creek in central Pennsylvania is a shallow spring creek with smaller substrate. When fishing shallow riffles in Spring Creek, a good drift might be just a bit slower than the surface current.

Situation 3: Deeper riffle larger substrate. A great example of this would be the Madison River (a.k.a. the 50-mile riffle) in Montana. The surface currents are fast and furious, but much of the Madison River's stream bottom is strewn with large boulders. These boulders create cushions for trout to hold and feed, despite the raging surface currents. In these situations, a good drift (indicator or tightline) is watching your visual strike aid moving significantly slower than surface currents. Going back to the Madison River example, usually I'll see bubbles flying past my visual strike aid, meaning my suspender or sighter is moving drastically slower than surface current. Remember, the larger the substrate on stream bottom, the slower the current will likely be.

Here I am getting some guidance from Steve Hoovler while fishing a Pennsylvania tailwater. Remember water speed stratification will increase with an increase in water depth. So there's usually a greater difference between surface and bottom current speeds when fishing deeper water. Adding larger substrate to stream bottom will only increase the difference in speeds. PHOTO BY CHRIS DANIEL

Amidea Daniel works a shallow riffle dumping into a trough. The drift started fast at the shallow rift but almost slowed to a halt before the boulder. The boulder created a hydraulic cushion that drastically reduced the top and bottom current speeds. In such situations you'll find your drifts moving in at least two speeds: usually fast at first and slow at the end.

No large substrate = less cushion for sigh to hold.

Large substrate = enough cushion for fish to hold comfortable in raging water.

Pay attention to the substrate size on stream bottom. Substrate laying on stream bottom will likely cause a soft hydraulic pocket or cushion of equal size above and below. This cushion allows a fish to rest without having to fight the current. This is important to notice since so many anglers pass over faster-moving water thinking the current is too fast for fish to hold. Even if the surface looks like a raging torrent, trout will hold immediately below this whitewater if there's large enough substrate to cushion the blow of the current.

Situation 4: Fast shallow riffle dumping into a slower run. Just understand drift speed may differ greatly during the same presentation. For example, think about a shallow riffle dumping into a deep run or pool. The first half of the presentation is going to move faster as the nymphs drift in the shallow riffle. Then the drift may drastically slow down as the nymphs enter the slower and deeper pool section. Just another variable to consider when your nymphing rigs move through various water types during the same presentation. Attention to small details like this make for better results.

Situation 5: High water. One important consideration on where trout move during high water is where the hydraulic cushions will occur. Using Spring Creek as an example again, on average this is a lower-gradient stream with small substrate. In other words, there's less structure within the stream to protect fish during high water. Although there are some cushions midstream, I feel many fish on Spring Creek are forced to the banks, where slower current speeds exist.

There are several other streams containing large natural cuts on stream bottom (a.k.a. bowels) along with large substrate to offer holding areas during extreme high-water events. Yes, many fish are still forced to banks

Large substrate create larger hydraulic cushions above and below the surface. Be prepared to fish your nymph extra slow when drifting close to large boulders, as you see here in this western freestone river.

Don't be intimidated by what you see on the surface. Although raging above, the currents below are bouncing back and forth between large submerged boulders. These boulders create plenty of holding spots for trout to feed and rest. If you see a boulder approximately 2 feet in diameter, it will likely create a cushion (sometimes called a pocket) of equal size above and below—more than enough space for a trout to hold in heavy current.

during high water but not as many you may think. For example, while fishing the White River in Arkansas during flows exceeding 15,000 CFS, I've seen several locals fishing in the middle of the river while tourists like myself were only fishing the banks. That's what makes fly fishing so amazing. Every stream has its own set of rules and you can spend your entire life trying to figure out just one system and still never dial it in.

Drift Depth

We've heard many times that if you're not losing flies or hanging up on bottom occasionally, you're not nymphing correctly. The question is how deep does my nymph need to drift or how many times should I be getting stuck on stream bottom? Again, situational awareness will provide guidance regarding the depth you need to drift your flies, but here are some variables to consider.

When a hatch is on and trout are frequently lifting off bottom or suspended higher in the water column, I feel you should not be hitting stream bottom at all. Fish your flies where fish are feeding. A shallow dry dropper rig is perfect for these conditions, where the nymph may not drift more than a foot below the surface. When fishing during the spring season in central Pennsylvania, optimal water temps exist starting midmorning, and there may be a feeding lull in early morning. This is when I may need to drift my nymphs near stream bottom, where I'll occasional catch stream bottom. Then the warmer air temps begin to warm the water in late morning, causing aquatic insects to become active. A trout's means of survival is noticing this change in activity, and they will change position based on where the greatest concentration of insects is moving.

Another example of fishing shallow is when fishing small streams. I often fish a shallow dry dropper rig on sterile mountain streams, since there's no need to go deep when hungry fish are willing to move for a fly. The times I fish deep on small mountain streams are situations where trout won't move far, which may include a cold snap where falling water temps have created sluggishly feeding trout.

I feel the only time you should frequently be losing patterns is when fish are stuck to the stream bottom. Other than that, you should occasionally connect with stream bottom but not as often as you may think. During peak hatch season in central Pennsylvania, when trout are looking up for food, I may only lose two or three nymphs in a day's outing due to snags. During the winter that number may double. Unless you're fishing a heavily wooded river section, you should not lose more than a half dozen nymphs a day. If you are losing more than that, you may be fishing too heavy of a rig.

Fishing Multiple Flies

I think that it is a myth that fishing two flies will double your chances. Two flies may increase your catch rate, but it will also certainly triple your chances of tangling. While I do fish double (rarely triple) nymph rigs, the majority of my time I spend fishing a single nymph. Because I usually place my weight near tippet's end, any fly added on a dropper will ride higher in the water column. I feel it makes little sense to fish a fly higher in the water column if fish are not lifting to eat. So I find myself fishing single fly rigs during periods of low trout activity. Plus, single nymphs are easier to cast and tangle less.

Also, the weight within my rig (e.g., the one nymph) is focused in one area. Since the mass within the rig is falling in a single direction, I feel it sinks faster. When adding a second weighted nymph (although sometimes absolutely necessary), these patterns may play tug-of-war with each other during the descent, especially when nymphing dynamic hydraulic areas, where multiple currents are moving in different directions. Therefore, I may use a single weighted nymph in fast pocket water, and if I need extra weight, I may opt to add a small split shot or piece of tungsten putty rather than adding another weighted nymph. If you don't believe me, try fishing two dry flies (e.g., 20 inches apart) together in pocket water and watch the amount of drag occurring between the two patterns. The same type of drag occurs when nymphing multiple patterns in pocket water, but rarely can we see it with our eyes as we can with the dry fly.

There are some considerations when deciding to add a second nymph. First, where is the heaviest pattern (if there is one) going to be placed? Personally, I like to add the heaviest fly on the point (end of tippet) and add a lighter nymph to a dropper 15 inches or more above the point fly. Even though some counter drag will occur when adding a lighter-weight nymph to the dropper, the heavier fly on the point should keep the rig anchored toward stream bottom while providing a deeper natural drift. You may find the sink rate of your rig slows down

A good example for when I fish a single fly: a small stream during the winter. Cold temps on this freestone stream had fish staying close to stream bottom. A single-weighted euro nymph fished near stream bottom was a good choice that day, as Amidea Daniel landed a handful of fish that afternoon.

if you fish two flies of equal weight. This would be similar to two similar-sized humans (weight and strength) playing tug-of-war with a rope, which is why I want a stronger/heavier fly with the rig to pull the other in the intended direction. The less resistance that pattern has during the fall, the greater the sink rate.

I think about my elementary gym class when thinking about the number and spacing of my nymphs. Specifically, I think about playing tug-of-war when the class is divided into two opposing teams and asked to grab onto the rope. The idea is to work together each time to attempt to pull the other team toward them rather than getting pulled or moved toward the opposing team. In other words, you have two teams pulling away from each other in an attempt to pull the opposing team toward them. At first, it's a slow, drawn-out process as both teams are pulling violently away from each other, where little movement or progress is made from either team. Nymphing with multiple flies in a dynamic current is similar due to drag. It's probable each nymph will eventually become positioned in opposing currents, creating an underwater tug-of-war between each other. This results in drag, which creates a slower descent toward stream bottom and an unnatural drift.

If I do decide to fish multiple flies in pocket water, then I'll place all or most of my weight (within the nymphing rig) in one fly along with one or two light to unweighted patterns. You create two anchor points when you fish two flies of equal weight. In other words, you're creating two opposing teams that will pull against each other when fishing water with multiple currents. This concept isn't as important when fishing water with uniform currents as these even current directions should drift multiple flies in relatively the same direction.

This will allow you to cover two levels: near stream bottom and 15 inches or more higher in the water column. If you want to fish both flies closer to stream bottom, then you can add a dropper closer than 15 inches. Given the influence competitive fly fishing has on modern euro tactics, we always hear about spacing your flies 20 inches apart, but this is an international rule, not a rule for the recreational angler. I know some excellent anglers who position their point and dropper patterns within 8 to 10 inches of each other. Find what works for you, but also think about the trout's feeding level and how that affects the distance between the heavier point fly and the lighter dropper.

I try to keep my weight focused in one location when dealing with dynamic currents. This picture shows a stream section full of tight/narrow seams moving in a variety of directions. I feel using one anchor point (e.g., one heavier nymph or split shot placed close together) keeps the nymphs drifting slower and deeper within a single seam.

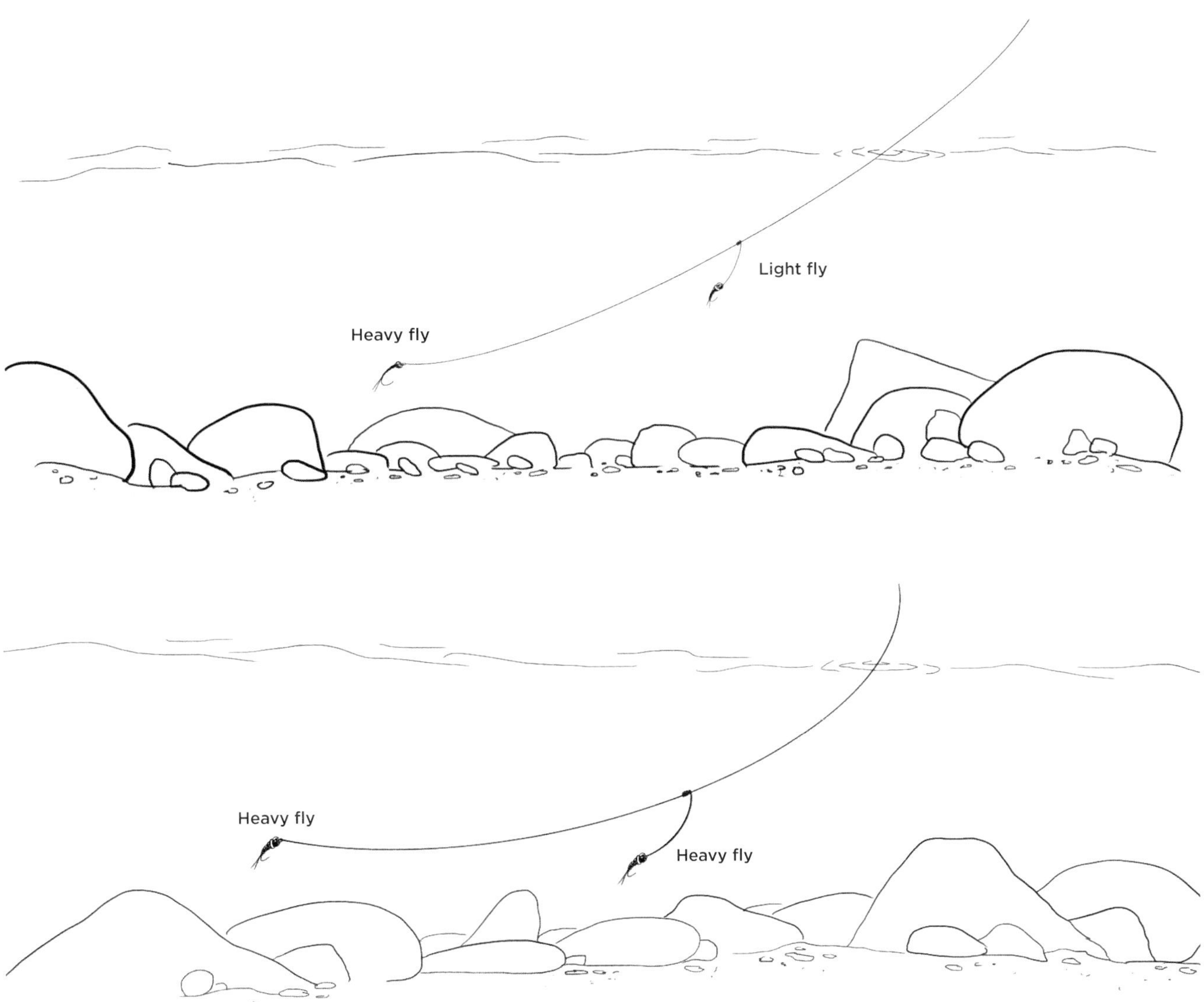

I like one anchor point when nymphing. I want most of the weight within one location instead of being spread over the tippet. I feel this gives me better control and keeps the entire tippet tight during the drift. For example, I like to place the heaviest nymph at the point position. If I decide to fish a second fly higher in the water column, I'll add a smaller or lighter-weight nymph to allow the heaviest point fly to maintain a straighter line within the tippet.

Another reason I like the heavier fly on the point position is I find the rig is easier to cast and tends to tangle less when casting compared to placing the heavier fly on the dropper and lighter fly on the point. This is what works for me.

However, there are situations where large and heavily weighted patterns are needed. Anchor patterns are larger/heavier nymphs used in euro nymphing tactics to quickly drop the nymphing rig in the strike zone. The use of split shot is prohibited in most fly-fishing competitions, so anchor patterns are used instead to achieve depth. At times, trout will eat these larger patterns, but usually anchor patterns are sacrificial and used solely to sink the nymphing rig. I like using larger nymphs for added weight and ease of attaching to tippet.

Only use anchor patterns if trout will eat them. It's important to know that not all euro nymphs are large and heavily weighted patterns. We'll later discuss tactics that allow you to achieve depth using small and lightly weighted patterns, which I find to be more successful on my home waters.

For years I replaced split shot with these larger/heavier patterns, but I would seldom catch fish on my home waters using these larger patterns. I no longer needed to follow international competitive fly-fishing rules, yet I was still sticking to these guidelines. Medium to smaller nymph patterns work better than larger ones on my home waters. For example, #16 is currently my most productive size nymph. And if I'm going to fish two nymphs, I want both of them to have a high probability

Large/heavy anchor flies are excellent choices when fishing high and dirty water. But I only use larger anchor patterns when there's a chance to catch a fish on them. Pictured is an angler drifting a large stonefly while drifting a Montana freestone stream during runoff—a perfect time to use larger patterns. PHOTO BY CHRIS DANIEL

of success. Usually there's enough weight in both #16 nymphs (tungsten bead and a few wraps of lead wire) to achieve proper depth. If the smaller nymphs lack the adequate weight, I'll add shot/putty to the rig instead of adding an anchor fly. Trout in some river systems will consistently eat larger flies, so the use of anchor patterns works for both catch rate and depth control. However, I've found smaller patterns produce better results on my home waters. Find what works best for the waters you fish and plan accordingly.

CHAPTER 4

Suspension Tactics

I use the term "suspension" when describing fishing nymphs under a buoyant device designed to hold or suspend the rig at a specific height in the water column. For years suspension rigs were extremely popular, especially on western waters. When suspension tactics were en vogue, anglers would say that tightline tactics were old-fashioned and only used by traditionalists. Today, as euro nymphing has gained popularity, I hear anglers saying there's no use learning suspension tactics. Both mindsets are incorrect. It's important to understand both tactics work and should be used based on stream conditions. While I personally believe euro/tightline tactics are more effective on a day-to-day basis, there are still countless times during the season where suspension tactics are clearly the best choice. My suggestion is to learn both.

Compared to euro tactics, I believe suspension is more challenging. Casting a buoyant/wind-resistant tool attached to your leader, the use of split shot, along with mending line on the water requires skill. Despite the increase in casting tangles, I wouldn't approach any trout stream without being prepared to suspension-nymph. Below are several common occurrences when I may switch to suspension tactics.

Working the flat/calm edges along the Madison River is a great choice for a dry dropper. The calmer and slower currents won't drag the suspender dry as much as the faster currents midstream, allowing me to drift my nymph. However, I would immediately switch to a euro/tightline approach if fishing the faster currents farther away from the bank.

If using a drop shot/bottom-bouncing tactic in turbulent water, try to keep the shot close together but without touch. Even an inch of separation between the shot acts like a chain dragging along stream bottom versus an anchor.

Downstream Presentation

As we'll discuss later, euro tactics often involve casting upstream, allowing the nymph to settle to the correct depth, then either leading or hanging the nymphs with the rod tip during the drift. However, there are times when you can't cast directly upstream. When a downstream drift may be the only or best tactical option, I'll switch to a suspension tactic. Maybe the section you're fishing has shallow water with nervous trout, and casting any nymphing rig over their heads will result in spooking the fish. Maybe there's an overhanging limb positioned directly over a prime lie, where an upstream cast is not possible. So, one option may be to cast above the limb from an upstream location and allow the suspension device to drift the nymph under the limb.

Although a shorter downstream drift can be achieved with euro nymphing, there are situations where the only possible presentation is a long downstream drift to a fish. For example, a recent trip to Tennessee's South Holston River during low flows made euro tactics in the flat water challenging. First, the slower bodies of water had skittish fish that spooked when getting anywhere within 50 feet. Second, the gentle disturbance of even a single lightweight nymph hitting the water surface was more than enough to send all nearby fish fleeing for cover. Third, even the thin euro leader (held off the water) created enough of a shadow to alert all fish. The only practical option I came up with (I'm sure there are others I didn't think of) was to locate a pod of fish or identify a good-looking lie well downstream of my position, suspend a small lightweight nymph under a dry fly, and present the fly 20 to 30 feet above the target. Once the cast was made well above the fish, I would kick out slack onto the water to allow the rig to drift downstream of the fish. Eventually this downstream presentation began producing fish, since the impact of the initial presentation was far enough away from the fish. Also, the downstream presentation created a situation where the fish sees the drifting dry dropper rig first rather than the fly line.

This also includes fishing while drifting from a boat. I will use euro tactics from a boat in fast, turbulent water, when I can fish at short range (a.k.a. directly under the rod tip). When I need distance from a boat (e.g., shallow or slower/gin-clear conditions), I'll switch to downstream suspension tactics.

Heavy Hatch

It's important to present the nymphs at the trout's feeding level, and I'm more confident in a suspension tool's ability to hold a fly at fixed height in the water column than with my ability to do so with a euro approach. Secondly, fish feeding higher in the water column are more likely eat a dry fly, so why not double your chances with fishing a nymph off a dry fly? I believe you can fish too deep during heavy hatches, as you may be presenting the fly below actively feeding fish. Let the trout's behavior dictate the level you fish your flies, which is why I fish shallower suspension rigs during heavy hatches.

Sometimes a downstream approach is your only option. On this section of the Yellowstone River, deep water below prevented Amidea Daniel from getting into position from below and casting upstream, so this downstream approach using a suspension device was the only option. Be prepared to nymph from any angle.

Another example where a shallow dry dropper rig will produce good results in fast/deep water. During the peak of the day, warmer water temps help jump-start a trout's feeding mode, creating a scenario where trout will lift 3 feet or more to take a drifting insect.

Small Streams

Small-stream fish are often aggressive, moving considerable distances to chase down food. Small-stream fishing during the peak season and time of day is when such aggressive feeding occurs. They often feed desperately due to the lack of food. When fishing small western trout streams, I've seen small trout lift 5 to 7 feet off stream bottom to eat a small nymph tied off the bend of my dry fly.

This is when I opt for a dry dropper presentation, where I use a dry fly buoyant enough to suspend a weight nymph but still small enough to represent the actual insect they're feeding on near the surface. One example is fishing smaller mountain streams, where the chance of taking a fish on both surface and bottom are about equal, so why not use a dry dropper rig, allowing you to cover both levels?

The only times I fish euro tactics on small streams is during the winter months, the morning after an unseasonably cold night during peak time, or immediately after any cold snap.

Windy Days

I spend several weeks every summer visiting western waters to fish. One major difference between central Pennsylvania waters and many of the larger western waters is the challenge of nymphing in strong winds. There comes a point when the wind becomes too strong to effectively keep line and leader off the water with a higher rod tip angler when euro nymphing. Even holding the rod tip 3 feet off the water creates enough surface area within the leader to blow the leader and sighter around like a kite. When the wind becomes too much for euro nymphing, it's time to switch to suspension tactics.

During these extreme windy conditions, suspension tactics allow me to keep the rod tip and line closer to the water surface, where the wind can blow the line around like a sail. While casting suspension rigs may be challenging during windy conditions, the advantage of this approach is the rod tip can be lowered toward the water's surface after the cast is made. The wind effect is lessened when both rod tip and suspension device are positioned low on the water surface compared to a

Charles Boinske fishes a small Montana mountain stream. Although the average water depth on this section is 3 feet, Charles used a shallow dry dropper rig and caught countless fish on both flies. On average, smaller streams tend to be more sterile and fish within them more willing to move for food. So when fishing these waters during peak trout activity, I tend to fish shallow nymphing rigs as trout are willing to lift up to eat. This approach also reduces the number of flies I lose to snagging stream bottom.

Strong winds begin to pick up during the late morning and afternoon on many western waters. When the wind becomes too strong to effectively euro nymph, I'll make the switch over to suspension tactics. PHOTO BY CHRIS DANIEL

higher rod tip and line/leader lifted off the water as is the case when euro nymphing.

Suspension devices with mass/weight like air lock, Thingamabobbers, or cork style provide additional momentum when casting in strong winds. Such devices will create a greater disturbance on the water, but strong winds will create a greater impact on the water's surface, which often mitigates this hard-impacting presentation. This is why I rarely use any light/wind-resistance suspender (like bushy dry flies or wool and yarn) when dealing with strong winds as these tools lack the punch needed to cut through wind—even with excellent casting.

Distance

Euro tactics have a limited range one can cast and control the drift. Personally, I feel approximately 25 feet is a maximum range I'm comfortable casting and fishing a euro rig. I'll switch to a suspension tactic anytime I need to fish beyond that distance. Maybe the water is too deep to wade into close position or low-water conditions are forcing you to keep greater distance between you and the fish. Whatever the reason, I'll use suspension tactics when my presentation cast exceeds 25 feet. It doesn't happen often, but when it does you need to be ready to present your nymph long-range.

Stillwaters

I enjoy fishing stillwaters for trout feeding immediately below and on the surface. A common practice is presenting a shallow dry dropper rig well ahead of a cruising trout. Depending on conditions, a short pull on the line wakes the dry fly on the surface. The wake hopefully attracts (rather than scares) the trout. The trout may take the dry fly but usually takes the low-hanging nymph. Again, this is all about fishing the correct depth, and during peak callibaetis and Trico hatches on western lakes, I find a shallow dry dropper is a great way to go. While I don't consider myself a strong lake angler, I do appreciate the fact that fishing lakes requires patience. Instead of just blindly casting a dry dropper rig as you might in moving water, I may not make a cast unless I have targeted a cruising fish. Random casting on glassy water usually results in nothing but spooked fish. Fishing lakes can be just as productive as fishing moving water, but presentations usually need to be intentional. In other words, don't cast unless you have a visual on a cruising trout.

Rigging for Suspension

Suspension rigs require more weight to achieve depth. Anytime you place a larger surface area object on the surface, currents will immediately begin pulling the

Jason Randall making a long-distance presentation while fishing the Driftless area during the late season. Distance is required when dealing with low water, so switching from a euro to a suspension rig may prove more valuable when you need to cast beyond 25 feet.

Sometimes fishing a static dry dropper presentation (i.e., casting and letting the nymph suspend for an extended period of time on the water) is more effective than continuously presenting and recasting a dry dropper rig when fishing stillwaters. Pay attention to where you see fish rise. Often, you'll begin to recognize lanes/highways trout will travel on these stillwaters. These are the areas where you want to fish a static presentation.

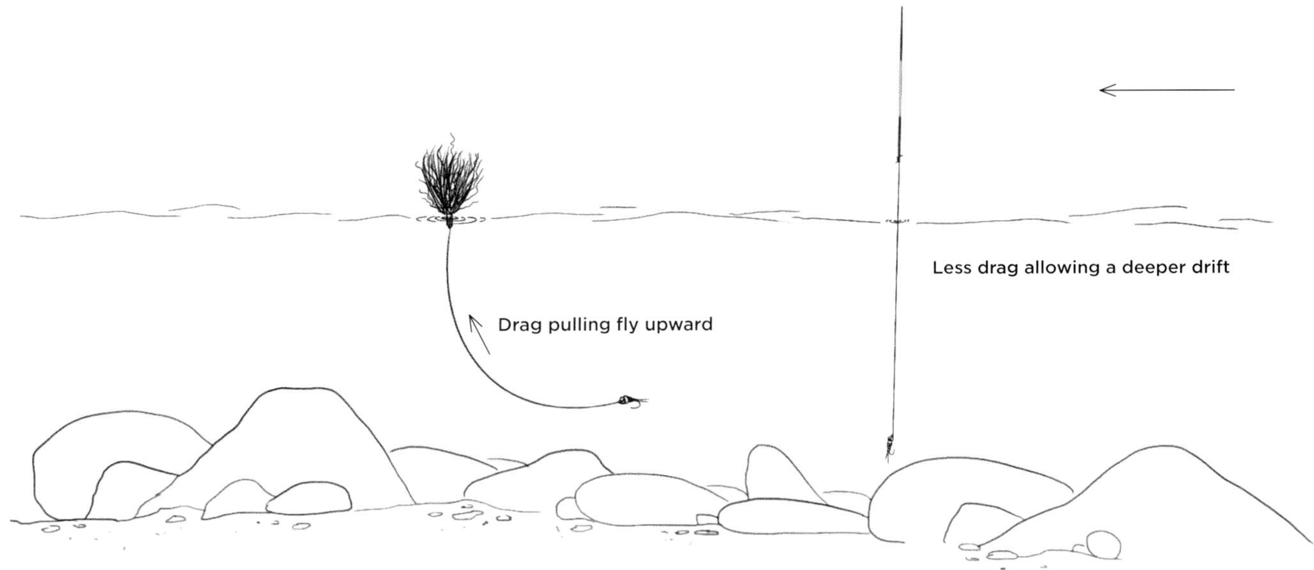

This illustration shows the same weighted fly with two approaches: euro and suspension. Notice the drag setting in on the suspender's larger surface area compared to the limited drag meeting the thin tippet of the euro rig. Additional weight is needed if a slower, deeper presentation is needed with a suspension rig. The distance between the suspender and the fly is often one to two times the water depth. Continue to adjust the distance until the suspender is moving more slowly than the surface current or when you occasionally catch the stream bottom.

suspender downstream, causing drag. This results in the suspender dragging the nymphs too fast and/or too high in the water column. Additional weight is placed on the leader to counter this drag. Larger suspenders create more drag, which is another reason I use as small of a suspender as I can get away with. Unless you're intentionally fishing higher in the water column (e.g., shallow dry dropper rig), you'll likely need to use additional weight in the form of split shot or putty to get your nymphs to the desired depth. This is the same reason why less weight is used when euro nymphing (i.e., often just the weight of the nymph). When euro nymphing, line and leader are lifted off the water, where only the tippet meets the surface currents. Compare the surface area of a 5X–6X tippet versus a balloon-style indicator—the difference is huge. This results in the need to add supplemental weight to the suspension rig.

Leaders

Some suspenders are easy to cast (like cork and plastic bubbles) while lighter/wind-resistant types (NZ Wool or large dry flies) will present casting challenges. I prefer using a tapered leader anytime I plan to use suspension tactics, especially when casting wind-resistant rigs. A shorter and thicker tapered leader will help generate energy during the presentation, and they are easier to mend. If you feel your casting skills are good but develop frequent tangles when suspension nymphing, a shorter and more powerful leader may reduce such occurrences.

I also like to use a shorter leader anytime casting light suspension or wind-resistant rigs. For example, I rarely use anything longer than a 12-foot leader when fishing NZ Wool systems. I prefer using the fly line mass and the leader's powerful butt section taper to aid in presenting the flies. Too many times I've attempted to cast wind-resistant suspension rigs with a long euro leader, which resulted in constant tangles. The more wind-resistant the suspension device, the shorter the leader, and vice versa. For example, I'll attach a large dry dropper (e.g., #8 Chubby Chernobyl Suspender) to tippet, then drop a shallow nymph off the bend of the dry fly. If casting #14 PMD/Sulphur Dry Dropper, a longer 9-to-12-foot 5X leader can be used. The #14 PMD/sulphur is considerably smaller, less wind-resistant, and needs less force to turn over. Learn what leader taper/length works best for the patterns you intend to fish.

Casting and Presenting Suspension Rigs

It's critical to maintain contact between suspender and nymph during the presentation. You want to have the nymph directly below or upstream of the suspender, as this position reduces slack and provides quick alerts to strikes. Nymphs drifting downstream or to the side of the suspender often result in slack, which hinders strike detection. You can intentionally place slack between suspender and nymph to decrease tension and allow a rapid sink rate. However, there's a time you want slack and a time when you don't want slack.

The problem with placing slack in the system is a total loss of strike detection. I prefer to make the first couple drifts with a tight connection between suspender and nymph. The tension between the two may not allow the nymphs to drop as fast, but at least I have strike detection in the event a fish takes the fly higher in the water column. This is especially true in pocket water, shallow riffles, or during a hatch. Trout are active in these situations, and so many anglers miss strikes as the result of creating slack in the system to allow the nymphs to drop.

After the first couple of casts, if I fail to move a fish or feel the need to drift deeper, I create just enough slack to allow the nymphs to drop into the strike zone, but not so much that I can't quickly regain control before the pattern drifts through a primary target.

For immediate control, I'm looking for the nymphs to land just upstream of the suspender. The surface currents immediately drag the suspender downstream, which begins tugging/pulling on the nymphs. No worries if the trout refuses to chase down the faster/higher-riding pattern—at least you have strike detection. If you don't detect a strike during these tensioned drifts, begin putting a little slack in the presentation to allow the nymphs to drop deeper. All you're doing is working the layers from top to bottom.

Finally, pay close attention to where the nymph enters the water in relation to the suspender. If the nymphs

Amidea Daniel fools a resident brown trout on a Montana meadow stream with a dry and dropper rig. An underpowered cast allowed the nymph to land below the suspender and drop fast due to the slack between nymph and suspender, getting the fly in the strike zone.

This shallow water section is ideal for creating contact between suspender and nymph the very moment of presenting the fly. Trout will often strike the moment your fly lands in this water. You may miss a trout take if you place slack (between suspender and fly) at the beginning of the presentation. PHOTO BY CHRIS DANIEL

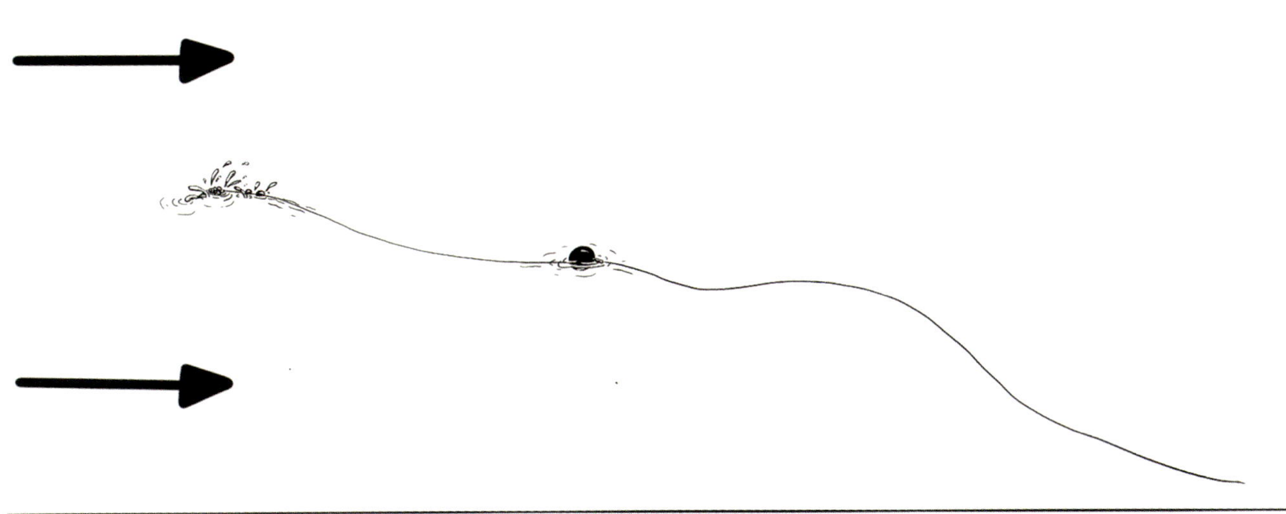

Contact between suspender and fly immediately occurs when I see the nymph plop directly upstream of the suspender. This creates immediate tension, where the suspender begins pulling the nymph downstream. This is a good approach when fishing shallow water and active feeding trout.

Amidea Daniel holding a rainbow trout taken while fishing a dry dropper rig. This fish was in 8 inches of water and took the nymph within 2 seconds after the rig landed on the water. A tight connection (i.e., nymph landing immediately upstream of the dry suspender) creates immediate tension and control, allowing Amidea to see the immediate strike.

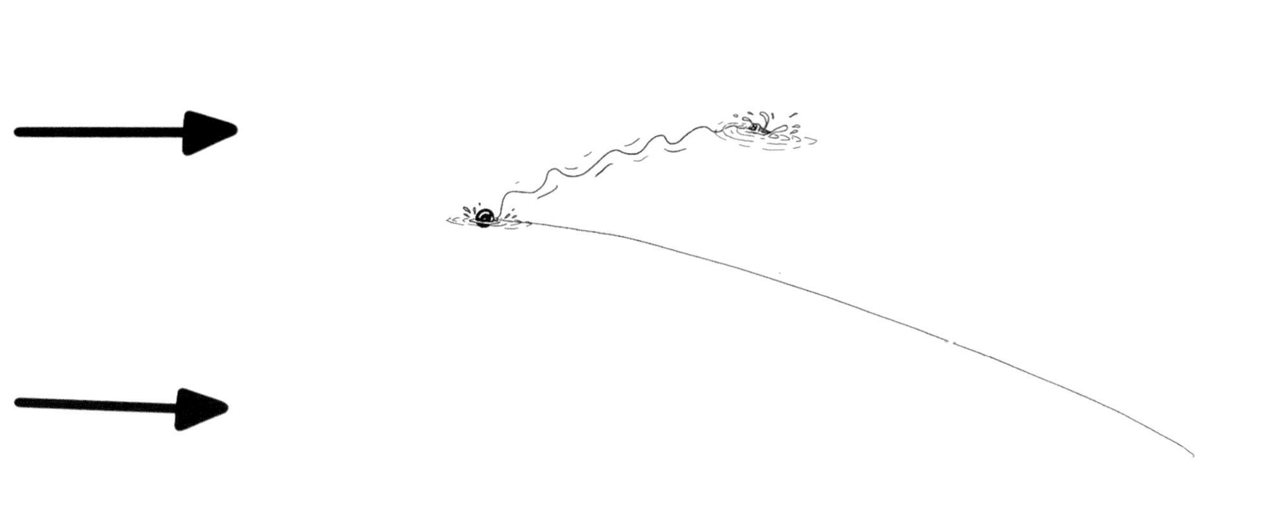

Slack and a loss of contact with nymph occurs when the fly lands below the suspension device. Eventually, control is regained as the fly settles toward stream bottom while the suspender drifts directly overtop the nymph, regaining tension, and begins to pull the nymph downstream. This is sometimes a desired approach, especially when trout are feeding deeper in the water column. Yes, there may be a few moments of slack, but that slack will decrease tension between suspender and nymphing, allowing the rig to settle deeper into the strike zone.

land immediately upstream, the rig will be tight from the beginning of the presentation. If the nymphs land downstream of the suspender, slack will occur for a few moments until the suspender moves directly above or downstream, eventually regaining tension. Again, this may be ideal if you're intentionally wanting a rapid descent. I like to call these moments of slack "sacrificial drift" as you're giving up a few seconds of strike detection to achieve a desired depth. This is like counting down with sinking lines while fishing lakes. Sometimes a few moments of slack is the only way to achieve the correct depth. As my mentor Joe Humphreys always says, "If what you are doing isn't working, change it!"

The least ideal situation is when the nymphs land off to the side of the suspender. Control may never be regained in this situation, or the nymph lands in a faster speed current and drags the suspender across current. This is when I'll use the reset technique to realign both suspender and nymph, where the rod tip pulls the suspender and nymph into proper alignment before continuing the drift. The good news with nymphing (unlike dry fly tactics) is you can usually recover after a bad cast. I cannot stress how important practicing your casting is to ensure you position the rig exactly how you want it to land on the water.

Some anglers have a keen eye and can see where the nymphs land in relation to the suspender. If you can't see where the nymph lands, you'll need to read how the suspender reacts during the drift. For example, we discussed the NZ Wool system earlier where the tall tuft of wool acts as a directional tool. The point here is to understand what the suspender looks like and does during a good presentation, and vice versa.

Still one of my favorite methods of nymphing is with a dual indicator. The idea is to fish two different-colored suspenders 6 to 8 inches apart (give or take a few inches). The suspender closest to your fly is considered the "top," while the other is called the "bottom." A good presentation (i.e., one drifting and under control) is when the top suspender is directly upstream of the bottom—in the same speed current. This perfect alignment indicates the nymph, tippet, and suspender are positioned in the same speed current. It also indicates a tight enough connection to signal a trout take. If the top suspender begins pulling to the side, it may indicate the nymph is positioned in a faster speed current than the suspender. For any number of reasons, a disconnect between suspender and nymph occurs during the drift.

When the top indicator begins dragging across current, the angler can use the reset tactic to realign the rig. Whatever the reason, the angler can reposition the suspender to resume control. This is a popular downstream tactic when fishing from a boat but can be used in other situations. Keep the downstream cast short so you can easily see and reposition the rig into the correct feeding lane, then you can kick out slack as the rig drifts downstream. Also, if you make a bad cast and notice the nymphs kick far off to one side, you can use the rod tip to pull back on the rig (regaining tension between fly and suspender) and then continue to drift under control.

Some water is simply too fast to use suspender tactics, in my opinion. Once landing on the water, currents

You can fish close to the boat in broken water, and using a longer rod will allow you to occasionally lift and reset the suspender on the water, allowing just enough slack for your nymph to drop. Pictured is the author drifting down a heavy riffle on an eastern tailwater as Steve Hoovler controls the boat. PHOTO BY CHRIS DANIEL

will immediately begin dragging the suspender. A little drag is OK, but excessive drag is not desirable. Current speeds near stream bottom are slower than surface currents, so a little drag by the surface currents is normal. To counter this drag, we use weighted flies or supplemental weight. However, some river sections have two extreme differences in speeds. For example, take the river section immediately below Quake Lake on the Madison River in Montana. Much of this section has raging whitewater near the surface but larger boulders on stream bottom creating slow pockets. While I've used indicator tactics in this section before with success, I feel I must use excessive amounts of split shot to counter the surface currents, and it makes for a clumsy feel while casting. Despite the excessive split shot, it takes several seconds for connection between fly and suspender to occur, which is not ideal when your drifts are short to begin in. Unless you're looking for a higher column drift in

this water type, my suggestion is to use a euro/tightline approach to decrease surface drag, allowing the nymphs to quickly settle toward stream bottom.

However, if you do not want to tightline, you can sometimes simply lift the suspender off the water to break the tension, allowing nymphs to quickly drop toward bottom. In other words, you're going to high stick the suspender off the water by lifting it off the water. The key is to lift upward just enough to peel the suspender off the water while not pulling on the nymphs. This approach is best at short range when the rig is directly under the rod tip, so the rod tip can lift the suspender directly vertical. If this tactic is attempted when the suspender is positioned far away from the rod tip, any lift of the rod tip will drag the suspender toward the angler. We don't want to pull the suspender in any direction—we simply want to lift it vertically to reduce tension so the length of your rod and hand extension will determine how far out you can do this tactic.

Depending on conditions, you can keep the suspender lifted off the water and treat the suspender as a sighter during the presentation. This is a great approach when fishing heavy pocket water with a suspension rig. Or you can lift the suspender off the water for just a short period of time, allowing the nymphs to settle to

Guy Murray uses the lift-and-reset suspender tactic. A low profile allows him to get close to the fish, while a full extended hand and 11-foot rod allow him to vertically lift the suspender from a distance.

In order to perform this lift-and-reset suspender tactic, you need to be close enough to the fly so you can lift the fly vertically straight up (or even slightly upstream). If you're too far downstream of the fly and lift the rod tip, you'll drag the fly downstream and create more tension. The idea is to cast upstream, allow the suspender to drift downstream, and lift the dry fly or suspender vertically off the water surface when the fly is directly under the rod tip. Just a short vertical lift of the rod tip is needed to break the tension between suspender and nymph. After a short couple-second delay, reset the fly on the water to continue the drift. It may take a moment for connection to occur again between suspender and nymph—a sacrificial period of slack that is sometimes needed to achieve depth.

the correct depth, before resetting it on the water surface. Sometimes only a few seconds of lift is all that is needed to achieve depth.

Mending Line and Leader

When it comes to suspension tactics, mending the line without causing additional drag is a necessary skill. Learning to mend is like learning how to cast. It takes time and practice, and the best time to practice is when you're not fishing. Practice on a local pond or any moving body of water without a fly attached. Practice the fundamentals of mending before fishing. Doing so will quicken the learning curve and reduce frustration on the water.

Limit as much line on the water as possible. Excessive line and leader on the water creates additional drag and requires mending. Suspension tactics are synonymous with mending tactics, but when possible try keeping as much line and leader off the water as you can. This may include using a slightly longer leader, but not too long. Remember, the most important function of the leader is its ability to present the rig. After developing better casting tactics, lengthening the leader's butt section several feet will still allow excellent presentation skills and a reduction with surface drag. A few additional inches or feet of fly line on the water doesn't seem like much, but it matters greatly when it comes to surface drag. Developing good casting skills that allow you to cast longer leaders with suspension tactics will greatly improve the presentation.

The first concept to good mending is a high floating line and leader. Clean mends that minimize suspender movement are not possible with a sunken line and leader, since these items need to break the surface tension before being repositioned on the water. Sunken line and leaders not only pull on the suspender but create additional noise during the mend. This is one reason I like to keep the loops on my fly lines as the larger surface area aids in keeping the line afloat. I'll also add floatant paste to both fly line tip and the leader's butt section to keep both items floating as high as possible. A high floating line and leader easily peel off the water during the mend.

The second concept to good mending is a clean fly line that slides through the guides. Mending requires kicking slack line on the water. A dirty or cracked line acts like Velcro going through the guides, which creates drag and pulls on the suspender. On the other hand, a slick line can easily pass through the guides without pulling on the suspender. It's only been within recent years that I've become disciplined when it comes to cleaning and maintaining my fly lines. Along with good

Mending line on the water is a necessary evil with suspension tactics. You need slack within the line and leader to allow a natural drift, but you need to tighten all that slack when setting the hook. This often means a longer/more aggressive hook set to tighten all the slack during the hook set. Pictured is Chris Daniel lifting as high as he can go with the rod tip to set the hook on trout, positioned directly upstream of a large boulder.

I like to roll my wrist toward the suspender while mending the line. But remember, the movement is like a roll cast, where the hand begins to lift the rod tip upward and allows a small belly to occur behind the rod tip. Then roll the wrist toward the suspender. Keep the movement short. This short movement creates just enough energy to move the line without moving the suspender.

Charles Boinske beginning to lift the rod as he prepares to mend the line while suspension nymphing. Notice the slack between his rod hand and reel. This slack allows him to move the rod tip and reposition line without dragging the suspender during the mend.

mending techniques, a clean line makes the mending process go smoothly.

The third concept to mending is having slack line off the reel to feed on the water surface to mend. Strip line off the reel before the presentation cast, but don't cast the entire length of line. After presenting the nymph rig, the slack line laying on the water needs to be positioned outside the rod tip (a.k.a. kicking out slack). Accelerating the rod tip across the water's surface (just on the surface) creates an anchor and pulls the slack line outside the rod tip. If the rod tip drags along the surface 6 feet, you pull approximately 6 feet of line outside the rod tip. I use this approach in faster water (where dragging the rod tip will not spook fish) when I need to quickly kick line outside the rod tip. The mend is made as soon as the slack line is laying outside the rod tip. A stealthier approach (but not as fast) to kicking line outside the rod tip is making short wristy casting motions with the rod tip pointed at the water's surface. Think of this movement as if you're making a sidearm cast just above the water's surface, but with just enough power to move the slack line from off the reel to outside the rod tip. Another tip is using the line hand to hold the line above the stripping guide before kicking out slack. This allows gravity to take effect, allowing the line to pass through the guides with less resistance. Remember, both methods of kicking out slack require an accelerated movement. You're not just moving the rod tip, but you're accelerating the tip just as you would when casting.

Use a high rod tip position when mending line. Think of mending as an underpowered roll cast. A higher rod tip angle holds line off the water, creating less surface tension when the rod tip accelerates forward to make the mend. Line also needs to hang behind the rod tip (similar to forming a "D" during the roll cast) to load the rod prior to making the mend. Again, the setup is almost identical to the roll cast, except less power is used during the forward acceleration. The goal is to use just enough power to reposition the slack off the rod tip onto the water's surface to achieve a natural drift.

I attempt to place the slack immediately above the suspender to provide a natural drift. If the line is positioned too far below or above, drag is likely to occur. When casting upstream (i.e., current is moving suspender downstream toward me), I'll aim the mend directly at the suspender. Since the suspender is a moving target, the mend lands just above, providing an ideal line/leader placement. You may want to aim below the suspender when mending in faster currents to compensate for the fast-moving suspender.

Only place enough slack on the water to provide a natural drift. Slack is good, but too much slack creates an inability to set the hook during the set. Think

The use of a switch rod and the right line allows for easier mending. Pictured is Amidea Daniel suspension-nymphing with an 11-foot 4-weight switch rod and a 5-weight long belly steelhead/salmon taper. I like to "go up" one line size, as the increased line weight makes short-distance mending easier due to the rod being under greater tension during the mend.

Mending requires practice, so think of the best practice when you're not actively fishing. You can't be sloppy when mending—the movements should be clean and with as little impact to the water as possible. Pictured is a beautiful brown taken with a suspension rig in low water on a central Pennsylvania trout stream.

about the distance the rod tip can travel—that length is about the maximum length of slack you can pick off the water during the set, along with using the line to aid in the strike. The perfect mend is applying the minimum amount of slack to provide an excellent drift but manageable in terms of setting the hook. Practice on the water until you're able to create that happy medium of getting a good drift but still able to set the hook when a strike occurs. Pay attention to the movement the suspender takes when you practice setting the hook. If there's a significant delay or if the suspender barely moves when setting the hook, you have too much slack.

Preventing Tangles

The combination of nymphs, split shot, and suspender attached on the leader is a recipe for a tangled mess during a bad cast. Tangles occur even with the best anglers. It's just part of playing the nymphing game. However, there are some casting and fishing tips that help reduce them.

SLOW DOWN!

Suspenders act like a sail on your leaders, slowing the passage of the cast. This means the pause between the backcast and forward cast is longer with indicator rigs then with a dry fly. Additional time is needed to allow the rig to straighten out before making the forward casting stroke. How long? A good tip is waiting until you feel the weights pull or tug on the backcast. Once you feel the weights tug on the backcast, then you know it's time to make the forward movement. A tangle will likely occur when attempting to cast prior to feeling the tug. You cannot rush when casting these rigs. Take your time. Wait for the tug on the backcast and you'll encounter fewer tangles.

SMOOTHING OUT THE CAST

By nature, I like to use short wristy casting strokes. However, wristy casting strokes with suspension rigs tend to tangle, so I adjust and use more forearm and lengthen and smooth out my stroke. At least for me, using the forearm smooths out most erratic movements within the cast, which results in fewer tangles. When I rely on my forearm, the cast looks more like I'm throwing a ball than tossing darts.

OVAL CAST

A regular cast where the rod tip moves in a straight line back and forth is a great cast for most situations, except for when casting super-heavy nymphing rigs, especially those with indicators. The issue I have casting heavy rigs straight back and forth is often a hard sideways kick on

Setting the hook requires a greater range or motion and power by the angler to not only lift excessive line and leader off the water but also to create enough force to set the hook. Remember, short lengths of line and leader on the water require less energy during the hook set than when fishing long lengths of line. In this picture the author had to use excessive force during the lift to secure a hook set when this trout took the nymph over 50 feet away. PHOTO BY CHRIS DANIEL

the backcast. Accuracy when casting heavy rigs is pretty simple—the weighted rig needs to be 180 degrees to the target before making the forward casting stroke. In other words, point your rod tip to where you want to cast the weighted rig. Look to see where the butt end of the rod is pointed behind you. That is where the rig needs to be positioned before you make the forward casting stroke. You can use a straight back-and-forth casting stroke, as long as there's no sideways kick. If the heavily weighted rig kicks off to one side, then accuracy will be lost on the forward casting stroke. One reason the heavy rigs kick on a regular cast is the weight moving fast and coming to a sudden stop, where the rig unrolls and kicks back on itself. Enter the oval cast.

The oval cast allows speed and momentum to occur on the cast without the kickback. Instead of moving the rod tip through a straight back-and-forth path, the rod tip basically moves in a half circle (i.e., 180-degree arc) on the backcast. The rig never fully unloads. Instead, the rig remains under rod tension during the entire cast and reduces any sideways kick. This allows the angler to carefully position the rig 180 degrees to the target. Once the rig swings straight behind the target, immediately use the forearm to make a smooth forward casting stroke. If you wait too long or don't wait long enough and do not allow the rig to swing out straight behind you, accuracy will be lost.

USE LESS POWER DURING THE HOOK SET

Hook sets are another culprit of tangled suspension rigs. This goes in line with the tip directly above. Excitement occurs when we see the suspender shoot under the surface. We quickly set the hook but miss the fish. However, the rig lifts off the water and moves in the direction we set the hook. Instead of allowing the rig to fully straighten out behind us, we get anxious and quickly attempt to redirect the rig back toward the missed fish before the rig straightens out behind us. The result is a collision between suspender, shot, and fly. If you set the hook and miss the fish, you need to let the rig straighten out behind you before recasting. Or just let the rig fall on the water or bank behind you before making the cast. You may need to walk back to the bank to pull your nymph rig off a low-hanging limb, but that's usually easier and quicker than trying to untangle a botched rig—pick the lesser of the two evils.

An ideal hook set is one where just enough power is used to lift the suspender off the water but keep the flies and shot below the surface. As my friend Mark Antolosky says, "all you need to do is move the fly several inches fast" to create enough power for a hook set. Easier said than done. There's little to no chance of tangles occurring if both nymph and shot remain below the surface during the set. However, the chance of tangles increases the moment both fly and shot break the surface tension. You don't want to drag or skate the surface with the indicator during the set as the drag of the suspender against the currents will slow down the hook-set speed. Instead, the ideal set is lifting the indicator just off the water and moving the rod tip downstream to set the hook. My best advice is to practice the hook set on moving water with just the shot and suspender. Pay attention to the movement and force needed to move the nymph several inches fast but without lifting the suspender off the water.

CHAPTER 5

Tightline/European Tactics

If allowed only one fly-fishing tactic to simply catch the greatest number of fish, then I would choose European nymphing tactics. Nymphing success is about getting your nymphs down to the fish as quickly and as naturally as possible, and I believe euro tactics accomplish those tasks better than other nymphing tactics for most fly-fishing situations.

Compared to suspension tactics, where the currents drag the suspender, the only drag occurring with euro is where a thin tippet slices down through the water column. This reduction in drag allows the nymphs to quickly drop to the strike zone faster than suspension tactics. This rapid decent is essential in situations where the drift is short, such as in pocket water. Another advantage of drag reduction is when fishing raging surface currents, where any larger surface area touching the faster currents will result in immediate drag.

Although drift length is shorter compared to suspension tactics, I feel this nymphing tactic is the most efficient method to achieving a natural drift near stream bottom, along with how quickly the nymphs enter the strike zone. While drifts with indicator tactics tend to be

Euro tactics involve the use of a thin line/leader, weight flies, and a long/limp rod. This combination creates one of the most effective yet fairly straightforward approaches to catching fish. Amidea Daniel euro nymphs a run on an Idaho freestone stream.

longer, it also takes longer for the nymphs to settle into the strike zone.

The term "euro" nymphing is a new term for an old tactic. While many of the tactics are the same (casting upstream and lifting line and leader off the water with a higher rod tip), modern equipment has revolutionized this tactic's ease and effectiveness. As a result, I use the terms euro nymphing and tightline nymphing interchangeably.

Lastly, in the past many of the European-style nymphing methods were categorized according to country (e.g., Polish, Czech, French, Spanish, etc.). Each tactic has its own nuance, mostly related to conditions found within that country's waters. Today, these tactics are clumped together under one tactic called "euro" nymphing, and each angler's rig is adjusted to match the conditions on the water. For example, when fishing raging pocket water, a shorter leader with heavier flies may be used. Or a long leader with ultra-thin tippet is called for when fishing low-water conditions with spooky resident fish. The tactics of casting, line control, and reading the drift are all the same. The only thing that changes will be tweaks within the rig, patterns, and casting approach.

I first learned to euro nymph with larger/heavier nymph patterns. I would cast upstream, allow the nymph to settle, and begin dragging it along stream bottom. While at times this is a successful approach in fast and turbulent water where trout have little time to react, I was still dragging my nymph. Dragging any pattern on the surface or below is still an unnatural presentation. I was finding my success rate dropping while attempting to drag heavy patterns in slower and clearer water conditions where trout become more selective or have a better view of your presentation. Later I learned the finer points of using a light euro setup (i.e., light line and leader) to drift lighter-weight nymphs. You are not pulling or leading the nymphs during the presentation. Instead, the nymphs drift naturally in the current while you use the rod tip and/or line hand to manage slack as the rig drifts. The result is the nymph drifting naturally with the currents rather than being pulled. This drift often means strikes are sometime seen (e.g., seeing the sighter twitch or pause) rather than being felt. Think about drifting your nymphs like drifting a dry fly—do you usually feel the strike when presenting a dry fly? The answer is likely no. The ability to drift light nymphs is the highest form of nymphing presentations. It truly is a natural drift. Learning how to detect strikes while drifting ultra-light euro rig will produce excellent results.

In this chapter I am first going to discuss a basic approach that I teach that breaks down the cast and presentation into simple steps. This simple system is what I've used for teaching countless anglers over the years to develop good presentation skills. After discussing the core concepts behind this simple four-part approach, I am going to cover certain points in more detail.

You can use any rod for euro nymphing tactics, but using a longer and limper rod allows you to keep more line off the water, while the softer tip allows for less-stressful casting on your hand while casting "thinned-out" leaders and light flies. Pictured is one of my favorite nymphing rods that allow for casting longer leaders and lighter nymph rigs with ease.

Here's the ideal presentation: This picture shows the mono rig traveling to the target, so some slack is occurring. Then the nymph lands and anchors near stream bottom while the mono rig tightens before I begin controlling the drift. This presentation gives me control from the very moment the flies land. If you're finding yourself catching fish only near the end of the drift, there's a good chance you have slack within the system during the first half of the euro nymphing presentation.
PHOTO BY JUSTIN IDE

Euro nymphing involves close-range casting. Sometimes maintaining a lower profile allows you to get closer to the fish—closer meaning better line control and greater casting accuracy. Pictured is a US Youth Fly Fishing Team member working a small Pennsylvania spring creek.

A Simple System

Breaking the casting and presentation movements into four separate movements forces you to slow down and focus on each individual movement to achieve accuracy and control from the beginning of the presentation to the end.

First, slow down your casting approach when learning to euro nymph. I think one of the biggest causes for poor casting is when recreational anglers watch top-level competitive anglers euro nymphing with speed. Not all competitive anglers are good casters. However, if you observe the best competitive anglers, you'll notice they possess the ability to make fast/rapid presentations in a controlled manner.

This combination of speed and control just doesn't happen overnight. It takes time to develop. I see so many

euro nymphers today casting and fishing way too fast. While they look impressive with the speed they cast and deliver the fly, their presentation is far from impressive. Meaning, the accuracy is off and excessive slack is placed within the leader due to a lack of control. This reminds me of a quote from legendary basketball coach John Wooden, who said, "be quick but don't hurry!" Develop good casting technique first and then work on increasing your speed. This may seem a bit robotic and unnatural, but it works, especially for those who feel anglers rushing the cast. Eventually, you can work on speeding up the process to allow more casts in a shorter period, but only once you've developed the foundations of a good nymphing cast.

SQUARE UP TO TARGET

Casting, similar to many other sports that involve throwing, requires that you align your body in the same direction as your target. Squaring your shoulder and pointing your toes in the direction you would like to cast helps you present the fly in a fluid movement. There are always exceptions, but squaring up in this manner allows for smoother, more controlled casting movement toward the target.

Using a water-tensioned cast (as mentioned below) is a good starting point as it forces you to slow down and allows time to complete each step without hurry. Then you can switch to a traditional nymphing cast (i.e., keeping the rig in flight during the presentation cast). Hurrying up the cast is the number-one cause of tangles with nymphing rigs.

Once squared to the target, extend your hand outward toward the target as if you're throwing darts. The rod hand wrist (either with finger or thumb on top) is cocked back so the rod tip is angled straight behind. We're going to start off using a tensioned cast, where the flies are positioned downstream of the angler and placed under tension by the water surface. The rod tip is cocked backward but remains high so the nymphing rig hangs at the surface. If the rig is positioned too deep below the surface, the cast will likely fail due to the energy required to break the surface tension. Make sure the rig is positioned at or near the surface before making the forward casting stroke.

THE CAST

Now it's time to make the forward casting stroke with the hand extended toward the target and wrist cocked backward. The forward cast is nothing more than a short but accelerated flip of the wrist.

Success with euro tactics involves accurately presenting the fly while maintaining contact with the nymphs. Let me stress the concept of maintaining contact with the nymphs! When nymphing with suspension tactics, the nymph rig drops toward stream bottom while the suspender pulls the rig downstream. In other words, the suspender controls the drift. You can recover from the aftermath of a poor cast while suspension fishing (e.g., excessive slack placed in leader and tippet) as the nymph eventually tightens up to the suspender and corrects itself. However, with euro tactics, the same concept of self-correction doesn't occur as easily. In other words, if a bad cast is made while euro nymphing, it's difficult

Control is gained quicker when your nymphs enter the water with momentum. Increasing the speed of the fly entry by using a double haul helps create a tighter connection earlier in the presentation. Brian Wilt shows a control presentation after rocketing his nymphs into the water.

or sometimes too late within the drift to regain control. On average, euro drifts are shorter than suspension drifts, so control needs to occur at the very beginning of the presentation. Therefore, excellent casting skills are essential for maintaining contact and control with nymphs while euro nymphing

An ideal European-nymphing drift is when sighter is lifted off the water and under control at the very beginning of the presentation. I like to call a good euro cast "sticking the landing." Think about an Olympic gymnast's perfect dismount as they stick their legs onto the matt, with little movement and an upright position. This is exactly what I'm looking to do with a euro cast. Yes, there are times when the sighter needs to be placed on water's surface, but often the sighter should be held off water. One advantage euro nymphing has over suspension tactics is the rapid sink rate, which is largely due to less surface drag. Having only the thin tippet section meeting water surface reduces drag, allowing the nymphs to quickly drop. Placing 0X–3X sighter on the water (compared to 5X–7X tippet) increases surface drag and slows down the sink rate of your rig. It may not appear to be a big difference, but I can assure you it is, especially when fishing light nymphing rigs common with euro tactics. Additional drag sets in anytime sighter is placed on water. I know I've made countless bad casts where I placed sighter on water's surface, then had to lift sighter off water. I could immediately see my drift slow down the moment the sighter lifted off the water.

Lastly, a sighter held off the water is easier to see than one that is lying on the water. Accidentally laying sighter on the water may delay both strike detection and line control.

The best casting advice I can give to help in keeping sighter off water is to simply look above your target. The rod tip usually travels in the direction your eyes look. For example, if you look down at the water, you'll likely aim your rod tip downward during the cast, placing leader and sighter on the surface, along with placing unnecessary slack in the system. Accidentally placing sighter on water often results in a quick reaction to rip the rod tip upward to lift leader and sighter off water. This quick upward reaction to correct the cast will likely pull the descending nymphs back up toward water surface, delaying the time the nymphs drift in the strike zone.

After years of on-stream instruction, I can accurately forecast if an angler is going to dump both rod tip and sighter on the water by looking at their head and body position. If you find yourself hunched over and looking downward at the water, it's likely you're going to make a

This brown was taken during a cold snap, which creates lethargic feeding from the local trout population. Using a euro rig keeps my flies near stream bottom while floating from a raft. PHOTO BY BRIAN WILT

If you lean or drop your shoulders downward during the nymphing cast, you'll place excessive slack into the presentation. This may be an ideal scenario for some dry fly applications, but it kills strike detection while euro nymphing.

bad euro presentation. Instead, think about good body posture your mom would be proud of, with your back straight and your head looking outward. It's amazing how much better a nymphing cast turns out when you start with good posture. Again, the ideal presentation is when the leader/sighter is laid out straight while being held off the water.

Another advantage of a good nymphing cast is it allows you to fish the nymphs on the fall. By fall, I mean having strike detection as the nymphs drop toward stream bottom. I never realized how many strikes I missed on the fall until I began "sticking the landing" with my presentation. Trout gorge themselves during peak insect activity on my home waters, frantically moving up and down, inhaling drifting insects. Countless times I've seen trout lift several feet off stream bottom to take a newly presented nymph. These sudden or impulsive takes are missed if there's a lack of control within the presentation. However, strikes are registered if you stick the landing, especially during hatches and when fishing feeding lanes like shallow runs or pocket water.

One last point about sticking the landing is having the leader, sighter, and tippet lay out with little slack. One common mistake I've seen myself and others do is rotating the hips side to side during the cast. The beauty of euro rods is how little energy is needed to cast. Unless you have a physical injury, where you can't rely on your wrist/forearm to cast, then you may want to rock your hips back and forth to aid in casting.

As mentioned above, sticking the landing involves the nymph anchored in the depths while the sighter and leader are lifted off the water. This tight connection occurs when the nymphing rig is anchored in slower speed currents. The sooner the rig breaks the water's surface tension and becomes anchored, the quicker you're in contact and control with your nymphing rigs.

Heavy rigs can be lobbed into the water and anchor fast due to the weight within the rig. The oval cast is a great option for heavy flies to reduce kickback as the flies straighten out behind while catapulting the rig high over the rod tip on the forward casting stroke. However, I feel the oval cast is not as good of a casting option when casting lighter rigs. Heavy rigs can penetrate the surface current faster than light rigs, creating a faster anchor and connection.

If a light nymphing rig is casually lobbed in the air and gradually falls toward surface currents, a delay will occur before the nymph anchors in the slower

Former US Youth Team member Mike Komara shows excellent casting technique as he is squared to the target with hand extended outward while making the cast. When it comes to casting euro rods/rigs, I feel less movement is better.

When casting light euro rigs on a modern nymphing rod, you need every ounce of energy you can garner. While I don't apply this idea to other fly-casting tactics, having the reel pointed at the target helps the light tip turn over lighter rigs. This isn't necessary if you're casting excessive weight, but it does help when casting ultra-light euro rigs.

Try to keep the elbow bent during the cast. This keeps the casting stroke short and moving in a straight line, causing an increase in power. This short stroke is a subject my mentor Joe Humphreys always stresses with me. For years I thought I had a short casting stroke until I watched video of myself casting. It's only been within a few years where I feel Joe would be proud of my casting stroke.

currents to provide the angler with a controlled drift. One way to speed up the process is to speed up the cast to shorten the time it takes to create a controlled drift. Speed increases when you travel through a straight line rather than moving through an arc, which is why I feel a short, powerful casting stroke is the key to shooting your nymphs into the water column.

This is not a new concept, as my mentor Joe Humphreys talked about the short stroke for years. One of the biggest impressions Joe made on me was how he was able to shoot his nymphs into the water like he was sending heat-seeking missiles into the stream and gain immediate control. It took years, but eventually I began shortening up my casting stroke and started seeing better presentation results. Before I was using too long and too wide of a casting stroke, moving the rod tip into a wide arc during the cast. The wider casting arc slowed the rod tip path and resulted in the rig traveling with less momentum before entry. I thought I was achieving more by moving my rod hand in a longer and wider stroke, but this resulted in a slower rod tip path, slowing down my presentation cast.

One of the best tips I can give you is to keep the elbow bent and use nothing more than a short, powerful snap of the wrist. If your hand straightens out on the cast, the rod tip moves through a wide arc and slows the path of the nymphs. Instead of straightening out your hand as if you're throwing a ball, think about making a short, powerful boxing jab. Keep the elbow close to the body while the casting hand moves in a short but straight movement that creates speed and energy. You create more power with a short and straight stroke than you do with a long and wide stroke. Remember to move the rod tip straight back and straight forward during this casting stroke. Any oval or curved movement will slow down the nymphing rig.

One more tip to increase speed is using a single or double haul with your nymphing cast. Speed is increased by using the line hand to pull on the line/leader on either forecast or backcast. Using a short casting stroke with the rod hand, the additional haul with the line hand will create the ultimate nymph cast, rocketing your nymphing rig deep into the depths. Again, I cannot emphasize short and fast movements enough. When done correctly, you'll look like you have short, stubby T-Rex dinosaur hands when making the cast.

My last tip to increase casting speed is false casting multiple times before making the delivery cast. The water-tension cast where you drag the flies in the water behind you and flip the cast forward works with medium to heavier rigs but not as much with light rigs. It takes a little more time to create momentum and speed with lighter rigs, so we need to false-cast several times before presenting the fly. Think of casting as nothing more than redirecting energy. In order to get this light fly moving fast, bounce it back and forth multiple times, increasing the speed and energy on each acceleration. And we do this with a short and powerful back-and-forth casting motion, waiting until we feel the rig straighten out and pull on the rod tip. I like the simplicity of the water-tension cast, but I find it difficult to use this cast with light rigs, so false casting has helped create enough speed and momentum for my rigs to shoot through the water column.

CONTROL THE DRIFT

It's time to control the drift. The goal is to limit slack between rod tip and nymph without dragging the

A good but simple casting tip with this tactic is to keep your back straight, hand extended toward the target, and your eyes looking outward, not downward. If you look down, you'll likely cast downward, placing leader and sighter on the water. The goal is usually having the sighter off the water, in view, and under control the moment the flies land. PHOTO BY AMIDEA DANIEL

presentation. The euro nymph drift is short. It is essentially the same length the rod tip can travel from the beginning of the presentation to the end. The drift is over when the rod tip can no longer travel downstream.

In the past I would lead and elevate the rod tip to manage slack as the current drifts the rig downstream. However, leading with the rod tip creates unnecessary tension that can pull the flies upward. Today, I rely mostly on the line hand to take in line with little rod tip movement. Using the line hand allows the rod tip to remain closer to water surface, reducing tension and allowing the nymphs to drop fast. I've found this tactic to be key when fishing light nymphing rigs in faster runs. The only way light rigs will drop to stream bottom is by reducing all possible tension. Of course the thin tippet attached to the fly creates a small degree of tension, but any additional tension (e.g., leading too fast with rod tip) delays sink rate.

Basically, you're pointing the rod tip directly at the flies during the drift. Keeping the rod tip pointed as level as possible, the line hand is stripping in line or performing a hand and twist. I prefer stripping with faster currents and hand and twist with slower speed currents. Sometimes I may start with a few long strips at first and then go into a hand and twist as the drift slows down. The goal is using the line hand to retrieve

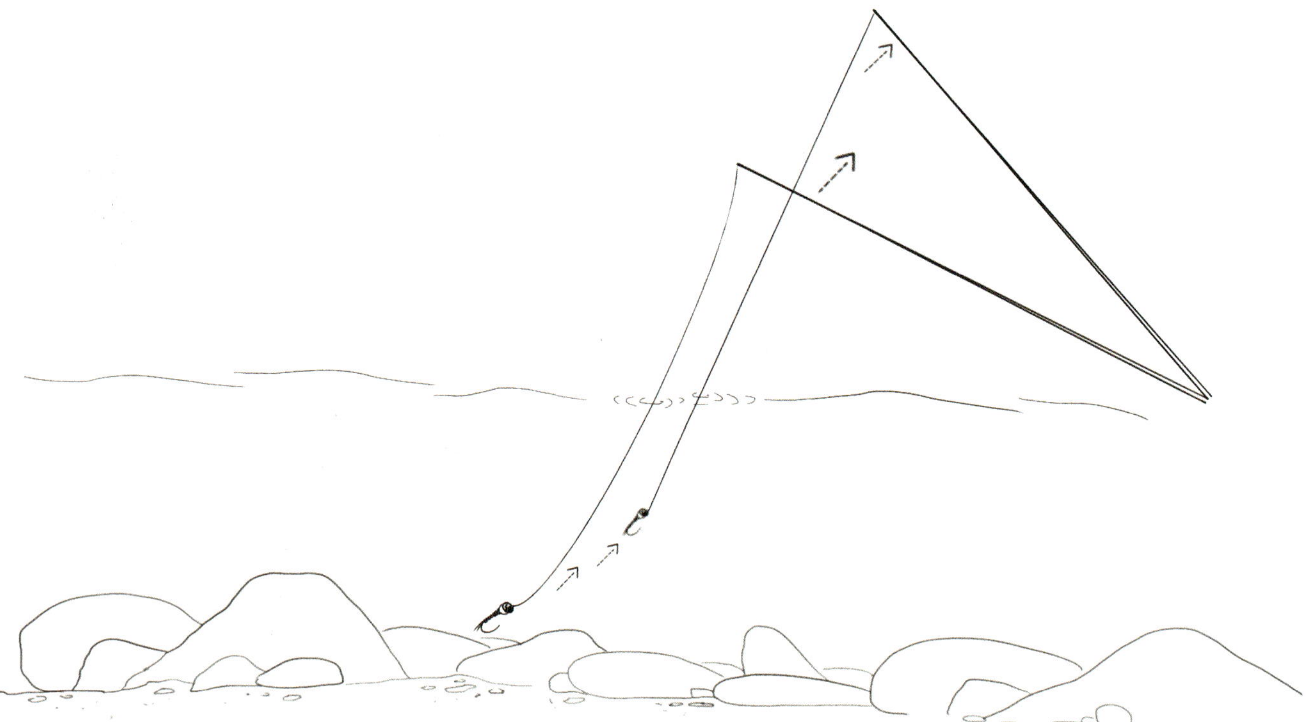

Lifting the rod tip high during the drift may create unnecessary drag, lifting your flies off stream bottom. Sometimes this induced drag is a good thing. For example, this upward tension can imitate emerging insects. However, it may kill any natural drift if you're attempting to drift your rig closer to stream bottom.

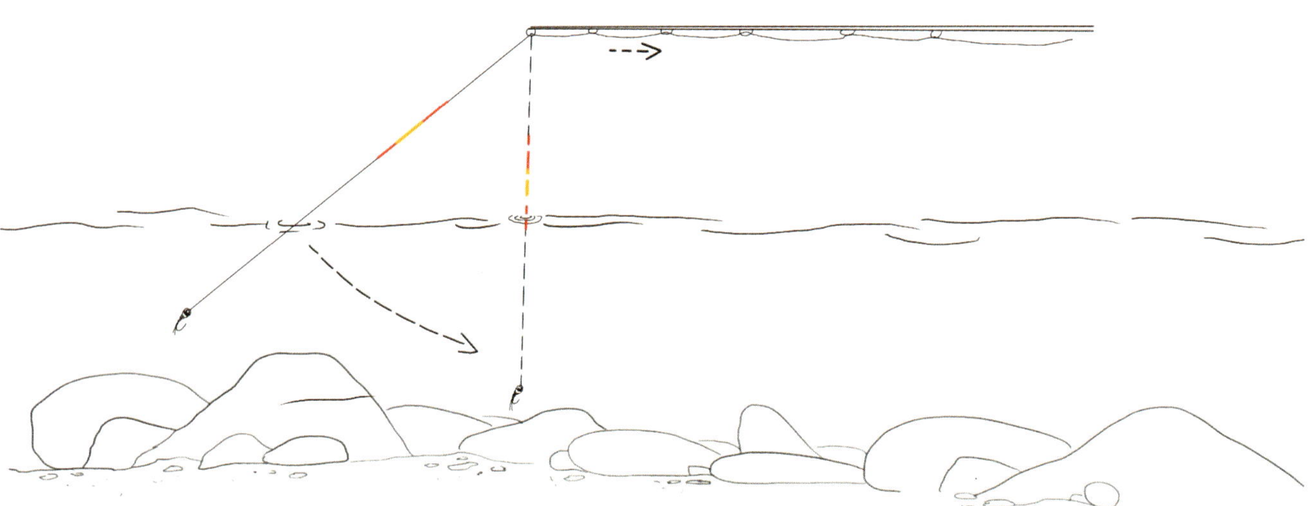

This diagram shows the ideal natural drift, where the rod tip remains pointing directly upstream toward the nymph, while the slack line is managed with line hand with a hand-and-twist retrieve or strip during the drift. And once the flies go vertical and are directly under the rod tip, the angler can keep the flies hanging directly under the rod tip for as long as possible.

the line at the same speed as the current. The rod tip may need to move downstream to control the drift if currents are swift. However, relying more on the line hand to retrieve slack (compared to rod tip) will allow a rapid descent.

The end goal is allowing the rapid descent until you see the sighter sweep to a vertical position (i.e., straight down under the rod top). Once the sighter dives to this vertical position, then the rod tip can move downstream as the sighter hangs directly under the rod tip. Hanging the sighter provides the most natural drift as the nymphs drift freely within the current. Also, strike detection is easily seen or felt as any strike will result in the sighter getting yanked directly toward the water's surface. This vertical position is only possible at short range and length is based on rod and reach length. Going vertical offers advantages with hook sets and fishing in windy conditions, which I'll discuss later.

Going vertical is important when trout are glued to stream bottom, as is often the case with this Pennsylvania limestone stream. Mike Pascareli prepares to go vertical as he points the rod tip toward the nymphing rig while stripping in line. Soon his rig will go vertical, where he can continue to hang the flies under the rod tip to achieve a natural drift.

SWING OUT, AND REPEAT

Now it's time to swing out the presentation. Swinging out your presentation performs at least two functions. First, a swung presentation speeds up and lifts the nymph toward the stream surface. Second, it positions the nymphing rig directly downstream of you, setting you up to repeat the process. Notice that your shoulders (sometimes your feet) are moving downstream following the fly during this swinging motion. Rotating your feet and shoulders allows for a controlled swinging movement. At the end of the presentation, you will have to reposition your feet and shoulders upstream before making another cast.

Eventually the rod tip and rod hand can travel no farther, resulting in the end of the drift. Now is the time to swing out your rig. I try not to swing out with suspension rigs as the larger bobber may create too much commotion on the water and spook fish. Also, I feel you can swing your patterns too fast (just like you can strip a streamer too fast) with added surface tension of the bobber skating on the water surface. As a result, I only swing out when euro nymphing.

Swinging out your rigs achieves at least two things. First, it positions the rig downstream, creating tension and setting you up for the forward casting stroke. Second, the swing lifts the fly vertically toward the surface and often creates a reactionary bite. The swing can imitate emerging insects, and I feel the swing is a huge part of my angling success during peak hatch periods. In fact, I would say approximately half my catch rate during a heavy hatch occurs on the swing.

However, I've been surprised to see how well the swing works during non-hatch periods, especially during the coldest winter months. Perhaps swinging out your flies represents a possible food item avoiding possible capture by exiting the water through the surface? Whatever the reason is, it works great during all times of the year.

While wet fly tactics are still effective, I tend to use a hybrid euro/wet fly tactic where I drift a nymph closer to the stream bottom and swing out my presentation with emerger of soft hackle patterns on droppers. I feel this allows me to effectively cover two feeding levels and likely double my chances of catching fish. Basically, you're casting upstream as you would with a euro approach but may have one or two emerger/soft hackle patterns tied on droppers above the point fly. Casting upstream allows the nymph to settle deep before

Control is everything with euro nymphing. If you feel as if you have no control/connection with your flies, just slow down your cast. Logan Daniel works a western river while euro nymphing at age 8.

Casting and fishing with euro tactics isn't difficult. In fact, I think it may be the easiest way for people to catch fish, especially for beginners with no prior experience. However, if you've fly-fished your entire life and are attempting to try euro nymphing, you're going to have to reprogram the way you cast. Logan Daniel is pictured showing off the results of good casting and line-control tactics.

Most nymphing casts require very little energy. Overpowering the cast is a common mistake I made while learning to cast and fish modern nymphing rods. These rods are designed to cast with little effort on your part. The finger on top is a favorite grip of mine, and I use it when casting short distances as I feel it gives me more accuracy and control during the cast.

drifting back downstream. Tension occurs at the end of the presentation to swing both nymph and emerger toward the surface. There are two types of swing that I use, which I will cover in more detail below.

Do not try casting while attempting to reposition your shoulders and feet back upstream. This erratic change of direction causes the rod tip to move in a sideways arc, increasing the chance of catching nearby vegetation and tangles. Let the fly swing out directly below and keep the fly anchored on water surface below you as you begin to square back up and position your rod hand to make the next cast.

Some Finer Points

Now I want to cover some finer points about casting, body position, line control, and reading drift as it relates to euro nymphing. I believe there are no secrets to successful fly fishing. Instead, I believe in the accumulation of executing the smallest of details. In over 25 years of teaching nymphing, I believe these are some of the most important details to master.

LOCK AND LEAD

Shoulder strain is common when euro nymphing, but it shouldn't be. There are situations where you need to fully extend your rod hand to lift over nagging currents. However, most shoulder strain is the result of the angler using their arm/shoulder to control the drift instead of using their largest muscles (i.e., hip and shoulders). In other words, use your hips and legs to control the drift rather than rotating just your shoulders. Before making the cast, extend your hand toward the target and position both elbow and hand in a comfortable position—one that you can hold for an extended period. Now lock that position. Once locked, use the short wrist movement to make the cast while keeping elbow and hand position locked. Begin to rotate the hips and rod tip downstream as soon as the cast made to control the drift as the currents move the rig downstream. Placing the heavy workload of controlling the drift on the hips reduces shoulder and upper-body strain. There are situations when you must extend your hand during the drift, but only do so when using the hips is not an option.

Not only does the lock and lead reduce shoulder strain, but it provides a smooth and controlled rod tip movement during the nymphal drift. A fatigued shoulder will shake while controlling the drift, and by extension the sighter will shake during the presentation. The goal is to have the sighter under total control (i.e., tight with no wobble) so any hesitation will be registered as a possible trout take. The point I'm attempting to make is to experiment with both body and hand positions that feel comfortable while casting and controlling the drift. Remember to hold those same positions while fishing and casting, which will lead to less fatigue, better line control, and greater enjoyment on the water.

I cannot stress the importance of the elbow position during the presentation. I've seen excessive drag and slack occur due to the elbow either pulling back or drifting forward after the cast is made. This is not to say the elbow can't move, but you need to move it in a direction and speed that complements the drift. For example, I've seen countless anglers making a nymphing cast with fully extended hands and suddenly pull back their elbow (and by extension the rod tip) to get into a comfortable position to control the drift. The elbow pulling back actually dragged the nymphs across several currents closer to the angler. Then I've seen the opposite scenario with hands close to the body during the cast, then the angler straightens out the hand/elbow for better reach. Unfortunately, the reach movement toward the fly is too fast, so slack accumulates. You get the point, but the concept here is recognizing whether moving the elbow position is helping or hurting the drift. This is why I like the "lock and lead" concept where the elbow is already in position to control the drift before the cast is made.

GOING VERTICAL

Going vertical uses a lower rod tip angle and helps with better hook sets and greater control during windy conditions. By better hook sets, I'm referring to the fact that both rod tip and hand position are lower during the drift,

Going vertical only applies when you're physically close enough to go vertical. Longer-distance presentation won't allow you to go vertical unless you have a 20-foot euro rod. Photo is Cory Cuje demonstrating excellent technique with a longer-range euro drift—a lower rod tip position—while relying on his line hand to manage slack.

Take time to become familiar with a comfortable elbow and hand position you can employ while controlling the drift. Find a position you can hold for a long time without getting fatigued or developing injury. Pictured is the author comfortably controlling the flies while euro nymphing Utah's Green River. PHOTO BY KEVIN LANDREN

which allows both to move a greater distance when setting the hook. Poor hook sets occur when the rod hand and rod tip are fully extended (i.e., can't move any more in any direction). This often occurs when the line control is done with mostly rod tip—elevating the rod during the drift to manage slack. How many times has a trout taken your fly at the end of the drift when the rod tip and rod hand were fully extended? For me, too many times, and I know I've missed numerous fish or had a weak hook set as the result of this rod tip and rod hand position.

A lower rod tip position also helps with reducing the effect wind has on the euro rig. A higher rod tip creates a bigger sail within for wind to blow upon the line/leader. By keeping a lower rod tip and relying more on line hand to manage slack, there's less line for the wind to blow upon. I would say this is my number-one tip when others ask how I euro nymph in windy conditions. This is also a great concept for when euro nymphing smaller streamers, where low-hanging limbs may prevent using a higher rod tip angle to control the drift. In fact, I often use a strip set when euro nymphing in small streams. When euro nymphing, you're setting the hook with sighter movement—compared to dry fly tactics where you see a trout take the surface pattern. For me, this means countless more hook sets while euro nymphing small streams than with dry fly. The fly or nymphing rig is likely going to exit the water when using the rod tip to set the hook. This is not an issue on most waters where there's plenty of room for the rig to unroll behind the anglers. However, less space is available on smaller streams, and the chance of hanging your fly increases anytime you're using the rod tip to set the hook. This

Although I prefer using a hand-twist retrieve for constant control, you can use the line hand to strip in and manage slack during the drift. I typically use the strip when dealing with faster currents, resulting in the need for faster slack line management.
PHOTO BY JUST IDE

is the reason I've been relying more on strip sets when euro nymphing smaller streams or any location where low-hanging obstacles are present.

CONTROLLING THE DRIFT VERSUS LEADING THE FLIES

Within the last two years, I've revamped my fly-fishing vocabulary to better communicate concepts with clients and students. For years I used the term "leading" the nymphs with the rod tip. The issue is we don't always want to lead the nymphs with the rod tip due to the tension created between rod tip and nymph. Increased tension decreases sink rate and likely drags your nymphs unnaturally within the currents.

Rod tip angles play an important role in determining how much tension is placed on the rig. For example, tension occurs when the rod tip is held a steep angle away from the rig. This is why I think the term "high sticking" is misleading. The concept with euro nymphing is to keep as much line and leader off the water as possible, which can be done without always having to hold the rod tip too high. Experiment with hand and rod tip angles to see the minimal angle you need to hold the rod to keep line and leader off the water. The rod tip can almost be held level with shorter presentation but requires a higher angle when more line and leader is placed outside the rod tip.

Another common issue is positioning the rod tip too far ahead of the nymphs during the drift. Tension occurs when the distance between nymph and rod tip increases. Just staying ahead of the drift to maintain control is one thing, but leading too far ahead of the rig is no different than dragging a dry fly. Focus on keeping the distance between rod tip and nymph as short as you can, while relying on your line hand to control most of the drift.

One thing you can do to get a sense of how tension affects drift and sink rate is to practice with tracer nymphs. Using bright-colored patterns like eggs, mops, and worm patterns allows you to see how rod tip angle affects how fast the nymphs drop to stream bottom. Too much tension, and you'll notice a terribly slow sink rate while the nymph remains higher in the water column. If you don't have any tension, then you'll notice a rapid descent. This is the best visual I know of to understand how rod tip movement affects sink rate and nymphal drift. Once I understood this concept, I began relying more on the line hand to manage slack while striving to fish the sighter vertically directly under the rod tip.

This shot was taken two years ago, before I fully committed to relying more on the line to manage slack while keeping a lower rod tip. There's no need to hold the rod tip this high. It puts more strain on my shoulder, gives me less leverage to set the hook, and creates a bigger surface for any wind effect. PHOTO BY CHRIS DANIEL

If you "lead" a euro rig with only little weight, you'll pull it from stream bottom and cause it to drag in the mid- to upper-water column. Amidea Daniel demonstrating what "leading" looks like—a high rod tip pulling the nymphs downstream.

SEEING THE STRIKE

You will both see and feel the strike while euro nymphing. It doesn't take long, but learning to recognize strikes takes some practice. I believe repetition is the best teacher for seeing, recognizing, and reacting to a strike. Position yourself in a fishing situation where you'll have the opportunity to experience countless strikes. For me, this has meant fishing local farm ponds and stillwaters full of panfish. Panfish are usually not shy and provide endless action.

What I like to do is practice euro/tightline tactics on panfish waters while using bright-colored nymphs, like mops and worm patterns. Not only do fluorescent oranges, yellows, and chartreuse patterns attract panfish, it usually means a strike occurs when the fly vanishes. Simply observe how the sighter behaves anytime the fly disappears, and you'll quickly learn to recognize what a take looks like. Sometimes the strikes are aggressive while other times they're soft. Practicing seeing the strike on panfish waters (or similar scenarios) provides the repetition needed to develop confidence in recognizing and quickly reacting to any strike.

When fishing heavy flies, you'll likely feel the strike versus seeing the strike. Heavy flies create additional tension within the leader as the heavy mass pulls harder downward toward stream bottom. When a fish takes the fly with this high degree of tension, you'll likely feel the strike. On the flip side, the lighter the nymph(s) used when nymphing, the less degree of tension created, which results in less sensation of feeling the strike. Don't get me wrong, modern nymphing rods and ultralight line/leader systems enhance your ability to feel the strike. However, a trout taking a lightly weighted

Having tags built into our sighter helps with visibility. Do whatever you need to do to increase your ability to see the strike.

Lightweight nymphs create little pull down (a.k.a. tension) during the drift. Very often you'll see the strike within the sighter due to the light tension rather than feeling the strike. PHOTO BY JUSTIN IDE

Softer-action euro rods enhance strike detection. You can actually see the sighter vibrate and hesitate better with modern nymphing rods. Today, you don't have to break the bank as there are so many great modern nymphing rods available at all price points.

Heavier flies like those shown here create greater pull on the tippet, increasing the tension within the line and leader. This results in you feeling the strike due to the tension within the system. Pictured are two favorites: the Chewy Caddis and SOS nymph with 5/32 tungsten beads. You'll likely feel the strike when fishing such heavy flies.

drifting nymph (rather than dragging) is more likely to be seen rather than felt. I feel this concept of drifting versus dredging is one of the most important concepts I've learned within the last couple years.

DEPTH CONTROL

As mentioned earlier, I've greatly reduced the weight within my rig during the presentation in order to drift rather than dredge. The feature I look for during the drift is for my sighter to twitch or vibrate during the presentation. What the twitch tells me is my nymphs are anchored in the slower current (near stream bottom) while the surface currents pick at the thin tippet like a guitar string. It's almost as if you're trying to play a musical note for the fish, but that vibration indicates the nymphs are likely positioned in the strike zone while the currents interact with the thin tippet section. It's likely I'm using too much weight or not enough weight if I see no signs of twitching, so adjust until you get that twitch. I also feel the vibration adds movement to the flies, similar to a drop-shot tactic where the shot bounces along stream bottom and sends vibrations up the leader.

Using tag ends on your sighter helps in seeing the twitch! When a strike occurs, you are just as likely to feel the strike as you are to see the strike, so set the hook anytime the twitching sighter stops or suddenly gets pulled downward. Remember, this twitch is when you're attempting to drift lighter rigs near stream bottom. You won't likely see the twitch occur when dredging heavy flies along stream bottom or when drifting a lighter-weight rig immediately below the surface.

The top of the run that Amidea Daniel is fishing is shallow, so the sighter is held a foot or so above the water's surface to keep the nymph from hanging on stream bottom. However, as the drift continues into the deeper water, Amidea will lower the rod tip with a slow and controlled forearm movement, dropping the flies a little deeper as they approach the deeper cut. Near the end of the drift, Amidea will lift the sighter off the water as the bowel shallows out. The beauty of euro nymphing with a sighter is it allows you to control the depth of the presentation—from start to finish.

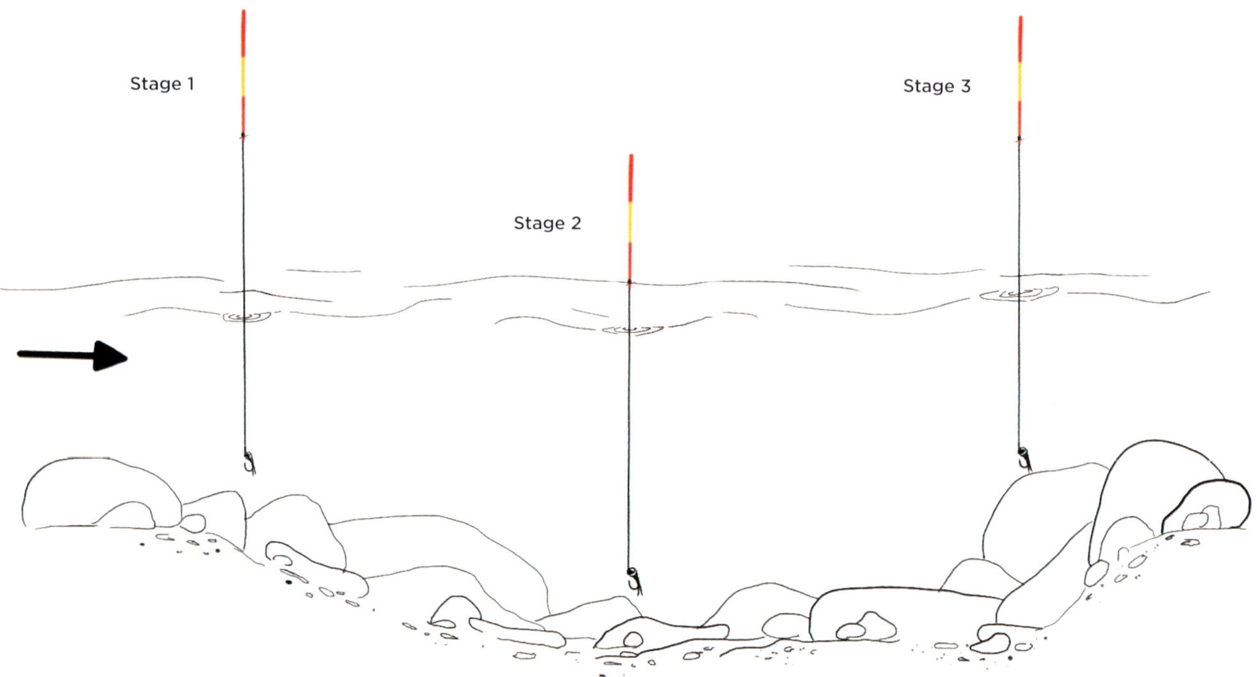

This illustration shows a cross-sectional view of a bowl depression within a stream. Notice how the beginning of the presentation starts in shallow water, then floats into deeper water, and finally shallows out at the very end. Euro tactics excel in these water types as the ability to control the depth of your presentation from start to finish is essential when fishing uneven stream bottoms as shown.

This section is as dynamic as nymphing water comes: slow, fast, shallow, and deep. This isn't difficult water to fish, but it does require a thoughtful approach. Pictured is the author fishing the Salmon River in Idaho.

Amidea Daniel places the sighter tip on the water's edge. Unless your sighter is ultra-thin (e.g., 4X or smaller), try to avoid putting it in contact with the surface currents. Placing larger-diameter sighters like 0X is going to cause excessive drag. It may not seem like a big deal, but it is. You may need to lengthen the tippet if you find yourself placing sighter on surface current. I'm not worried about the color of the sighter spooking fish. I'm concerned about the drag it creates.

To get to the proper depth, focus on the height of your sighter off the water. If you feel your flies aren't deep enough, then lower the sighter several inches for the next several drifts. If you're hanging up every cast, then lift the sighter several inches higher during the next several drifts. Often the difference between a good day and an OK day nymphing is correctly adjusting speed and depth. And what makes euro nymphing so exciting is your ability to correct the depth from start to finish.

Streams are dynamic systems and are constantly changing in speed and depth. Some stream sections run a uniform depth, so sighter height will remain constant throughout most stream reaches. However, some streams vary dramatically within a short distance. This means you must be aware of the stream's approximate depth before deciding how high or low to hold the sighter. This is another reason why I prefer to use a consistent tippet length so the hard drive between my ears doesn't have to constantly recalibrate. If you know your tippet length is always 4 feet long and your fishing 3 feet of water, then your sighter should be approximately (and I stress approximately) 12 inches off the water. The point is to use a system that allows you to make adjustments without overthinking it.

Usually all that is needed is adjusting the sighter height during the drift. If you feel your sighter is at the correct height during the drift but still not feeling connected (i.e., seeing a twitch or occasionally coming in contact with stream bottom), then a weight adjustment is needed. One size of bead can make a difference when it comes to naturally drifting your nymphs. You want just enough weight to stay anchored but light enough so the currents can move the nymphs down current. So, it's important to carry a small selection of confidence nymphs but tie them in a variety of sizes. Today there's a great variety of bead sizes so if you don't plan to use supplemental weight to achieve correct depth, make sure you tie your favorite patterns in three or four different bead sizes.

SWINGING

There are multiple ways of swinging out your pattern. I'm going to provide two basic swinging concepts: arching swing and parallel swing.

An arching swing is when the rod tip pulls the nymphs and emerger patterns across currents. This is a great way to fan out your presentation and cover a larger area of water. At the end of the presentation, the rod tip

Don't neglect swinging out your patterns after every drift. At certain times of the year, the swing accounts for many of my strikes.

During peak hatch season, the swing may account for half of my strikes. After swinging out, make sure to square back to the target before casting back upstream. Avoid casting and turning simultaneously.

begins pulling the flies toward the bank. It's important to swing out your pattern at a speed that creates a positive response from the fish.

One of the best lessons I learned from legendary angler Davy Wotton was slowing down the speed of the swing. Like so many others, I have the bad habit of hurrying the swing. This is no different than a streamer angler stripping their streamer pattern too fast, creating a presentation where the trout doesn't want to chase down the fly. Only experience and time on the water will give you a feel for the correct speed, but my suggestion is to begin with a slower swing and use the rod tip to move the flies across the current in a natural manner. Most insects gradually rise to the surface or swing toward the stream bank to emerge. Rarely do insects shoot up toward the surface or toward the stream bank at Mach 5 speed. Instead, they swim, drift, or wiggle their way up or across currents. As a result, we need to do a better job imitating this movement with a slower-speed movement by slowing down the rod tip movement during the swing.

You should also seek movement/liveliness with your swing, letting the emerger and soft hackle patterns dance within the current. Dragging your patterns across currents is not ideal. Instead, slowly control the swing with a slower rod tip and provide the occasional pause before continuing to lead the patterns across current. I'll tap the rod blank with my index finger to send vibrations down the leader and give the patterns even more movement during swing.

I was taught to swing patterns across the currents, not with the currents. Then 10 years ago a Connecticut fly-fishing guide named Antoine Bissieux traveled to Pennsylvania to take a lesson from me. I think I learned more from him during our two days together, and the greatest lesson was watching him swing out his patterns parallel to the flow of water. Instead of pulling the rod tip and flies toward the bank at the end of the presentation, Antoine would hold the rod tip over the seam he wanted to cover and allow tension to swing the patterns upward and parallel to the flow of water. Basically, he would control his nymphs during the drift and suddenly put the brakes on his presentation (i.e., stropping the rod) over the seam he wanted to swing out. He would first elevate his rod tip to tighten the rig and reduce any slack as he set up to swing. As soon as the sighter and flies swept under the rod tip and began drifting downstream, he would slowly lower his rod to reduce tension, allowing for a slower upward rising of the flies.

As he mentioned to me, emerging insects don't rocket to the surface. Instead, they slowly rise, so he would intentionally lower the rod tip during the parallel swing to slow down the speed of the upward-moving patterns.

Floating the Sighter

Although most euro nymphing discussions involve keeping the sighter off the water, there are situations when the sighter can placed on the water to be used as a suspension tool. By their physical makeup, sighters are thin and have little surface area, which results in little buoyancy. This means sighters should lack the ability to suspend medium to heavy rigs but can be used for drifting light rigs. Examples of light rigs could include a 3/32 brass bead pheasant tail nymph, 5/64 tungsten bead zebra midge, or a non-beaded wet ant. The idea of floating the sighter is drifting light rigs immediately below the surface or somewhere in the middle water column. I recommend using a buoyant dry fly or manufactured suspender if you need to go heavier or deeper.

Floating the sighter is also a good option when you need to make a quick tactical switch from a deep drift to a shallow one while using a euro nymphing system. Use fly floatant grease (e.g., Loon's Payette Paste) to help float the sighter. Packing fly floatant grease on the sighter's bunny ears (a.k.a. leaving long tippet tags) also helps float. I use a shorter tippet section below the greased sighter to maintain control during the drift. I find using tippet lengths longer than 3 feet difficult to control when floating the sighter. I prefer lengths of 24 to 36 inches. ■

Antoine Bissieux demonstrates the parallel swing on the Farmington River in Connecticut. Basically, he'll control the drift downstream until he can no longer control the drift with the rod tip. Then he "stomps on the brakes" to stop the rod tip immediately over the seam he wants to swing out. A short lift of the rod tip and/or stripping in slack line he places the flies under tension, causing the deep drifting to lift toward the surface.

This angler is setting up for a parallel swing. This is a great example of a section where you may want to keep your nymphs parallel to the seam you're nymphing. Basically, I'll use this approach when fishing very defined water or a likely seam. The longer I can keep the fly riding in that seam (drifting or swinging) the better.

The name of the game is keeping your fly within a trout's strike zone as long as possible. Amidea Daniel notices the deep cut on the opposite bank, so she keeps the rod tip extended outward and holds the tip over the cut during the swing. This is a good swing-out position for this water.

Pictured is Amidea Daniel swinging out in the same water but now pulling the rod tip toward the bank. Notice the shallow water Amidea is standing in—our day's fishing revealed that few fish were holding that shallow, especially during the height of the sun. While this swing out does set Amidea up for a forward cast, it pulls the flies into nonproductive trout water (at least it was for us this day). The better option would have been to keep the flies swinging parallel in the deeper water, not in the shallower water.

Unlike suspension tactics, there's less slack to tighten up while setting the hook. Nothing more than a short downstream (not downward) movement of the rod tip—moving parallel to the flow of water—is needed to connect. Cory Cuje uses a short snap of the wrist to set the hook while euro nymphing Pennsylvania's Spring Creek.

The author using a reverse bow-and-arrow cast to drop a large mop fly along the opposite bank. Fully extend the hand outward and pull the rod tip back with the nymph held under the rod. This not only allows the sighter to be off the water during the beginning of the presentation, but this upward trajectory allows you to shoot distance with your nymph into cover.

Bow-'n-Arrow

Eventually you'll encounter nymphing situations where no backcast is available. Roll casting is usually an option but difficult when fishing with an all-mono rig due to little to no mass to unroll. A modified bow-'n-arrow cast might be your best option when euro nymphing in tight brush. By modified I mean the angle the rod tip unloads. As mentioned before, one goal of a good euro nymphing cast is having the sighter off the water and in view from the start of the presentation. If you hold the nymphing rig above the fly rod as you load the rod back, the rod tip will shoot downward toward the water, laying leader and sighter both on the water. This may be excellent for dry fly tactics but not for euro nymphing, where you want to see the sighter lifted off the water. Instead, hold the rig underneath the rod during the pullback. When released, the nymph and sighter will have an upward trajectory, allowing you to begin the drift with sighter already lifted off the water. ■

Trout usually hook themselves whiling swinging out your presentation due to excessive drag being placed on the line and leader. If you do set the hook, try to do nothing more than lift the rod tip with a soft forearm lift. You're likely going to rip the fly out of a fish's mouth if you aggressively set the hook on the swing.

This resulted in a slow and controlled upward swing. I noticed he would do this in areas with distinct seams, like pocket water or well-defined current lie. The idea was keeping the rig drifting and swinging in the primary water. There was no need to swing across current and cover water as he knew exactly where the fish were. This simple logic of keeping the patterns closer to feeding fish is one reason this tactic works well when you know or suspect where trout are located.

SETTING THE HOOK

You can look at euro nymphing in at least two ways: drifting with little tension and swinging under greater tension. Basically, a shorter and more powerful movement is needed when the flies are freely drifting. As my friend Mark Antolosky says, "move the fly 1 inch fast." Understand that many of today's euro-style nymphing rods possess a soft/flimsy tip so the rod tip needs to move a greater distance to move the fly "1 inch fast." I try to use more of a level downstream hook set (not downward) with the forearm rather than the wrist. The idea is to keep the flies below water's surface and simply slide them fast downstream without breaking the water's surface. It may be a good idea to use bright tracer patterns to see how far and fast the flies travel when setting the hook. This visual will be helpful in letting you know how much power is needed to set the hook during the drift.

Creating a forceful set is important when drifting nymphs. However, less power is needed when setting during a swung presentation since the rig is already under a high degree of tension. Often just a short lift of the forearm is all that is needed to set the hook on a swung presentation. I tend to overpower my swung hook sets due to the aggressive takes, but I have gotten better over the years. Another important concept is never pointing directly at the fly during the swing. The rod tip should be used as a shock absorber, to cushion aggressive strikes, so create an angle (45 to 90 degrees) between rod tip and fly. Much of the force is taken up by the flex of the rod, which is essential when euro nymphing with ultra-fine tippet. Usually, the trout hook themselves. So just remember to use less energy on a swung presentation and you'll find yourself with more landed fish, rather than short strikes.

PART II

Dry Fly

The art of dry fly fishing is truly an art of stalking. The best dry fly fishers stalk the surface like a special-force sniper stalks their prey. A dry fly fisher studies the currents between them and their prey just like reading the green of a golf course. Fishing dry flies may be the most challenging tactic. Trout suspended or moving higher in the water column are on high alert, and your presentation must be spot-on. Drag or any unnatural movement often goes without a take and your casts must be accurate and not line the fish.

Because the angler is casting an unweighted fly (unlike many nymphs and streamers), a weighted fly line taper and tapered leader are used to present the fly. And this often means that line and leader are placed on the water. Unlike with nymphing when a cast is made and the angler can pick line and leader off the water, most often the dry fly angler needs to let the line and leader lay on the water from start to finish. This means there's little chance to mend or reposition the line after the cast. So much more thought goes into studying the currents between the angler and the fish to ensure line and leader are positioned in a manner to achieve the best possible drift. For me this means less casting and more time thinking about my presentation cast. Dry fly casting is like the carpenter's rule "measure twice and cut once."

Make your first cast count. Spend a few additional moments reading the currents and dialing in your rig before presenting a dry fly to selective surface feeders. Over the years I've learned the best dry fly fishers are usually some of the most patient anglers I've met. You can't rush your dry fly presentation like you can a nymphing cast. Surface feeding trout are far from forgiving. Pictured is an angler choosing a dry fly while fishing the Owens River in California.

CHAPTER 6

Dry Fly Tools

I may only spend 20 percent of my streamside time fishing dry flies, so I take that into account when I carry gear. This means I may carry few dry flies in comparison to the number of nymphs and streamers I carry. Also, in seasons like late fall and winter when dry fly opportunities on my home waters are scarce, I may opt not to carry any dry fly gear at all. What you see below is my short list of essential dry fly tools. If I spent more time fishing dry flies or lived closer to waters that offer greater dry fly opportunities (e.g., the Missouri River in Montana), my list might be expanded.

Rods

It's great if you enjoy collecting and fishing countless fishing rods. For years I always wanted a fly rod to handle every conceivable fly-fishing situation. Up until 3 years ago, I owned and fished more than 60 fly rods throughout the year. While this was enjoyable, I would say it wasn't efficient. The issue was in becoming reacquainted with each rod. Fishing a fly rod is like having a relationship with another human being: It takes time to learn how to work together.

Pictured is Amidea Daniel casting to a rising trout on the Yellowstone River with her favorite 10-foot 4-weight trout rod.
PHOTO BY CHRIS DANIEL

I've gone mostly to all 3- and 4-weight rods for most of my trout fishing. This creates some level of simplicity, and using fewer rods means I have a better feel for the few trout rods I use. Again, using the sniper analogy: Usually a sniper won't be switching back and forth between many rifles. Instead, they use few but develop a deep connection and understanding of how that gun performs under a wide range of conditions. They are dialed into the weapon's performance and know exactly how to adjust for any slight changes, such as shifting wind direction. They don't have to think too much about making adjustments—they simply react given the excessive experience they have with the weapon. Basically, the rifle becomes an extension of themselves.

I understand this is an extreme example, but I feel the same is true when using any tool, including fly rods. Every rod has its own action and performance, and it takes me time to get to know exactly how to get maximum performance out of my fly rods. This is why I now attempt to limit the number of trout rods I fish with. I know some anglers who can pick up any rod at any time and make it work great, but it takes time for me to learn how to get the maximum performance out of each rod.

Based on where I fish and my love affair with longer rods, my euro rod doubles as a short-range dry fly casting rod. Given the softer tip actions found on most euro rods, these rods are excellent for casting up to 30 feet but lack the power needed for casting longer distances and when casting into strong winds. When I need additional power, I'll use a 10-foot 4-weight with a medium action tip. If I need to use a shorter rod, I pick a shorter rod with a very similar taper so it has a similar performance as the longer rod. For example, a year ago I began switching over to all three and four rods for trout fishing, and a friend sent me a beautiful 7½-foot fiberglass 4-weight for small-stream fishing. The issue was the taper and therefore the rod action on this full flex fiberglass was drastically different than with my medium action tips. This difference in rod action always took some time to become familiar with, which developed into frustration when I failed to correctly present the fly during critical circumstances. Everyone is different but familiarity is an absolute must when dry fly casting accuracy is needed, so I stick to similar action fly rods for all my 3- and 4-weights.

The other advantage of the medium action rod (compared to a softer tip) is the ability to lift line off the water for the hook set. Of course, I've seen excellent dry fly fishers play big fish on light tippets with fast action fly rods, but I admit to having a heavy hand and find myself breaking off too many fish when using such rods. The medium action rods provide me with enough shock absorption, while fishing lighter tippets, but possess enough power

Softer action rods protect lighter tippets when playing big fish. Use as heavy a tippet as you can, but realize some situations demand lighter tippet, and having a rod with some cushion in the tip will help land quality fish on such tippets. Amidea Daniel proves that large trout can be landed on light tippets in a timely manner. PHOTO BY CHRIS DANIEL

Avoid aggressive/short tapered fly lines if you plan to mend, both in air and on the water. Although considered "old-school," I find double-tapered fly lines are excellent for repositioning line in air and on the water. In this photo I am attempting a long-reach cast while fishing downstream to a rising trout on the South Holston River in Tennessee.

to quickly lift 20 to 30 feet of fly off the water during the hook set. Again, find what works for you and your style.

Another reason I favor medium action dry fly rods is that I prefer fishing longer leaders. Often I'm casting more leader than actual fly line, so I need a rod that can load while casting minimum amounts of line outside the rod tip. Trying to cast longer leaders (with little line outside rod tip) with a fast action rod takes too much work.

Fly Lines

Call me old-school but I still prefer a double taper line when dry fly fishing. So much of dry fly casting involves control while casting and mending in the air. I feel a slight loss of control with accuracy and aerial mends with weight forward. Although lacking power, lines with rear taper (like double tapers) appear to have a more delicate turnover while offering the ability to reposition line in the air during the cast. I feel mending in the air with various aerial mends is one of the most important skills to have, but the right taper line is needed to aid in this strategy. In short, if you need to reposition a section of line in the air, you need mass. For example, if you are casting an aggressive weight-forward line with most of the mass built into the first 30 feet, it will be challenging to make a 45-foot-long cast and expect to reposition the last 15 feet of running line in the air. Although most manufacturers produce weight forward fly lines with a rear taper, I still find these lines lack control with both accuracy and mending. A smooth energy transfer within the fly line without any hinge effect is key to accuracy and aerial mends, and I have yet to cast any weight-forward line that offers the same control when presenting the dry fly.

As for color, I opt for one I can easily see on the surface for at least two reasons. First, I want the ability to use my peripheral vision to locate an area's excessive slack. For example, casting upstream to a rising trout, most focus is on the trout and the dry fly itself. As the currents bring fly, leader, and fly line back downstream, I desire a visible fly line color so I focus on the dry fly drift, but I'm able to use my peripheral vision to know when too much slack is accumulating. Slack allows a dry fly to drift naturally, but excessive slack will lead to a loss of control when attempting to set the hook when a trout takes the fly. Much of dry fly fishing involves casting line and leader on the water. While some anglers

My 94-year-old mentor, Joe Humphreys, lands a fish on a Pennsylvania limestone stream. Joe uses bright-colored fly lines so he can see what is going on, and you could say he doesn't have problems catching difficult trout.

claim a brighter-colored fly line may spook fish (in a few scenarios, I've seen this to be true), I would rather have a brighter-colored line allowing me to see when slack occurs and noticing any belly, which could indicate a current causing drag. In my opinion the line weight and how the angler places the line on the water has far more potential to spook fish than line color.

A slick shooting line is a must when casting for accuracy and slipping line while mending. A line that sticks and catches within the guides during the cast causes kickback, which leads to a loss of accuracy. Research what the best mode to clean your manufacturer's line is and make it a weekly habit. Smoothness within the cast and fly line leads to accurate casts.

Leaders

Leaders are an extension of your fly line. They are especially important when dry fly fishing where the leader needs the energy to deliver the fly to the target while allowing the angler to control where the leader lays on the water, allowing for the longest drift without drag. Whereas in nymphing corrections with line and leader placement can often be made after the cast, the dry fly angler has fewer opportunities to correct the presentation after line and leader fall on the water, and the initial cast needs to be done correctly from the start.

Compared to previous years when I was constantly experimenting with new leader designs, today I fish with only several tapers. For me, this simplification creates greater confidence in my presentation casts and allows me to carry less gear. There are so many excellent dry fly leader systems but my intent is to share with you the handful of dry fly leaders I constantly find myself using. There's always a time and place for experimentation, but when I'm fishing prime dry fly time, I fish with what I am familiar with and experiment in the off-season.

Pinpoint accuracy is a must when dry fly fishing technical trout water. A well-designed leader and good casting skills help improve your odds when dealing with finicky trout. Trout living in food-rich trout streams don't need to move far to eat, so the ability to place your cast exactly where you want it to go is essential. Choosing the right leader for the conditions helps.

THE LINE AND LEADER CONNECTION

Before discussing my favorite dry fly leader systems, I think it's best to highlight the importance of creating a strong connection between fly line and leader and avoiding any hinging effect. I believe the connection between fly line and leader ultimately makes or breaks the energy connection during the cast. Any hinge lessens the energy transfer from fly line to leader, so it's important

An angler presenting an accurate downstream cast to a rising trout. PHOTO BY CHRIS DANIEL

When building leader, you're not engineering rocket ships, but I suggest adding a heavy butt section to create a continuous taper from fly line to leader. I feel this continuous taper creates better energy transfer, making your dry fly presentations accurate and more efficient. If you're buying manufactured leaders, check to see how their butt section matches up with the fly line tip. Some manufacturers use a large-diameter butt section, so you may not need to add a butt section. I don't worry about taper with nymph and streamer tactics, but I swear by it when casting and presenting dry flies.

to maintain some form of continuous taper from line to leader. In simple terms, avoid any significant gap in diameter between line and leader. Whether you use a nail knot connection or a loop-to-loop connection may dictate using a different diameter of leader butt section.

With the current cost of fly lines and the rate at which I change leaders, my preference is to keep the fly line loop. The larger-diameter loop does help the floating line tip float better due to its larger surface area. For years I was advised to cut the fly line loop off for two reasons: First, the loop would eventually come apart, and second, the loop caused a hinge between line and leader. This was true then but not now as fly line loop technology has advanced, and rarely has one of my loops come undone.

And as for the hinge effect, that was also true but only so due to the diameter of the leader butt material I was using. I grew up in central Pennsylvania and for years used the original George Harvey leader formula, which called for a .017 butt section, which I feel is on the thin side. This thin .017 butt section, when using a loop-to-loop connection, creates a hinge. The solution was to cut off the loop and attach the thin .017 butt section directly to a thinner fly line tip, which created a sturdier connection and better transfer of energy from line to leader. This also works, but I found my fly line tip would sink more often and that made it challenging to frequently switch leaders.

If you decide to keep the fly line loop and use a loop-to-loop connection, start off with a larger-diameter butt section material. For example, I use Orvis 60-pound (.025) mono for most of my dry fly leader butt sections. I feel the larger diameter creates a better hold between the line and leader, reducing any hinging and allowing for a smooth transfer of energy and increased accuracy. If you're just starting out in fly fishing, you may not even notice this slight disconnect. If you're a seasoned fly fisher, then I feel you will notice greater leader turnover and greater accuracy by using a heavier butt section connection between line and leader, when deciding to use a loop-to-loop connection. Some leaders (e.g., Scientific Anglers 14-foot 5X Absolute Trout) already have a heavy butt section so no additional butt material is needed to reduce the hinging effect. Again, the key is to reduce the diameter gap between line and leader loop. Sometimes a thicker butt section is needed—sometimes you won't need to add anything—but maintaining a gradual taper between line and leader will increase both energy transfer and accuracy during the cast.

FAVORITE LEADERS AND TIPPET

During my 36 years of fly fishing, I've changed my opinion on using only hand-tied leaders for dry fly tactics. While growing up, options were limited and performance of the typical manufactured leader was average, so I did what most anglers did, I tied my own leaders to match conditions. My preference has changed within the last 5 years for several reasons. First, I find it easier to carry a small variety of manufactured leaders instead of carrying spools of various diameters of monofilament. Secondly, the variety and performance of specialty leaders on the market today is incredible. Leaders ranging from aggressive to mild to delicate turnover are now available in a knotless design. For this reason, I'll carry a handful of knotless leader designs to handle a variety of conditions.

My preference is to use a nylon leader with a nylon tippet while dry fly fishing, although I use fluorocarbon as tippet when nylon isn't available. Nylon floats on water's surface better and is supple. For tippet-shy trout, I degrease the tippet with mud, sand, or several manufactured decreasing agents. A tippet section floating high on water's surface is likely to reflect light. A tippet section that rides within the surface is less likely to reflect light and may offer a tactical advantage, but only when dealing with fussy fish. I only degrease my leader when fishing flat, calm water.

Here are several examples of manufactured leaders I carry with me. I may add a butt section to increase length or adjust tippet diameter, but I feel comfortable dealing with any dry fly situation with the two following leaders as a base to work from.

Here's an example of the small variety of leaders I use for fishing dry flies during sulphur season in central Pennsylvania. I cover all my bases from a shorter 7½-foot 4X leader all the way to a 35-foot 6.5X leader. Water clarity, available casting room, and size of fly will determine the length and tippet diameter.

When using any manufactured leader, I'll cut 12 to 20 inches of the original tippet off and replace it with a fresh tippet. I do this as a precaution because I think that there is something about the extrusion process that appears to weaken the tippet material. This extra step isn't always necessary as it depends on your situation. For example, if you purchase a 7½-foot 4X tippet for fishing small-stream trout that don't weigh over 1 pound, this extra step doesn't matter. However, if you purchase a 12-foot 6X tippet for large selective trout on the Delaware River, then I feel switching to a fresh 6X tippet will make a difference when hooking and playing larger fish. Use discretion to choose what is best for your situation.

My standard dry fly leader base is an Orvis or Scientific Anglers 7½-to-14-foot leader rated from 2X to 6X. For fishing big bugs like hoppers or eastern green drakes, I'll often start with a 7½-foot 3X. Shorter leaders aid in turning over big bugs, but sometimes selective trout or shallow water demand a longer leader. In that event, I simply add a butt section onto the current leader to provide the additional length I need (see below). When fishing the sulphur hatch in Pennsylvania during regular higher May flows, I'll start off with a 9-foot 5X leader. Again, if I find the leader is too short for the conditions, I'll simply add a longer butt section to extend the length. When fishing Trico spinners in late August, when water levels are often at a season low, I'll start off with a 12-to-14-foot 6X–7X leader. When low water dictates a leader longer than 14 feet, then I'll add a longer 4-to-8-foot butt section. What I like about this system is keeping just a handful of leader lengths/diameters and one butt section spool. This system allows me to carry a limited number of leaders while being prepared to deal with just about any dry fly situation. There are only a few situations where I either build or purchase specialized leaders.

LEADER LENGTH

While dry fly fishing, my preference is usually geared toward longer leaders for several reasons. First, my belief is that line mass (in the form of line weight) has more to do with spooking fish than line color. A long, aggressive tapered leader will land softer on the water than any fly line, resulting in fewer scared fish.

Second, less mass on the water equates to a longer natural drift. A thinner-diameter object on the water creates less surface drag than a thicker-diameter object on the same body of water. This is also the reason I use 3- or 4-weight lines for most dry fly fishing instead of thicker 5- or 6-weight lines. The thinner diameters of the 3- and 4-weight lines allow for longer drifts to occur before drag sets in. By extension, this is the reason I also opt for using as long a leader as possible. The longer leader not only lands on the water softer, but the leader's smaller diameter (compared to more fly line on the water) allows for a longer drift to occur before drag sets in.

Lastly, the reason I like using euro-style rods for dry fly fishing is the fact that these rods possess softer tips, allowing me to cast long leaders with ease. Using long leaders isn't always the best option, but when I feel I can effectively use a long leader for dry fly tactics, I do so for the reasons stated above.

To increase the length of the leader, I'll simply add a long butt section to any of the above leader formulas. As mentioned previously, I prefer to maintain a taper from line loop to leader, so I'll add a section, ranging from 4 to 8 feet of .025 diameter.

When I find a leader taper I like, the only thing I do when making adjustments to length is adding or subtracting butt section. Rarely do I play around with the taper, only the butt section. Another reason for the heavier/thicker section is due to the fact that more energy is needed to aid in turning over longer leader. I've found a .025 diameter to be ideal for maintaining a gradual taper between line and leader while providing the power needed to cast longer leaders.

Although my dry fly tippet is 5X–6X, I do carry a spool of 0X–4X to maintain the leader's taper. The taper is essential for providing an energy transition from butt section to the tippet, in a manner that accurately presents the fly. It is an essential link and plays a huge role in getting the line, leader, and fly into the correct position. Pay attention during the cast. If the taper section hinges or sags during the cast, the taper needs repair.

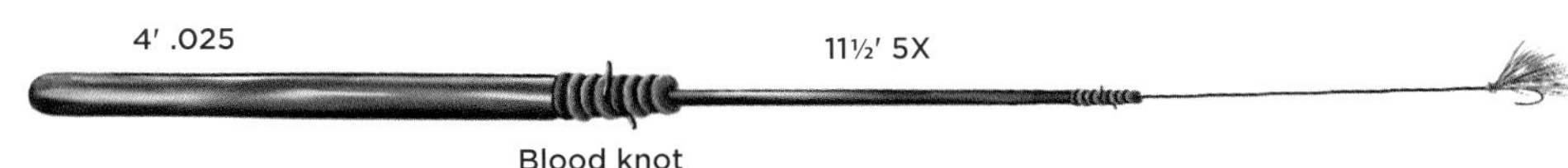

Just an example of only needing a handful of leader length/tapers to handle just about any condition. Depending on conditions, I'll add 4 to 8 feet of .025 to any standard leader. I'll use this 11½-foot 5X during regular flows while fishing sulphurs in central Pennsylvania. If water levels become low and clear, I'll fish as long as a 20-foot leader tapered to 6X.

My preference is for a shorter 7½- to 9-foot leader when fishing smaller streams and broken water. Reduced casting freedom sometimes will force you to shorten your overall leader length.

The taper will become too short after changing tippet so many times. You can discard the leader with too short of a taper and replace it, or you can do some maintenance to keep the leader performing. Every manufactured leader is different. Just pay attention to the approximate length of the leader's taper before fishing. Keeping similar specs (after repairing leader) will add longevity to your leader before needing replacement. Even taking a permanent marker and marking the taper length will provide some guidance when repairing the leader. Repairing a leader's taper isn't as complex as building a rocket ship, but keeping the repairs close to the original length will continue the life of the leader so you won't have to replace it.

One modification that helps while fishing in calm and flat water for spooky fish is to soften your leader. Years ago, I learned from my Portugal friends one way to soften your leader was boiling it in water for 5 to 7 minutes. The leader becomes softer the longer it is boiled, but this length of time is ideal. This modification helped while fishing calm and flat water for spooky fish. While I do find casting these soft and limp leaders challenging, I see its application in conditions where there's calm, flat water and little wind. Again, softening up the leader will make casting more challenging, and I rarely use this approach when casting during windy conditions or casting wind-resistant dry flies. I find this modification useful while fishing Tricos or any midge patterns on windless days while fishing flat water. For example, one of the few times I used a boiled leader was fishing the morning trico and callibaetis hatch on Hebgen Lake. The softness of this leader does allow significant additional drag free-float on flat water as the entire leader (not just the tippet) will lay on the water in a series of S curves.

These S curves are needed in most dry fly scenarios in my opinion, and that is one reason that I do not use leader straighteners. First, I prefer having some slack within my leader and tippet when dry fly fishing, as it provides a natural float. I don't want my leader to straighten out as this will decrease the length of any natural dry fly drift. Second, leader straighteners create friction when pulling the leader through, which weakens the leader. The best way to reduce excessive memory from your leader is simply stretching it with your hand. Stretching the leader for 10 to 20 seconds is usually all it takes to take memory out of your leader. If stretching doesn't work, then it may be time to replace the leader.

TIPPET

I prefer using the softest material for the tippet (not always the leader) to create the slack needed for a drag-free presentation. Although a good slack leader cast is essential for a good drag-free presentation, using softer tippet material will increase the natural drift before drag sets in. Check the limpness of both mono and fluorocarbon tippets to find which brands may allow for the best presentations. Most manufactured monofilaments will do the job, but very few fluorocarbon materials offer the limpness I'm looking for in a dry fly presentation.

Adjusting tippet length (based on the size and wind resistance of the dry fly being used) is as important as dialing in the correct weight on your nymph rig. With nymphing, the weight fishes the nymphs at the fish's feeding level, while with dry fly tactics, the correct tippet

Bob Williams demonstrates a beautiful low-angle presentation with a short 20-inch tippet section along with his favorite foam beetle pattern. It would have been difficult for Bob to make this cast if his tippet was 30 inches or more in length.

Matt Verlac choosing a Hex pattern to start off the night with. A shorter and stouter tippet is a must when casting large wind-resistant dry flies like the ones you see below. The general idea is the larger and more wind-resistant the fly, the shorter the tippet.

Fishing bushy, wind-resistant dry flies on high-gradient mountain streams doesn't demand long tippets. Using shorter 7½-foot 4X leader with short 20-inch tippet is usually all you need to get a good enough dry fly presentation.

Sometimes an extremely long tippet is needed when fishing glassy water conditions and small dry flies. For example, a 5-foot 6X tippet and #22 Trico spinner helped fool this Hebgen Lake brown trout.

Slack is good, but too much slack is counterproductive. I think the key is to use the least amount of slack to achieve a natural drift. Excessive slack may shorten the distance between fly line and fly, and requires more rod tip movement to set the hook. Pictured is what I consider to be manageable slack—enough to provide a natural drift but not too much to make setting the hook difficult. Shown is an ideal amount of slack.

Placing slack in the fly line helps lengthen a natural drift, but only if both line and leader possess slack. Drag will occur if you have slack within the fly line and none located within leader/tippet. Usually, the most important location to have slack is within the last 2 to 3 feet of tippet. Shown is slack in the incorrect location.

length allows the angler to accurately present the fly with the slack needed for a good drift. Dry fly patterns range from delicate midge patterns to bulky terrestrial patterns. Larger wind-resistant dry flies need a shorter and stouter tippet to turn over and deliver the pattern, while still offering enough slack in the tippet for a natural drift. Smaller patterns need a longer tippet to achieve a similar presentation. If your fly "hangs too high" when casting under tight brush, you may have a tippet that is too long for the wind resistance of the fly. Typically, longer 3-to-4-foot tippet lengths can be used for #18 and smaller dry flies, but you will need to shorten the tippet if you want to cast a larger/more wind-resistant dry fly under a low-hanging limb. Avoid presenting your dry fly until you can accurately present the pattern with a slack leader presentation.

If you feel you're making a good cast and the tippet falls on the water with excessive slack, then the tippet may be too long. Slack is needed in the presentation, but excessive slack can delay a hook set. I've also seen excessive slack laying too close to my dry fly turn off actively rising fish. Paying attention to how the leader/tippet unrolls/turns over shows you whether the tippet is the correct length. A sign the leader is too long is when the dry fly and tippet hang for an extended period instead of smoothly unrolling. Besides excessive slack and an inaccurate cast, the hanging effect won't allow you to unroll your dry fly under obstacles. In addition to poor casting techniques, too long of a tippet is another cause of not being able to cast under obstacles. So when in doubt, start longer with tippet as it's easier to cut back if your fly hangs during the presentation. Remember, smaller/less wind-resistant flies require longer tippets while larger/bushier patterns require shorter tippet lengths. Avoid presenting your dry fly until you can accurately present the pattern.

Mono Rigs

Mono rigs have become popular with European nymphing tactics, but many have also found this rig useful for dry fly presentations. Compared to fly line, mono has little mass so it lands softer on the water and provides a gentler presentation. The second advantage to less mass is the reduction in surface drag. In short, anytime you place two varying diameters of material on the water, the one with the smaller diameter will float longer before drag sets in. Hence, the thinner the fly line, or in this case the leader, you use, the longer your dry fly will drift before drag sets in. Within recent years I've found myself using excessively long dry fly leaders (up to 40 feet) where nothing but monofilament is being used to cast and present the dry fly. I know for some, the idea of casting a dry fly with nothing but a monofilament leader sounds impossible, but let me assure you it can be done with a little practice and with the correct tools.

It's worth mentioning that the conditions need to be ideal for using these excessively long leaders. First, I use these long dry fly leaders only when conditions are challenging. Low water, spooky fish, or situations where a long natural drift is needed are the few times I

Although it takes a little time to get used to casting mono rigs and dry flies, I feel this system offers the best dry fly presentation. Compared to a tapered fly line, a dry fly mono rig (like a Hends leader) is significantly smaller in diameter, resulting in a long drag-free drift. *Note:* A traditional line is a must if the wind picks up when casting a dry fly mono rig.

A longer rod tip movement is needed when fishing with a long and supple Hends leader. They have lots of stretch when applying pressure to set the hook, so you may need to lift your rod tip higher and faster. This was a common mistake I made when learning to fish mono dry fly rigs. You'll also need to apply more pressure with the rod tip while playing the fish, since there's more give in the leader. Trout will come unhooked if you don't maintain enough tension.

Small-Stream Leader

The one situation where I prefer a knotted leader is when fishing small streams while casting wind-resistant flies. When fishing small streams, or any area with tight cover, where I need to shoot my larger wind-resistant fly under obstacles, my preference is for a hand-tied leader with a hard nylon butt section. And when I say small streams, I mean streams with dense overhanging vegetation and little room to cast. This is one of the few times I feel a shorter hand-tied leader helps turn over bushier patterns in tight brush.

The more knots in the leader, the stiffer the leader becomes, regardless of whether you're using soft or stiff nylon material. For example, cutting sections throughout a manufactured leader's butt section and then reattaching with a blood knot will stiffen up the leader. You may want to do this if you're casting wind-resistant flies or casting in windy conditions. The time of your drag-free drift may be reduced by stiffening up the leader, but you'll at least be able to deliver the fly closer to the target.

Most small streams I fish in central Pennsylvania require nothing more than a bushy Elk hair Caddis, Hi-Vis Wulf, or stimulator pattern to catch fish. I need a leader that can shoot these bushier patterns under brush, and therefore my preference is for a hand-tied leader made of both stiff and softer nylon. Since small-stream trout live in environments with less food, they're more likely to move good distances when they do locate food. A long drag-free drift isn't always the priority with small-stream dry fly tactics—the priority is getting the fly into tight cover. Some find aggressive hand-tied leaders to be helpful for beginning anglers who may have trout turning over a cast. Other situations, including casting large patterns like large attractor dry flies or terrestrials, may call for using a knotted leader. Experiment and find what works best for you. ■

Although considered a small stream, I would consider this central Pennsylvania mountain stream to be somewhat "open" in regard to castability. I would feel comfortable fishing a 9-foot leader on the stream. Use as long a leader as you can, especially when dealing with lower flows as pictured here.

Perfect water type for fishing a dry fly on a mono rig. You can get close to fish in broken water, making it easier while casting a dry fly on basically a long leader. The major advantage is you can high-stick (i.e., hold leader and most tippet off water with a high rod tip) in broken water, allowing you to present your dry fly without mending.

ORVIS

Hi-Vis Hends Leaders

Watching for drag (e.g., in the form of a belly) within the fly line is easy, as fly line is usually brighter in color and larger in diameter. When a belly occurs, the angler can mend the fly or recognize what current is creating the drag, so a casting or repositioning adjustment can be made during the next presentation. However, seeing drag within the leader is challenging given the visibility and diameter of most nylon leaders.

Although I don't use them as frequently as I have in the past, using Hends fluorescent leaders will immediately tell the angler how the leader and tippet fall on the water, along with indicating micro-current causing drag during the presentation. Besides seeing where drag occurs within your leader, this hi-vis leader is one of the best tools for showing you where your leader falls on the water. If you accidentally throw a curve or make any casting error during the presentation cast, the hi-vis leader will highlight it for you while lying on the water. Too often I think I've made an excellent presentation cast, only to see my hi-vis leader telling me otherwise.

As for spooking fish, I still believe that disturbance of line falling on the water spooks fish more than line color. As a result, I feel using a hi-vis leader with clear tippet spooks very few fish while showing the angler exactly how the leader and tippet are lying on the water. The only way to correct a dry fly presentation mistake is first knowing it's occurring on the water. Using hi-vis leaders like this Hends product is one of the best teaching tools out there. ■

Using a loop-to-loop connection allows you to quickly change out leaders. I've reused this Hi-Vis Hends Camou leader dozens of times this season and it will likely last several more seasons. This leader's long aggressive butt section casts this 30-foot plus leader and small fly with relative ease. A 3-to-5-foot 5X–7X tippet deals with the most demanding dry fly scenarios. Again, a softer action rod helps cast these long leaders

use this system. This is a specialized system with difficult conditions, but it's important to know the limitations of such specialized systems. For example, wind speed needs to be little to none in order to cast dry flies with long leaders. Given the lighter mass when compared to a traditional fly line, this system is difficult to cast against heavy wind—there's just not enough mass to counter that of the wind. Also, these long leaders perform better when paired with smaller/less wind-resistant dry flies. Again, this system's mass may lack the power to efficiently cast larger wind-resistant dry flies like hoppers and green drake patterns. Instead, this long leader system is designed to cast small/less wind-resistant dry flies including midges and delicate CDC patterns.

Lastly, I believe many of the euro rods on the market today do a better job casting these leaders than traditional action rods. Most fly rods are designed to cast the weight of a fly line so a certain amount of mass is needed to help load the rod. When casting long leaders (not flipping but actually unrolling and casting leaders), a softer tip helps the rod tip load during the casting stroke. This is why I feel many of the euro-style rods (i.e., soft-tip rods) on the market today make excellent dry fly rods as well, especially when casting long leaders.

Casting nothing but a long leader requires a short, powerful, wristy cast. In many ways this cast is similar to a tenkara-style casting stroke, where the hand is extended out toward the target and locked in place, followed by wristy back-and-forth motion.

The advantage to fishing dry flies with this system is the extended time your dry fly rides before drag sets in. For example, my current mono rig dry fly leader consists of a 900 cm (approximately 30 feet) Hend Camou Leader in Fl Orange tapered to 3X. I then add anywhere from 3 to 5 feet of level 5X–7X tippet to the 3X. Another advantage of this leader is the ability to high-stick (i.e., elevate rod tip to keep line and leader off the water) in pocket water. This is the same principle as euro or

A high-floating fly line tip and leader is key to a quick and quiet fly line pickup. Pictured is my friend Bob "The Beetle" Williams setting the hook on large, private water brown trout, which took a beetle pattern off the bank. Bob routinely applies a grease floatant to both his leader's butt section and first several feet of his fly line. He's one of the best terrestrial fishermen I've ever fished with.

When fishing long leaders like this 30-foot-plus Hend Camou leader, I spend a few minutes greasing the entire butt and transition sections. The result is a high-floating leader I can mend on the water and identify when a belly (a.k.a. drag) begins forming in the leader. Seeing exactly where the belly forms allows me to know exactly where that drag is occurring. Pinpointing this location will allow you to make adjustments on your next presentation.

contact nymphing: keeping as much line and leader off the water as you can to decrease drag and improve the length of the drift. Compared to lifting fly line off the water, which sags and eventually creates drag, mono can be lifted off the water while creating little drag. So, this means you can high-stick dry flies in pocket water, and it also offers the ability to mend the leader on the water with minimal impact to dragging the fly, all due to the lack of mass within the leader. And yes, you did read me correctly when I said mending the leader: A properly tapered leader and a soft-tip fly rod will allow you to mend and reposition long leaders on the water.

While the leader takes a lot of work to get used to, I can attest that the effort is worth it as the time your dry fly naturally drifts is significantly extended. I cannot emphasize enough the point of using this long dry fly leader in tandem with a softer-tip rod. The soft tip will load easier and allow casting these longer leaders with less effort. Attempting to cast these leaders with a faster-action fly rod will result in frustration and possible injury due to the effort needed to cast these light leaders. Many of the dry fly tactics we discuss are applicable to the mono rig.

It's important to use paste on part of the leader and fly line tip. A sign of a loud pickup (i.e., lifting line and leader off the water) is a partially sunken fly line tip and leader section. A sunken leader or line section needs to be pulled through the surface before a cast is made, which results in a loud disturbance. I find surface-feeding fish are spooked easily and any loud noise/commotion may put a fish down. Using a paste (not a gel) to keep the fly line tip and leader butt section floating high will allow for a quieter pickup and reduce the chance of spooking surface-feeding fish. The last thing you want to happen is to rip the line off the water around a pod of rising trout. Greasing the line and leader aids in peeling (rather than ripping) line off the water in a quieter manner.

CHAPTER 7

Dry Fly Patterns

I enjoy fishing dry flies more than nymphs, but the opportunities to do so—and catch fish—are far fewer. Hence, I carry fewer dry flies than nymphs and the selection I carry is determined by season and geographic location. I may carry some generic patterns including a Griffiths Gnat, Parachute Adams, or some X Caddis, but most dry fly patterns I carry are designed to imitate a specific insect.

Unlike my nymph selection, where most patterns are categorized as suggestive (i.e., patterns that can imitate a wide range of insects), I split my dry fly selection from suggestive to imitative. I feel trout feeding on the surface look through their eyes with a magnifying glass. In other words, trout feeding on the surface appear to be more selective than trout feeding on the bottom, especially those feeding during an intense hatch.

As with any fly selection, your geographic location and the specific waters you fish will determine what patterns you may want to carry. Further, it's important for you to research the waters you fish to understand

If you're a guide and get paid to carry flies for every possible situation, then it makes sense to carry a wide variety of dry fly patterns during peak hatch season. My friend Matt Verlac is shown here looking through his Hex box before nighttime. Matt is a consummate professional and often carries more than ten styles/types of Hex patterns just to be ready for any situation.

This is Bob "The Beetle" Williams's terrestrial box—not exactly a convenient box to stow in any chest or waist pack. Bob uses this box to store the bulk of his patterns and keeps it home or in the vehicle. He'll pull a handful of flies from this box and place them into his working box. After fishing, he'll likely return unused flies back into this storage container. Only bring out the patterns you intend to fish.

Just because you own thousands of flies doesn't mean you have to carry them everywhere you go. Think about where and when you're fishing, and pick the patterns you believe you'll use during a single day, not the season. Place those selected flies into a working box—a smaller box containing only the flies you plan to fish with within the immediate future. Pictured here is Bob "The Beetle" Williams looking at his terrestrial working box.

which insects play an important role regarding dry fly tactics. For example, the famous sulphur hatch offers some of the best dry opportunities near one of my local streams, while another stream offers little opportunity 20 miles away. And just because a hatch occurs on the water doesn't mean you should carry corresponding dry flies, as some hatches seem to go unnoticed by trout. Learn the essential dry fly patterns to reduce clutter and keep your boxes organized. Keep pattern selection simple and carry only the patterns applicable for the current conditions you face. For example, no need to carry ant and beetle patterns while fishing a Montana tailwater during the month of January.

Instead of going into every dry fly I carry, I'm going to provide the short list of dry fly patterns I carry during a typical season. I feel this is more useful as you can use this as a template and simply adjust the size and color for the hatches you encounter. The following dry fly patterns make up around 90 percent of my dry fly arsenal.

Everyone has a system for organizing gear and patterns that work for them. For myself, I like to carry one working dry fly box, while all remaining patterns are placed in a large fly box with dividers. Although loose in the dividers, the patterns are organized according to insect type and size range. The large dividers allow me to store my dry fly pattern without smashing the pattern when not in use. When I need a certain dry fly in storage, I'll pull out all of the dry flies within a divider and pick through the ones I wish to use. This allows me to keep a somewhat accurate inventory of all my dry fly patterns, so I don't waste time tying patterns I already have adequate inventory for. When I'm done with a pattern type, I'll double-check to make sure it's still usable and doesn't have any moisture. To reduce the chance of placing moisture in the box, I use a small fan to dry off any pattern before placing it back in the storage box.

Dry Fly Emerger/Crippled Patterns

This is likely one of the most important styles of dry flies to carry. By emerger dry fly or cripple pattern, I'm describing a pattern that imitates an emerging insect (often partially sunk) trapped within the surface before taking flight, or an insect that is injured (at any life stage). I use the term emerger and cripple hand-in-hand since I believe many emerger patterns can imitate a crippled

Drying Dry Flies

Despite high floatability and ease of tying, modern dry fly materials eventually sink. A simple system can be used to reduce the frustration of a sunken dry fly and keep it floating if possible. Dry fly patterns are meant to float within or ride above the surface to mirror the same level the natural insects float in the water. Failure to mimic the same drift level as the natural insect will likely result in failure, so be prepared to do the necessary maintenance to keep your fly floating correctly.

I carry several types of floatants: gel for both traditional and CDC dry flies, paste for floating leaders and lines, powder desiccants to wick moisture, and brand-name paper towels to soak up waterlogged flies.

After a fly has been used well, I'll use quality brand-name paper towels that will absorb the bulk of moisture from the fly, then treat it with powder, which will likely take up any remaining moisture, followed by a gel treatment. Amadou is fungus used as dry fly drying patches. This natural material is excellent for absorbing moisture, but there are several downsides. First, amadou is expensive. Second, once fully soaked (e.g., falling in the water or standing in a rainstorm), the patch appears to lose all its absorbing capabilities and cannot be revived. One useful dry fly accessory I carry is high-quality paper towels in a ziplock bag. Although the shelf life is short, the cost is cheap and it appears to work just as good as amadou. This is especially useful when fishing with CDC-style patterns. I unzip the baggie, drop the dry fly into the baggie between two sheets, and squeeze. This wicks the bulk of the moisture of the dry fly, where I can then place additional desiccant or apply dry fly liquid to revive the pattern. It works great as long as you use high-quality paper towels that absorb moisture. I've tried many of the cheaper paper towel brands and found those knockoffs won't work.

Another great tip for pulling moisture from your dry fly, specifically CDC-style patterns, is placing a rubber band around the dry fly bend and plucking the moisture off your fly. The idea is simple: Place a rubber band around the dry fly bend, then hold onto the tippet and the rubber band (so the dry fly is hanging under tension between band and tippet). I like to hold the tippet and rubber band with my thumb and middle finger of both left and right hands, then use my index finger to pick (like a guitar string) the tippet. This springy action of the rubber band helps your fly shed water like a wet dog shaking off. This is often the first step I take when dealing with a fully saturated dry fly. ■

If you fish CDC flies, make sure to use a floatant that can work with CDC feathers and all other materials. Loon's Lochsa is just one of numerous floatants that will work with all dry flies, including CDC.

Using a rubber band to shed moisture is a great first step before reapplying floatant.

Sometimes simple flies work the best. The snowshoe rabbit emerger has become a favorite over the years. I like to use a buggier-looking dubbing, like the Trout Hunter CDC dubbing pictured here, as it takes on a mangled-insect look. Plus, these patterns take only a few minutes to tie. This handful of emergers was whipped up in less than 30 minutes.

insect and vice versa. Countless literature is available regarding the importance of emerging style patterns, so my discussion here will be brief.

As I'll mention throughout the book, through countless years of evolution, trout are masters of efficiency. An emerging insect usually offers some of the easiest meals, since many insects remain helpless for a brief time before taking flight. One factor determining how long an emerging insect remains on the water is current weather conditions. Periods of precipitation (rain or snow) along with high humidity often lengthen the emerging insect's stay before taking flight. I get excited about wet and damp days as these conditions often provide some of the best dry fly fishing of the season, even though most anglers stay home and wait to fish when "weather improves." Insects like the blue-winged olive are known for hatching during foul weather, and I feel the reason these tiny insects create excellent dry fly opportunities is their emergence often coincides with foul weather. Trout recognize when the emerging insect's flight is delayed due to foul weather and will likely then begin feeding on these helpless insects.

On the flip side, some insects hatch during periods of warmer/drier weather—these insects can quickly dry off and take flight. As a result, these fast-drying emerging insects may go untouched by trout. While other factors play a role in whether trout focus on emerging insects, I feel weather conditions are one key variable. Remember, wet, damp, and uncomfortable weather can produce some of your best dry fly conditions.

Below is a short list of my favorite emerging/cripple-style patterns. I carry more emerger-style patterns than I do actual fully hatched adults, so this list will be more extensive than the others.

The most unpleasant weather can provide some of the best dry fly opportunities of the year. For example, blue-winged olives are known for hatch during wet and cold conditions, even during snow events. Although unpleasant for the angler, this cold and damp weather keeps freshly hatched insects on the water longer before taking flight, providing an easier target for trout to pick off. PHOTO BY CHRIS DANIEL

X CADDIS

The trailing shuck, low profile, and hi-vis deer-hair pattern is a favorite for dealing with any caddis emerger or adult. I tie this pattern up to a size #10 (often imitating the large October caddis) all the way down to #20 for several micro caddis I've encountered on the East Coast. Rarely have I had to cut the trailing shuck off for imitating fully hatched caddis adults, but the situation has presented itself a few times over the years. The point here is the X Caddis doubles as an emerger and adult caddis, so this means carry fewer caddis adults. When no caddis hatch is in sight, I still carry several sizes of a gray or tan X Caddis for a general searching pattern.

PUFF DADDY

This simple CDC soft hackle pattern does a great job imitating any emerger (caddis, mayfly, or midge). Although I use this pattern mostly as a dry emerger, I feel this pattern does well imitating crane-fly adults as well as spent mayfly spinners. For dead drifting on calm waters, I'll use a quill or a thin thread body. Anytime I intend to pulse or twitch the pattern, I'll use Trout Hunter CDC dubbing to increase floatation. No matter how you tie the puff daddy, I feel the key is to start off using high-quality CDC. My idea of a high-quality CDC feather is a thin/limp stem for easy winding around the hook shank while possessing dense CDC fibers. Creating a thick CDC collar with quality CDC feathers is important for keeping the fly afloat.

One of my favorite ways to fish this pattern is what I call the "puff and twitch"—a tactic I learned about while competing across the pond. The concept is to create tension and pull the puff daddy emerger just below the surface a few inches, then reduce tension to allow the pattern to pop back up toward the surface, imitating an emerging insect breaking the surface film.

X Caddis

Hook: #14 dry fly hook
Thread: 8/0 tan uni thread
Tail: tan antron
Body: tan beaver dubbing
Wing: elk hair

Puff Daddy

Hook: #18 dry fly hook
Thread: 8/0 light olive uni thread
Body: olive Trout Hunter CDC dubbing
Collar: Dun Trout Hunter CDC

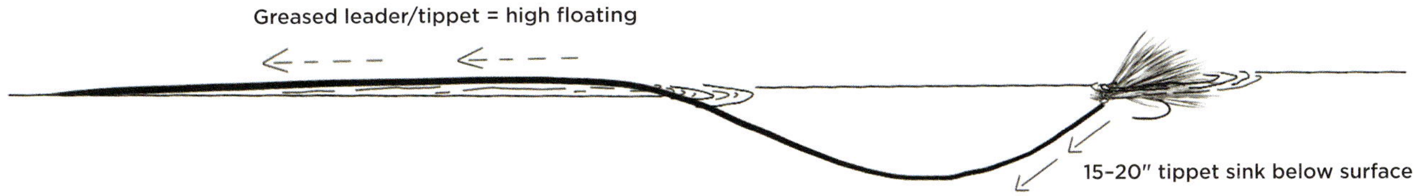

The very last tippet section needs to sink for this to work. A degreasing agent or rubbing mud can make this happen. Think of the sunken tippet as a sink-tip fly line trying to pull a buoyant streamer under the water with every strip. The high-floating emerger will travel the path of the sunken tippet when tension occurs. Remember to use only short strips—just enough tension to pull the fly below the surface (not into the depths). If you pull the dry fly too deep into the water, it may not resurface.

Here's a favorite setup when fishing the Puff and Twitch tactic:

Step 1: Use a dry fly paste to grease the last several feet of fly line, along with the entire leader, except for the tippet section.

Step 2: Use a decreasing agent or rub mud onto the tippet to aid in sinking the tippet. Using fluorocarbon tippet instead of nylon will help with sinking the tippet.

Step 3: Attach a puff daddy (or similar buoyant dry fly) to the tippet.

Step 4: An ideal casting angle is up and across angle. First, the main idea is to cast upstream to allow some slack between high-floating emerger and sunken tippet.

Step 5: Once slack is provided, the tippet will sink several inches below the surface.

Step 6: Use a short strip with the line hand or a short twitch of the rod tip to move the line and leader, creating enough tension for the sunken tippet to pull the puff daddy a few inches below the surface. Remember this is not a super-buoyant dry fly, so don't attempt to pull under more than an inch or two. If you wait too long and pull the puff daddy too deep in the water column, it will not have the buoyancy to pull itself back up to the surface. Often just a little flick of the wrist is all that is needed to pull the fly just under the surface.

Step 7: After the fly is pulled under the surface, reach or point the rod tip back toward the fly to place slack back in the leader. The moment you release tension, the puff daddy will pop back up to the surface, imitating an emerging insect. Often, you can create this ascending emerger action several times during one drift. The best way I can compare this approach is to a diving popper being used on a slow sinking line.

Other dry flies can be used for this approach. I've seen anglers using a poly wing caddis to achieve a similar effect. This technique does require some prep work and regular maintenance (keeping paste on the line and leader, degreasing the tippet, and adding dry fly desiccant to the puff daddy).

BALTZ PARA EMERGER

This fly is a similar concept to an X Caddis but imitates an emerging mayfly. Use a hi-vis parachute-style pattern for broken or disturbed water, when greater visibility and floatation is needed. This higher-floating emerger pattern is also a good candidate when deciding to use a

Baltz's Para Nymph

Hook: #18 dry fly hook
Thread: 8/0 olive dun uni thread
Tail: dark brown antron
Body: olive beaver dubbing
Wingpost: gray poly
Hackle: medium dun

dry dropper tactic, due to floatability and visibility. The parachute post can be tied in any color but the fluorescent colors Tom Baltz uses on this pattern are excellent for smaller-body mayflies, which are difficult to see.

SNOW SHOE RABBIT EMERGER

This simple no-hackle emerger pattern is a favorite emerger pattern when using a single pattern for challenging fish. The pattern is simple to tie, rides low in the surface, floats great, and just catches fish. For the body, I prefer using a Trout Hunter CDC dubbing to aid in with floatation. The CDC dubbing doesn't wind as tight of a body as other dubbing materials, and it takes on a roughed-up appearance, which I feel takes on the appearance of a trapped emerging insect. Remember your emerger patterns don't need to be a slim profile such as duns and spinners, so I don't mind having a little bulk with emerging-style patterns.

Snow Shoe Rabbit Emerger

Hook: #16 light scud hook
Thread: 8/0 yellow uni thread
Tail: dark brown antrol
Body: sulphur yellow beaver dubbing
Wing: dun snow shoe rabbit

In Michigan a hatching insect is referred to as a "hatcher." Trout will focus on this state when high volumes of hatchers happen, so you must be willing to fish patterns that represent the state of insect trout are focused on. Matt Verlac holds a Quigley-style Hex emerger—a favorite of his when dealing with Hex "hatchers."

Half-and-Half Emerger

Hook: #16 scud hook
Thread: 8/0 olive dun
Tail: dark brown antrol
Body: goose biot
Rib: small copper wire
Thorax: olive beaver dubbing
Post: gray poly
Hackle: dun

BWO Barr's Vis-a-Dun

Hook: #18 dry fly hook
Thread: 8/0 light olive uni thread
Tail: light Coq de Leon
Body: olive trout hunter CDC
Wing: black poly
Hackle: dun

HALF-AND-HALF VARIATION

The half-and-half is an emerger-style pattern designed for the lower half of the body to ride below the surface. I do prefer a heavier wire scud hook to aid in sinking the fly and use materials for the rear section that keep the fly riding deep. The version I use is a thinned-out Antron tail, thin pheasant tail abdomen or goose biot, ample ultra wire rib for segmentation, along with added weight. A hi-vis poly wing post provides visibility and floatability, while heavily hackled creates the illusion of splayed mayfly legs.

Hackled Adult Patterns

Use these patterns when fishing choppy or broken water, when needing a higher-riding fly. A hackled pattern is also a great choice anytime you intend to skate your pattern. Although the popularity and performance of CDC and no hackle-style patterns has surpassed traditional hackle patterns, it still pays to carry a small variety of these traditional patterns.

BARR'S VIS-A-DUN

This simplified thorax-style dry fly is a favorite when dealing with broken water or windy conditions. This is not a pattern I use when trout become selective. This is a pattern I use when fishing pocket water or a riffle, where the water is turbulent and trout have less time to decide. The larger profile upright wing on the pattern acts like a sail—just as the natural does in windy conditions. Instead of trimming the bottom half of the hackle, I leave it on (at first in case I want to skate) and use scissors anytime I feel a lower profile is needed. This pattern also makes a great indicator fly when using dry dropper or when fishing a difficult-to-see dry fly. Size and color depend on the mayfly you're trying to imitate.

Snow glare hampers your ability to see anything on the surface. Using a dark high-profile dry fly wing helps you locate your fly when dealing with glare. Pictured is an angler working a pod of trout eating blue-winged olives along the Firehole River in Yellowstone National Park.

A hi-vis wing can be added for better visibility. *Note:* Sometimes hi vis means a darker color like black. Glare on the water makes seeing any "hi-vis" pattern difficult.

A black wing post may provide you the only chance of seeing a dry fly on the water. Although I don't use them often, I will carry a handful of black wing post dry fly patterns for the most important hatches of the year. This black wing post Barr's Vis-a-Dun is a favorite, and I'll change size and color to match any mayfly hatch. Pictured here is a blue-winged olive version.

Colors like fluorescent pinks, oranges, and chartreuse bleed into the glare. Often the best way to combat glare is using a dark wing color (e.g., black). One example of where a black wing post is useful is while dry fly fishing when the banks are covered in snow. Snow reflects light and often can create a blinding glare. One of the best ways for your pattern to show up in the blinding light is to fish a dry fly with a dark wing post. Some insects like blue-winged olives are prone to hatch during foul weather (including snowstorms) so having a few black-winged dry flies will offer better visibility.

HARRY DRAKE

I came across this pattern while fishing the Grayling, Michigan, location. My friend and guide Matt Verlac adapted this heavily hackled pattern for any mayfly hatch, where actively twitching the pattern on the water is part of his presentation. Two of Matt's favorite hatches to use this pattern include the brown drake and the slate drake. I've seen this pattern coax larger AuSable River brown trout from the depths of slow-moving pools, when lower-riding patterns failed to rise a fish. Sometimes it takes a twitch to entice a dry fly strike, and the Harry Drake has become my go-to "skater" pattern for larger mayfly adults. One key part of this larger dry fly is the

ISO Harry Drake

Hook: #10 2X long dry fly hook
Thread: 8/0 light olive Uni thread
Tail: Coq de Leon
Body: gray beaver dubbing
Rear hackle: brown
Wing post: Dun Poly
Parachute hackle: grizzly

A variation of skating flies, this green drake version is an excellent choice when trout are keyed in on emerger/adults kicking and moving in the water. Plus it acts as an attention getter in low-light periods. If you notice trout eating the active adults moving on the water, use a pattern and tactic that mirrors what the trout are eating.

use of softer fibers like pheasant tail or Coq de Leon. These tail materials will bend/flex, allowing most trout to inhale your pattern. On the flip side, stiffer fibers (like moose mane) can make it challenging for average-size trout to inhale your pattern.

ELK HAIR CADDIS

This is still a great pattern, but I tend to use it in broken water or anytime I anticipate skating the dry fly as part of my presentation. The hackled body along with the deer hair make this a great pattern for skating presentations during a hatch. The skating presentation is also excellent when fishing small streams, during times when trout need additional encouragement to rise to the surface. For example, when small-stream trout are holding closer to stream bottom in the slower and deeper sections, sometimes that additional movement on the surface triggers a strike. Usually, the deeper or faster the water, the more aggressive the twitch. A #12–#16 brighter-yellow color is a favorite for prospecting small streams East or West. I've also begun using a purple body for small-stream patterns as well.

Elk Hair Caddis

Hook: #12 dry fly hook
Thread: 8/0 tan uni thread
Body: yellow beaver dubbing
Hackle: grizzly
Wing: elk hair

Twitching Your Dry Fly

A favorite approach to twitching any dry fly on the surface is incorporating a slight overpowered mend into the line and leader. The idea is to imagine sending an underpowered roll cast toward the fly line—just enough to send a ripple of energy through the line and into the tippet, moving the dry fly just a few inches along the surface. I prefer to send this shock wave outward since it not only moves the fly but also inserts additional slack into the leader. Compare this movement to when the angler pulls the rod tip back to move the fly. Pulling back on the rod tip to move the fly pulls out all the slack in the tippet, allowing drag to set in earlier after the fly is reset on water to drift.

The key to this outward underpowered twitch is just enough energy to twitch or skate the fly but without straightening out the leader. It takes a little practice, but it's well worth the work once you dial in the approach. A greased leader is essential to executing this movement as a partially sunken leader makes this tactic difficult to implement. In other words, a high-floating leader and tippet help skate the dry fly across the surface, where a sunken leader and tippet pull the dry fly underwater. This approach works for any surface presentation requiring additional movement during the drift. ■

Jac Ford, a living fly-fishing legend, holds a first-light Michigan brown trout, fooled by a drift-and-twitch Hex pattern. This fish came up from 4-plus feet of water to take the fly. The first two presentations were drifts with no movement placed in the fly, and they were refused both times by the fish. The third presentation was a drift and twitch, where the trout aggressively came up and smashed the fly. First change your technique if what you're doing isn't working. If that fails to catch a fish, then change fly patterns.

This is why moving or twitching your fly is so important during certain hatches. A struggling adult insect on the surface is sending the proverbial dinner-bell signal to the trout. This is no different than a wounded baitfish kicking and turning in the water—it's a trigger trout focus on. Pictured is an adult Hex pattern struggling on a Michigan trout stream. You'll never be able to match the exact ripple movement created by the insect, so the next best thing is using the rod tip to vibrate the fly in the water.

It's no secret trout love an easy meal. Cripple insects provide a "sure thing" meal for trout. Carry cripple patterns for every important hatch you encounter. Pictured is a cripple green drake dun that never took flight. Notice how the wings are spent and the body curved. This picture explains why mangled-looking dry flies work so well.

Bushy and high-floating patterns like the stimulator are excellent choices for high mountain streams, as these patterns are durable and usually require less maintenance to keep floating. It's common for anglers to catch dozens of fish in a short time period on these streams, so using a durable/high-floating pattern can keep you focused on fishing rather than applying fly floatant and desiccant after every fish. Pictured is Charles Boinske fishing one of his favorite small mountain streams in Montana.

STIMULATOR

Besides the famous western salmon fly hatch, there have been few times I've encountered epic large stonefly hatches on my Pennsylvania home waters. However, I still fish a version of Randall Kaufman's stimulator pattern as a searching pattern for late spring, when larger stonefly sporadically hatch on my home waters. It's still a favorite pattern for drifting and twitching along likely dry fly feeding locations, when sporadic larger stonefly hatches occur. Some of my largest dry fly trout each year come from blind casting and twitching these large, heavily hackled dry fly patterns.

Stimulator

Hook: #10 2X long curved dry fly hook
Thread: 6/0 fire orange uni thread
Tail: deer body hair
Rear body: dark brown hare's ear
Rear hackle: brown
Wing: deer body hair
Front body: orange hare's ear
Front hackle: grizzly

Stimulator patterns are also a favorite when fishing small streams. Twitching this large hackled pattern often can pull larger fish off the bottom, plus the larger pattern often prevents smaller/juvenile fish from inhaling the fly. When fishing small streams, it's common to catch first-year trout on smaller dry flies. I prefer not to handle these smaller/more fragile trout so using larger patterns reduces the chances of having to hook and release these small-stream gems.

No-Hackle Dry Flies

Doug Swisher and Carl Richards's book, *Selective Trout* (Skyhorse, 2018), was my early introduction to the "no hackle" pattern. Growing up in northern Pennsylvania, I cut my teeth fishing small streams with traditional patterns including the Adams and Wulff. Rarely did I encounter situations where my heavily hackled patterns, along with a decent presentation, wouldn't rise a trout. Then I moved to Pennsylvania's limestone region when I was 14. These hackled patterns that appeared to catch fish at will on the small mountain streams usually failed to convince a trout to rise. Although my dry fly presentation skills were limited at that age, I soon began catching more fish when I switched over to the no-hackle patterns, specifically the comparadun.

So much has been written about the reasons/effectiveness of no hackles so I won't regurgitate this information. Instead, I want to stress the importance of how your dry fly lies on the water. I feel the imprint the fly has on the water does need to match that of the natural. Many hackled patterns make your dry fly appear it's doing a pushup off the water, where all the trout may see is the hackle tips touching the water's surface, not the body. Many adult/terrestrial insects' bodies lie in the water while floating. By extension, the body imprints on the water's surface, where trout see the body in the view. Hackled patterns that lift the body off the water won't allow the body to imprint.

This may not seem significant, but through evolution, trout have learned how to discern food from folly, especially on waters rich in aquatic life where ample feeding opportunities occur. On the other hand, streams

High-floating patterns like the elk hair Caddis and traditional stimulator are great choices when fishing broken water. Pictured is an angler blind casting an elk hair Caddis on a Pennsylvania limestone stream during the famous grannom hatch.

I only use delicate dry fly patterns, like the Spanish dry fly, when I have no options. A Spanish dry fly is a good option anytime trout become selective or when fishing slow-moving water, where trout have an eternity to look at your pattern. Pictured are several streams and water types I frequently fish with a Spanish dry.

Silver Creek is an Idaho spring creek notorious for challenging dry fly fishing. Low riding/no-hackle dry flies are essential patterns when dealing with these fish. Sean Sullivan, a Silver Creek Outfitter guide, changes flies during the famous brown drake hatch.

possessing little food may force fish to become less selective, so no hackle patterns may not be as important for presentation purposes. Let the waters you fish determine how finely tuned your dry fly patterns need to be. Although I've gotten away from the comparadun-style dry fly, most of the dry fly patterns I carry are no-hackle styles. Below are a few of my favorite types for selective fish.

SPANISH-STYLE DRY FLIES

I first saw this dry fly style while competing in the 2006 World Fly Fishing Championships. This pattern is designed for the selective trout feeding in calm water. It's similar to a CDC comparadun but with a thinned-out floss-style body and an upright CDC wing split in half with a hi-vis yarn material. Unlike higher-floating dry fly patterns that remain afloat after numerous casts, this

Spanish Dry Fly

Hook: #16 dry fly hook
Thread: 8/0 olive dun uni thread
Tail: Coq de Leon
Body: 8/0 olive dun uni thread
Wing: dun trout hunter CDC
Hi-vis: yellow poly

Although gaining popularity, stillwaters are often overlooked fisheries that can provide fantastic fishing. Pictured a trico spinner fall on a well-known Montana stillwater, which has become one of my favorite places to fish dry flies during my annual western pilgrimage.

Although small in size, clusters of trico spinners on the water will encourage larger fish to feed on the surface. This large stillwater brown trout was located feeding on spent spinners 2 feet off the bank. PHOTO BY ALICE OWSLEY

fly has a shorter floating life—it needs more drying and dry fly floating maintenance. Therefore, I don't use this fly for blind casting when there's no sign of rising trout. Instead, this is a pattern to use when you're headhunting individual rising trout. The split upright CDC wings act as a stabilizer that keeps the pattern floating upright. Often a floss-like material is used for body and light dubbing for thorax around the CDC wing. Instead of a floss body, I often keep it simple and just use a thread body, but the key is to keep the body thin. Even with thread, it's easy to overbuild the body.

Too many of the traditional dry fly patterns' profiles are too thick, compared to the actual original. Remember, size, shape, and color are three variables to consider when tying a fly. More traditional-style mayfly patterns are all that is needed to consistently catch fish in most conditions. Such a delicate dry fly isn't needed, but there are times when this dry fly style is a must with finicky trout!

TCO CDC CADDIS

Tony Gehman, owner of TCO Fly Shop, developed this simple but deadly pattern in the 1990s when CDC was becoming popular in the United States. This simple dry fly is constructed of only two materials (i.e., dubbed body and CDC wing tied on a light wire scud hook). Although the original is tied without a tail and designed to imitate a caddis, I've used various sizes and colors to imitate mayfly emerger, duns, and spinners. I've added tails on these patterns to imitate crippled mayflies and found it's no more effective than ones without a tail, so I often opt not to tie in the tail. If I only had one dry fly to fish, for finicky trout it would be this pattern. This pattern lacks the sex appeal of other CDC patterns but it's deadly. Sometimes I think fly tyers overdesign patterns. This pattern is proof that simple is sometimes best. This pattern in both a gray body/light dun wing and with a black body/white wing are my go-to patterns for imitating the callibaetis and Trico spinners on western lakes.

Terrestrials

When it comes to dry fly tactics, I feel some anglers underestimate the importance of terrestrials, especially on the East Coast. In some ways, terrestrials may offer the only readily available food source for trout during the warmer months. For example, many of the small Pennsylvania trout streams I fish have little to no hatching activity during the warmest summer months. While aquatic insects like mayflies, stoneflies, and caddis are present, they are not active and by extension are not always readily available for trout. These periods of little insect activity are when I think terrestrials have the greatest impact on one's success on the water because it may offer the only chance of food during the day, especially on small, sterile mountain streams during the dog days of summer. Of course, terrestrials will produce during other periods, but I find fishing these patterns during late July and August (on my home waters) to be prime time for terrestrials.

Lastly, I feel terrestrial fishing may be more productive than fishing during most major hatches. The reason I say this is you're not competing against hundreds or thousands of naturals as you may during a major hatch. The number of naturals floating on the water during a heavy hatch makes it difficult for you to fool the fish with your offering. Unless a massive swarm of flying ants falls upon the water, or some other unique natural event, a terrestrial-hunting trout is more likely to eat a well-presenting pattern given the fish usually has fewer options to choose from.

Lastly, I want to mention I seldom use hopper patterns on my central Pennsylvania trout streams. While

TCO Caddis

Hook: #16 light scud hook
Thread: 8/0 tan uni thread
Body: tan beaver dubbing
Wing: light Dun Trout Hunter CDC

grasshoppers are present along our streams, I've found ants, beetles, and inchworms to provide greater success on the water. I would certainly carry more hopper patterns if I lived closer to many of the famed western waters, where hoppers may be the most important terrestrial insect. Here are two of my absolute go-to terrestrial patterns:

ARRICK'S ANT

This West Yellowstone Fly Ant pattern is a guide favorite, but I've found good use for this pattern anywhere either ants and/or flying ants come into contact with water. For an attractor-style ant, I'll tie a flashier body made of cinnamon, peacock black, or purple ice dub. I regularly use beaver dubbing in shades of black or

Arrick's Ant

Hook: #14 dry fly hook
Thread: camel 8/0 uni thread
Rear abdomen: black beaver dubbing
Front abdomen: brown beaver dubbing
Wing: white poly
Hackle: brown

The Arrick's Ant was designed to fish the broken/choppy water found near the originator's home waters of West Yellowstone, Montana. Low-riding dry flies can easily get lost in choppy waters, like this section of the Madison River. The high wing post on this pattern allows you to see your pattern and react the moment a trout takes. Even aggressive surface takes will go unnoticed if your eyes are accidentally fixed on another location 5 feet away.

cinnamon brown for a more natural-looking color. For larger patterns (e.g., #12–#16) I'll use poly for the wing. On patterns #18 or smaller, I usually use pearl flashabou or even a white CDC wing.

BEETLES

Ants or beetles? I use ants and long leaders/tippets when fishing calm and flat water, where delicate presentations are needed. On the other hand, I use beetles in situations

When necessary, create an impactful landing with your beetle presentation. Beetles are hard-bodied insects that create a "plop" when falling on the water. Using a forceful downward cast increases the force of the fly meeting the water. This is why I use wide foam beetles instead of narrow-bodied beetles. The wider profile creates a greater impact or slap on the water, getting the attention of the fish. As a general rule I'll gently present ants but aggressively present beetles.

Great example of a beetle "smacking" the water. This impact will be felt by any nearby trout. This is a must anytime trout are holding under deep undercut banks. These fish may not feel a delicate ant fall on the water, but they certainly will feel the impact of this presentation. Let the situation dictate your approach. Present a beetle with a little more care in shallow and calm water, but be aggressive in deeper or off-color water. Make these tactical adjustments before changing flies!

It's my experience trout will move greater distances in the summertime for terrestrials. While a few hatches will occur in central Pennsylvania during the summer, terrestrials are often your best bet for dry flies.

where I want my dry fly to intentionally create a "plopping" sound on the water. For example, I like plopping beetles on the water during windy days, when a chop occurs on the water and I want to create a disturbance. I may use a beetle when I feel a fish is tucked under an undercut bank, and I want a fly to create enough of an impact for the hidden trout to feel and come out to investigate. Also, if trout are holding near bottom in a deep pool, I sometimes think an aggressive plop may pull those fish from stream bottom. Again, I fish ants with delicacy and beetles with more aggression—that's just the approach that works for me.

Over the years my friend Bob Williams (a.k.a. Bob "The Beetle" Williams) introduced me to two styles of foam that create an excellent beetle body—dense foam designed to create a "plop" on the water. The truth is not all foam performs the same when it comes to creating impact, which is what I'm looking for when fishing beetles.

Natural beetles make a plop when they fall onto the water, which is exactly what I want when my beetle lands on the water. Because of the lack of available drifting food (above and below the surface), I've noticed trout moving great distances to hunt down a fallen food item. Hence, when approaching water types like this, I like to plop my beetle short, presenting the pattern on the inside of the drop-off. Trout will sense the fallen fly and will move to look. If you make too long of a cast, there's a chance you'll spook the fish. Also, due to area the plop covers, I work wider grids when placing the next cast. This means making one cast in a larger area, then moving on to the next grid. Rarely do I make more than one or two plops in an area. That is, beetle fishing is like fishing streamers—make a few good casts and move on.

You can accomplish this plop with an aggressive cast (e.g., hauling the line to increase speed) and/or use a dense foam and combination of materials that create a similar impact. Over the years, Bob introduced me to two excellent beetle foams, but sadly those manufacturers no longer produce those products. Currently, I'm using the densest (not thickest) foam I can find and spraying the sheet with a black metallic paint. The purpose of the paint is to add density and stiffness into the foam. This may sound extreme for making foam beetles, but I think it's well worth it.

CHAPTER 8

Casting and Presenting the Dry Fly

Good casting skills are important with all fly-fishing tactics but may be most important when delivering the dry fly. When dry fly fishing, often you're fishing your fly with line and leader on the water. This means the angler needs to lay the line on the water in a manner that offers the best natural drift. The ability to control where line, leader, and fly fall on the water is a skill that takes time to develop.

Dry Fly Casting Pointers

PICKING LINE OFF THE WATER

Any disturbance on water's surface can sound the alarms to a rising trout. Exercise caution while presenting the fly and picking line off the water. First, strip in as much line as you can before attempting to pick line off the water. I know this sounds like common sense, but this is not

Between you and your targeted trout, a lot of things are going on within the currents. Faster currents, slower currents, currents moving in different directions, and so on. The ability to understand the direction and speed of the currents between you, along with the ability to adjust your presentation, are the greatest skill sets a dry fly fisher can have. Pictured is the author casting to a rising trout on Utah's Green River. PHOTO BY FLYCRAFT

The result of picking line off the water too soon. Notice how long the rip line is on the water. This was because I began lifting line off the water with a low rod. In other words, the lower rod tip allowed more line on the water before picking up, which resulted in a greater disturbance.

Notice the rip line isn't as bad this time. This was the result of lifting more line off the water with an elevated rod tip, before lifting into the backcast. Be patient. If you want to spook fewer fish with your line pickup, lift as much line as you can off the water before going into your backcast.

Amidea Daniel making the first of three movements to complete the voodoo/snake roll pickup. The first movement is an accelerated undercut C shape with the rod, which lifts the line off the water. Once the tip of the fly line lifts off the water's surface, you can begin your backcast, creating less commotion as you pick line off the water.

common practice as I see anglers attempting to pick 30 feet of line off the water, creating a disturbance I can hear from a great distance away. The shorter length of line allows you to lift more line off the water by elevating your rod tip before beginning the backcast. Elevating the rod tip to lift as much line as possible (before beginning the backcast) minimizes the degree of disturbance as you pick line off the water.

Voodoo/snake roll pickup. If you need to quickly pick a long length of line off the water without creating too much impact, a snake roll pickup cast is one option. The purpose of this cast is to elevate line off the water before making the backcast. This allows for a quicker pickup of line. The typical pick-up and lay-down cast involves two parts: acceleration to a stop for the backcast and acceleration to a stop for the forecast. One more acceleration to a stop is added with the snake roll pickup before making the backcast: The rod hand accelerates downward while the rod tip remains horizontal to the water's level while forming an undercut series of C shapes before coming to a sudden stop. This movement literally lifts the line off the water in a series of coils. Once the line unrolls off the water, the angler can then proceed with the backcast. But remember to keep the rod tip angled outward while the rod hand accelerates during the circular pickup.

OVOID ROLL CASTING AROUND SPOOKY FISH

While the roll cast is a useful cast for locations with limited space for backcasting, the process of rolling line off

This is one water type I would never roll cast around. It's tough enough avoiding spooking fish with a delicate presentation on such water, but almost a certainty if you attempt to roll cast as the force of the line ripping off the water sounds the alarm.

the water creates significant disturbance on the water. Basically, I avoid this cast in any low or slow water situation, where trout are easily spooked by the commotion of the line rolling off the water. Try using a rolling switch cast (if enough backspace is available to form the loop). A regular roll cast involves line laying on the water in front of the angler, which then needs to be rolled out to the target. Instead of sliding the line on the water with rod tip and allowing line to lay on the water, the switch cast involves a half-powered backcast that carefully lifts line off the water and places a larger D loop of line behind the rod tip. The key is waiting for the tip of fly line to land on the water immediately in front or directly off the slide of the angler before making the forward stroke. The fly line tip needs to anchor on the water surface before making the forward cast. This pause (between setting up the loop and making the forward cast) is nothing more than a split second—basically a continuous back-and-forth movement.

SHOOTING LINE: STABBING THE LOOP

Again, little things make big things happen. Do anything you can do to reduce spooking fish. Another simple tip is shooting line on the final forecast rather than false-casting multiple times over a rising trout. Shooting line is nothing more than demonstrating simple physics with fly casting. The first part is understanding how much line is needed outside the rod tip to shoot line. Adequate fly line mass outside the rod tip is needed to pull other line through the guides during the presentation cast. Depending on the fly line taper used, you need to understand how much line you need outside the rod tip in order to shoot line on the forward cast. Short, aggressive triangle-style tapers require less line outside the rod tip, while mild tapers require significantly more line. Again, length of line outside rod tip and the speed in which you move the line through the air are two variables that determine your ability shoot line. Once you establish minimum amount of line outside the rod tip, the next step is mastering the concept of stabbing the loop.

Stabbing the loop is a concept I first heard from Lefty Kreh. The idea is creating an upward trajectory cast (with adequate line outside the rod tip) and coming to a sudden stop, allowing the line to begin shooting through the guides. If the rod tip remains high while shooting the line, the line has to climb upward though the guides. The line loses energy when climbing this high angle, so in order to allow the line easy passage, the rod tip is lowered when the line is beginning to shoot line. So in simple terms, stop the rod tip high during the forward cast, and begin to level out the rod while the line is shooting. This leveling of the line is creating the path of least resistance, creating maximum efficiency for the line to travel outward toward its target.

Pictured is an angler in an excellent casting position for the check cast—eyes focused upward and standing straight up. If you look down or have a slight downward bend in your back, you're likely going to slap the water with the line. PHOTO BY GEORGE DANIEL

The **check cast** (a.k.a. parachute cast) is a popular dry fly cast involving a high trajectory cast, then pulling the rod tip downward to collapse the cast. The collapse piles line and leader on the water to allow for a drag-free drift. Remember the rod tip usually travels in the direction your eyes are focused on. If you want to stop the rod tip higher on the check cast, don't look down at the water. Instead, find a target above where you want to cast and focus your eyes there. This will help you direct the rod tip upward during the forward-casting stroke, allowing you to stop the rod tip and drop slack ono the water.

While this cast is useful, it has many limitations. First, this cast is inaccurate as it is susceptible to even the smallest degree of wind. Think of dropping a feather onto a designated target. The faintest wind will blow the feather way off course. The same concept applies anytime you place your dry fly high in the air and give it too much time to fall onto the water.

Another situation for which I don't use the check cast is when casting across faster-speed currents. The mass of the fly will land before leader and tippet, since the tippet is attached to the wind-resistant dry fly. Drag will likely set in since fly line lands well before the leader and fly. This means the line and part of the leader will already be positioned downstream of the dry fly, before the fly falls on the water. A line and leader positioned downstream of the dry fly will cause immediate drag. The only times I use the check cast is when casting downstream (not across currents) without wind and when casting in a uniform-speed current.

Reach Cast

Every great dry fly fisher I know has mastered the reach cast. If you want to be a successful dry fly fisher, I suggest you learn the reach cast as well. It may be the single-most important dry fly cast. When given the chance, I prefer to mend in the air rather than on the water. It appears higher-level feeding trout are far more sensitive to a line mending on the water than a trout eating drifting nymphs closer to stream bottom. This is why I always try to set the line, leader, and tippet on the water in a manner that requires little to no mending after the cast. Although the reach cast has been extensively written and talked about, few have taken the time to practice and perfect this cast. I will say this: Every excellent dry fly angler I've seen has mastered the reach cast.

A reach cast is considered an aerial mend, a movement made after the rod tip comes to a stop. That is, the line begins traveling to the target after the stop, then the angler slides the rod tip to one side to direct where the backend of the line lays on the water as the fly approaches the target. The goal is to position line, leader, and, more importantly, the tippet on the water to delay drag.

Although not as much slack may be created with the reach cast as with the check cast, I feel accuracy is better. I would rather have a deadly accurate presentation with some slack than an inaccurate cast with lots of slack. This is especially true when casting to cruising trout on stillwaters or slow-moving river sections. Try not to give the fish too much time to investigate the pattern. So my approach is putting the fly just within the feeding window, so the fish must make a split-second decision. For a fish that is holding and feeding immediately below the surface, I may attempt to cast only 8 to 12 inches upstream from the fish. Additional distance is added if a fish is holding deeper in the water column. Or add distance if you feel placing the fly too close to the trout will spook. No hard-and-fast rules: Experience on the water is the best teacher.

Putting on the green. Often line and leader are placed on the water between angler and a rising trout. Remember, the dry fly is attached to the leader and fly line. If the line and leader begin to drag, so does the dry fly. If the line and leader drift naturally with the current, the dry fly is likely to drift naturally. I know this is the essence of all fly-fishing tactics, but I feel it is even more important when presenting a fly on the surface. For

It's called the reach cast for a reason. Notice how my casting hand is fully extended to my side as the fly line and leader land. The ability to properly position fly line on the water is one of the hardest casting skills I continue to learn.

The key to a good reach cast is aiming high and coming to a sudden stop. Moving the rod tip in a straight line (not a curve), drift your hand to one side of your body. Allow line to slip through the guides while making the reaching movement. This allows the line to gently and accurately land on the water. If line isn't allowed to slip, the line will likely backlash on itself, causing inaccuracy and excessive slack.

This beautiful Hex eater was the result of using a glow-in-the-dark fly line. Although the line does help suggest where your dry fly is, in complete darkness I feel its greatest purpose is seeing if any belly occurs in the line during the drift. This belly is causing drag, and even trout feeding on Hex in complete darkness will shy away from a dragging fly. My first cast to this rising fish (you're listening for the rise) resulted in immediate drag due to a current I couldn't see in the darkness. However, I corrected the mistake with a reach cast after pinpointing the location of the current causing the drag. Never in a million years would I have caught this fish without the visual help of the glow line. PHOTO BY MATT VERLAC

example, there are few situations where the angler can high-stick (keeping line and leader lifted off water as is done with nymphing) the dry fly presentation. The challenge is the dry fly angler's ability to read the hydraulics/currents that lie between them and their target. This is similar to how a golfer needs to study the green before putting the ball. Because line and leader are attached to the fly, the position the line and leader are placed on the water has a direct effect on how the pattern drifts.

While this simple concept is true with all tactics, I feel it's most important with dry fly tactics since "on the water" mending isn't as useful as with other tactics, including nymphs and streamers. Surface-feeding trout are on high alert, and any disturbance on the water (even a quiet on-the-water mend) often spooks a fish. My experience is mending on the water while dry fly tactics spooks more fish. This isn't true with subsurface tactics including nymphs, wet flies, and streamers but certainly when presenting flies to higher-level feeding trout. Therefore, it's important for the angler to have the casting skills necessary to correctly place line, leader, and fly in the best spot from the very beginning. In other words, place these items in a manner that requires no mending after the cast. I feel the carpenter's rule of "measure twice, cut once" applies well to dry fly fishing. Study the current between you and your target and attempt to make a cast that positions line and leader on the water for the best possible drift. And if the first presentation isn't ideal, identify the currents that are causing the unnatural drift and make the proper adjustments.

Reading the drift with dry fly tactics is more straightforward than nymphing. This means you can see the dry fly drifting naturally on the surface or dragging. However, reading the currents and possessing the casting skills to present a drag-free drift with a dry fly is one of the most challenging fly-fishing skills to master. I've seen several good nymph fishers who are poor fly casters, but every good dry fly fisher I've known is also a

Dam releases on Tennessee's South Holston River create clumps of submerged vegetation, which in turn create a dynamic hydraulic. Pay special attention to where drag occurs within leader, tippet, and fly line to determine where drag is setting in. This water is a lot harder to fish than what it looks like.

good fly caster. My suggestion is to practice these casts/presentations either on the grass or on the water without a fly. Master these fundamentals before approaching the stream-you'll enjoy your fishing experience more and experience less frustration.

Modifying your casting stroke for the best presentation. While leader construction and design play a role in one's dry fly success, I think the angler's ability to modify their casting stroke is just as important, if not more important, for delivering a good presentation. I spend time thinking about the taper and design of my dry fly leader, but spend more time adjusting my casting stroke to complement the leader's action. For example, I'll open my casting stroke to make a wider arc with the rod tip if I feel the leader is straightening out too much. If I feel the leader is lying on the water with too much slack, then I'll try to increase line speed with a haul, along with moving the rod tip in a straighter path during the casting stroke. Remember, casting is often about speed. The straighter the path the rod tip takes during the cast, the greater the line speed and quicker turnover of the line and leader. So if the leader straightens out too much without slack for a dry fly presentation, I'll begin casting in a wider arc. The wider arc slows down the leader turnover and will likely result in more slack lying on the water. In truth, this is why beginner fly casters often have the best dry fly presentations—they use too much wrist during the casting stroke, which results in additional slack in both line and leader landing on the water. Sometimes the leader is not the cause for too much or not enough slack . . . often it's the angler's inability to modify their casting stroke to complement the leader's performance.

Tightening up the loop with the haul: Although any tactic can be employed on small mountain streams, I feel the dry fly is synonymous with small mountain stream tactics. Typically, small mountain streams are less fertile, and trout are more willing to move for any food item. The ability to control the shape of the loop is essential for all conditions, but especially smaller streams where your delivery window is smaller.

In short, the rod hand and rod tip's path determine the shape of the loop. If the rod hand and rod tip travel in a straight line, the loop tightens. If the rod hand and rod tip move in a wider arc, the loop opens. I feel the biggest mistake I make while casting in small streams is attempting to force the cast too much with just the rod tip. Anytime I rely solely on the rod hand to make the cast, I tend to move my casting hand in a wider arc and open the loop. As a result, I tend to rely more on the line hand to haul the line and create the energy I need to make the cast. Basically the rod hand moves in a short but straight path (basically just holding on the rod) while the line hand hauls the line in a powerful but smooth manner. This reliance on the haul tends to smooth the casting, allowing the path to move in a straighter plane and tighten the loop.

Roll and Bow Cast

Years ago Joe Humphreys shared with me this modified roll cast. With a traditional roll cast, the rod tip needs to be angled upward and behind you, while the line hangs off the rod tip. Some fly-fishing environments don't provide the needed area to angle the rod tip backward, so we need to find a creative solution to load the rod. A roll and bow is a good choice when you need to keep the rod tip either directly above or in front of you (not behind you) when you have no room behind you to make a traditional roll cast.

Wiggle roll cast: With limited space behind you, another way to get distance is with this wiggle roll cast—another great lesson I learned from Joe Humphreys. A traditional roll cast involves sliding the line on the water as the rod tip is angled behind you at a higher angle, then the rod tip accelerates forward to lift line off the water and redirect forward. Traditional roll casting is still a great cast but it has two limitations. First, it creates an unwanted commotion on the water that can spook fish. Second, the angler needs to create enough energy in the cast to break the surface tension between line and water surface to move. The wiggle roll cast is an ingenious modification to get more energy out of the roll cast while creating less surface disturbance.

Downward Kickback Retrieve

There are times when you need to place your fly line and/or leader over a limb or branch in order to achieve a drift with a dry fly. Maybe the branch is too low to shoot line under so you have to place your line on top of the branch to give your dry fly a natural drift. The easy part is laying line and leader on top of the branch, but the challenge is when you must pick the line off the obstacle to recast. Trying to wiggle your line/leader/fly over the brush does work but only a percentage of the time. Instead of trying to wiggle the rig through the brush, why not lift it high over the brush to avoid any chance of contact between fly and brush? This is when the downward kickback retrieve helps.

The downward kickback retrieve is one of countless ways to retrieve a fly line lying on top of an obstacle. The basic idea is smoothly accelerating the rod tip toward you in a upward direction (Let's use a 45-degree angle for demonstration purposes), then suddenly accelerating the rod tip downward in the exact opposite direction. The movement creates a kickback in the line, causing a loop on the front end of the fly line to lift upward

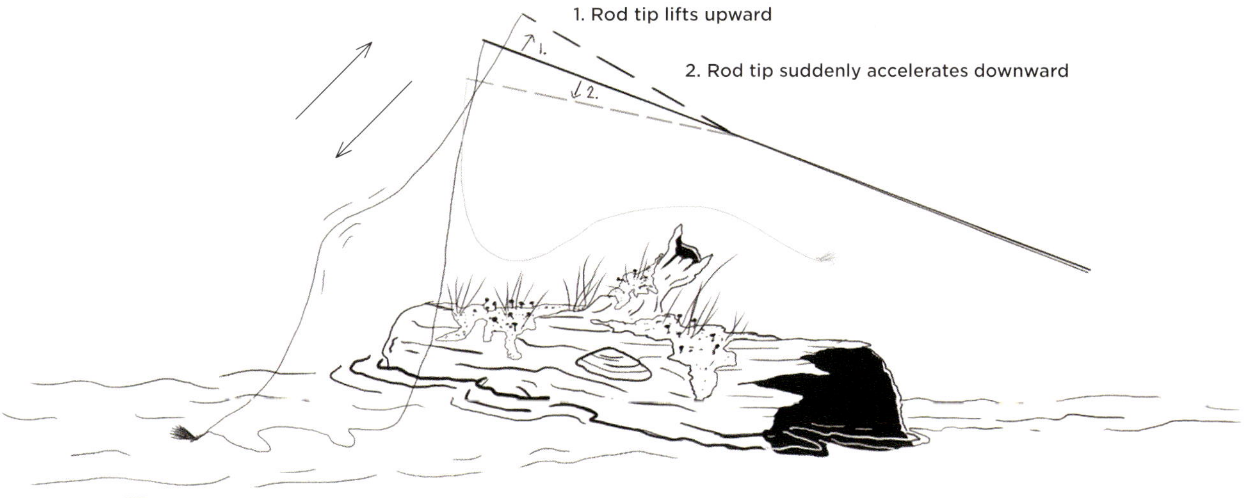

and toward you as it clears the obstacle. Remember both movements require an accelerated movement, first up at a 45-degree angle and then down the same 45-degree angle.

Casting under an obstruction. Overhanging tree limbs and vegetation are trout magnets. They provide both security from overhead predators and possible food sources, as terrestrial insects crawl on and fall off streamside vegetation. The ability to not only cast under obstacles but shooting distance under these obstructions to a trout's location is essential for success. Keeping it simple, we need to remember two key concepts when casting under an obstacle. The first concept is the loop forms where the rod tip stops on the forward-casting stroke. This means the rod tip should be near or below the height of the obstacle we want to go under, before

The biggest mistake when casting under the brush is dropping your shoulder during the cast. This opens up the loop, sending the fly into brush rather than under. Pictured below is the perfect tight brush cast. Notice how Bob is standing straight after the cast, his rod comfortably off to the side, and the height of his rod tip is below the obstacle he wants to go under. The result is a tight loop unrolling below the brush. Even after fly fishing for 36 years, seeing a cast like that gets me stoked!

coming to a stop. Second, if we want to shoot distance under the obstruction, an upward trajectory is needed in order to keep the line/leader/fly moving slightly upward the cast unrolls.

Dry Fly Presentation Tips

Let a bad presentation play out: Part of fly fishing is learning patience—a quality I'm still learning myself. When your dry fly presentation doesn't go as planned, just let it slowly swing out and away from your targeted area before attempting to pick up and recast. Attempting to pick line off the water around a rising fish will likely result in alarming the trout. Be patient and allow the line to drift away from your targeted area before attempting to recast.

Avoid casting over rising trout to other rising trout: Another common cause of spooking fish is casting over a pod of rising fish to target another pod of fish. I made this mistake with friend and Delaware River guide Rich Hudgens. While anchored up, I attempted multiple casts over several rising trout without rising fish. Without raising the trout, and due to lack of patience, I immediately began casting over the first fish to target a second trout that began rising. Within seconds, I spooked the trout and the surface feeding stopped abruptly. Rich looked at me and said, "Never cast over a rising trout!" Point well taken.

Although the current looks calm, these submerged weed beds will cause the creation of countless micro-currents within a short area. This is one scenario where I prefer to use the downstream reset tactic. Look at how wide the openings are between the weed beds. The slack within the leader and tippet should be narrower than the opening.

Sometimes you have no other choice than to cast around potential snags. Trout seek cover—it means protection. When casting near or over midstream obstructions, the downward kickback retrieve reduces the chances of snagging your fly during the pickup. PHOTO BY CHRIS DANIEL

CASTING TO A TROUT'S SHORT SIDE

Make a cast to the short side of the fish when you're not 100 percent sure of a trout's holding position. Nothing will spook a potential rising fish faster than placing line and leader over the trout's back. Again, I cannot overemphasize the importance of having excellent line control and fly casting accuracy skills. Even if you know where a trout is, make the first cast short and behind the fish.

FEEDING SLACK FOR A DOWNSTREAM PRESENTATION

Sometimes your only presentation option is casting downstream to a trout. This tactic is reserved for sensitive trout that flee or shut down the moment any fly line and leader lands within close distance. When these conditions exist, often a good choice is presenting the fly well upstream of a rising fish and feeding slack into the line, allowing the fly to drift naturally to a trout. The spookier the trout, the farther upstream the fly needs to be set on the water. A good cast places line, leader, and fly in the best position within the current to allow a natural drift. All that is needed to extend the drift downstream is simply kicking slack line outside the rod tip. The goal is to kick out slack without disrupting the drift of the dry fly.

DOWNSTREAM RESET PRESENTATION

Although I prefer an upstream approach, challenging fishing conditions may force you to present the fly downstream to a fish. For example, streams like the Henry's Fork or Silver Creek are two systems where casting either fly line or leader over a trout will likely result in spooking

The result of good reach cast. Amidea Daniel holds a beautiful Madison River brown. The trout rose on an Arrick's Ant pattern midstream, demanding several reach-cast attempts before fooling the fish.

Pictured is an angler lifting the rod tip upward to straighten out the line, leader, and tippet before sliding the rig to the side. Once the fly is positioned in the correct seam, the rod tip lowers to feed the slack downstream, allowing the line, leader, and fly to travel and tight seam without drag.

As mentioned before, create only the minimal amount of slack needed to achieve a natural drift. For example, if you create too wide of slack within your tippet while fishing between two weed beds, micro-currents will likely grab that slack and cause immediate drag. You're basically whiplashing the dry fly back and forth between the micro-currents. In other words, sometimes excessive slack (in the shape of wide loops) causes excessive drag.

the trout. On top of that, thick clumps of aquatic vegetation build up during the warmest months on streams like Silver Creek, creating a labyrinth of micro-currents for your line, leader, and fly to pass through. So not only does the fly need to land well above the feeding trout so as not to alarm it, but the line/leader/fly needs to drift through a narrow seam in order to achieve a natural drift. For example, clumps of aquatic vegetation will disrupt flow and create a series of micro-currents pulling in varying directions. Achieving a natural drift around thick aquatic vegetation is one of the greatest fly-fishing challenges, due to dynamic currents wanting to pull your rig in a number of different directions.

Usually, trout position in a *narrow* lane between weed beds. Basically, this is a narrow and linear micro-current seam moving between the weed bed. This is the one time when I will present the fly directly downstream and with little or no slack in the leader. While slack is usually a good thing to have in a dry fly presentation, if the leader/tippet slack is too wide (S curves), the micro-currents surrounding the targeted seam will likely play tug-of-war with your leader and tippet. In other words, you want to straighten out the leader/tippet as much as you can to slip it through the narrow seam. It's like crawling under a barbed-wire fence while wearing multiple layers of jackets and a backpack. The larger profile you create while

Pictured is Bob "The Beetle" Williams about to present a beetle several feet downstream of a rising trout. The hope is the trout will feel the fly land behind it, turn around, and approach the fly. This way the trout sees the fly, not the leader, first, increasing your chance of success.

This is where the downstream and reset presentation is so useful. First, cast to one side of your targeted location (well away from your target) and keep your rod tip low to the water. Then lift your rod higher and pull it back toward you, as this will straighten out the line. Finally pull or drag the straight line over the seam you want to drift down. This keeps your rig tight as it passes through any narrow seam, giving a great presentation. So yes, there are times when you must present a straighter leader and tippet during a dry fly presentation. And you can do this with a downstream presentation, as long as you feed slack into the drift.

attempting to slide under the fence, the more likely the fence is going to grab and pull back on you. The same is true when working narrow seams between weed beds or similar situations—you want to narrow the profile of line and leader to reduce the chance of a micro-current dragging your leader into a different direction.

The basic idea behind this presentation is to cast at an angle away from the targeted line, then elevate the rod tip to pull back on the line and leader to both straighten the line/leader along with dragging the line/leader into the exact seam you want your dry fly to drift down. The key is to reset the line far enough upstream in order not to spook the trout. Another advantage of this approach is the fact you will see the dry fly drag along the surface, which lets you know exactly where your dry fly is positioned. This is useful when fishing smaller/lower-riding dry flies that are hard to spot on the water. Even if you can't see the dry fly after the reset, you at least know the approximate location after seeing it drag into the targeted seam. Basically, this gives you full control of where you place line, leader, tippet, and fly.

Dry Fly Hook Sets

As we'll discuss with streamer and nymph sets in the other chapters, the goal is to move the fly in the direction and speed that provides the best opportunity to impale the hook into the fish's mouth. It's not as simple as lifting the rod tip. While a knee-jerk rod tip lift will hook fish, here are several common dry fly situations I find myself in when attempting to set the hook. The point I want to express here is to not only think about positioning for the best presentation but also plan out what options you have when setting the dry fly. Here are some things to consider:

1. Dry fly fishing often involves excessive line and leader on the water. With euro nymphing, most line and leader is off the water, and a short rod tip movement is all that is needed to set the hook. On the contrary, dry fly fishing often has line and leader off the water, so in order to get a good set, that line needs to be lifted off the water before snapping the wrist to set the hook. In my opinion, the last thing you want to do while dry fly fishing is have to drag the line along the surface of the water to set the hook. Dragging the line creates drag and slows down the time it takes for the excessive slack in line and leader to become tight before moving the hook toward the fish's mouth. So anytime line and leader lying on the water is part of your presentation, I feel a fully extending rod hand accelerating the rod tip upward (to first lift line off the water) is needed before snapping the wrist/rod tip to make the hook set. Any line and leader on the water will create drag and slow down the time it takes to set the hook. Think of your experience learning to cast on water. One of the first rules we learn, before making the backcast, is to lift the rod tip upward and lift line off the water before making the backcast. If you don't lift the rod tip first, then you end up ripping line off the water, which either spooks fish or causes too much resistance during the backcast.
2. Length of line on the water/distance fish is away from angler: The shorter the distance between angler and fish, the less time it takes to pick line and leader off the water to set the hook. So, when

The shorter the distance between you and the rising trout, the quicker the hook set and vice versa. Shown is Amidea Daniel connecting with a shoreline cruising trout. This fish quickly rose and ate her fly. A fast and swift lift of the rod tip was used to set the hook. PHOTO BY CHRIS DANIEL

Same lake a few minutes later, Chris Daniel patiently waits as a trout slowly lifts to inhale his ant pattern. Try to mirror the hook set the action of the fish. Chris delayed from setting the hook too soon, allowing the fish time to inhale the fly and close its mouth. Even small fish like one, will cautiously rise when in such clear and calm water environments.

Gulpers are usually quality sized trout feeding on the lake surface. They're called gulpers due to the sound their large mouths make while sucking in the fly. Often gulper takes are slow, as their weary trout have all the time to inspect your offering. The slower the rise and the slower the mouth closes on the fly, the longer you need to wait before lifting the line.

fishing short distances (e.g., 15 feet) and a large trout slowly opens its mouth and eats my fly, I'll wait for the trout to close its mouth before setting the hook. In New Zealand they speak the entire phrase "God save the queen" before setting the hook when a large trout eats their dry fly. This is an excellent concept, but I feel it works best when large fish slowly take a fly while fishing shorter distances. If you're fishing 40 feet away, then it's going to take additional time for you to pick up the extra line and leader before setting the hook. So when fishing from afar, you may want to begin setting the hook while you see a larger fish slowly take in your fly. My best piece of advice is to simply practice casting various lengths of line on the water and notice the time it takes to pick up the slack line and leader. It's not an exact science, but understanding how distance affects the timing of the hook set is essential for proper timing.

3. Size of the fish/speed of the rise. Larger fish become large because they've generally been selective when feeding. As a result, larger fish take the fly, often slowly opening and closing its mouth to inhale the fly. When this happens, the angler needs to pause a split second longer before setting the hook, giving the fish plenty of time to close its mouth on the fly. On the other hand, smaller fish are often rise to a fly with reckless abandon and attack the fly quickly and without much caution. These types of takes require an immediate lift of the rod tip. This is easier said then done. I know my emotions and adrenaline increase when a trout rises on my fly, and my nature is to simply overreact. This overreaction is fine with small fish, as they take the fly fast, but detrimental when a larger fish takes my fly. This was a huge learning curve from me when my family moved from north-central Pennsylvania (home of small stream brook trout fishing) to central Pennsylvania (home of larger brown trout). It took several months for me to break my overreactive hook set I developed on the brook trout streams. Eventually, I learned to become more patient with the cautiously rising brown trout and began hooking fish. And with time on the water, you will too and more likely learn a lot faster than I did.
4. Angle of presentation (upstream, across stream, downstream). The ideal hook set is moving the fly in the direction of the fish's mouth, so the hook has a better chance of catching. I know this is common sense, but so often I've made many hook set errors by setting the hook in the wrong direction. So, my suggestion is to think about your hook set based on the angle of your presentation. For example, I break my presentation into three categories: Upstream,

Cutthroat and grayling are labeled as lazy risers. When fishing grayling or cutthroat waters, be prepared to wait a little longer to set the hook when seeing a trout take your fly. Pictured is Amidea Daniel hooking into a large Yellowstone cutthroat trout, after a delayed reaction to set the hook.

Whether within the continental United States or internationally, I'll intentionally fish dry flies anytime I know grayling are present. But just as with cutthroat, grayling almost kiss the fly during the take so be extra patient when presenting dry flies to grayling.

up and across, and down and across. When casting upstream I try attempt to move the rod tip in the same direction that water is flowing. Since trout face upstream, this downstream set will likely pull the fly directly toward the fish's jaw. When presenting up and across stream, the set is high and slightly downstream. When fishing directly downstream, I'll first wait for the fish to close its mouth and then attempt to lift high and off to one side. But I find the key to the direct downstream hook set is waiting a split second longer, allowing the trout to fully inhale the fly before setting the hook. *Note:* This is assuming the fish is taking the fly while positioned into the current. However, there are occasions when a fish will let the fly float overhead and carefully follow the fly downstream before rising. This is an exception but does happen so understand the system I'm discussing doesn't always work as they're always exceptions to the rule.

5. Fly rod action: This concept is geared toward the individual who frequently fishes various rods for dry fly fishing. The main point is faster-action rods not only create more energy during the cast but also create more energy while setting the hook. Meaning, less energy is needed with the rod hand to set the hook when fishing a faster-action rod, when compared to a softer/slower-action rod. For example, when dry fly fishing with my soft noodle actioned tenkara rod, the hook set movement must be far more aggressive when compared to tradition action fly rods. In summary, slow-action rods delay the hook set, so you may have strike sooner or harder than what you would with a faster-action rod. Again, knowing your gear's performance is part of a successful outing.
6. Limpness and length of leader: As I mentioned before, I occasionally fish a long Hends leader on flat/calm water. This leader is soft and lands with lots of slack, plus there's a lot of stretch in the leader when playing and setting the hook. Because of the leader's elasticity, the hook set must be more aggressive than while using shorter/stiffer leaders since the leader absorbs a good bit. In fact, the hook set is often a very aggressive lift or the forearm with a hard snap of the wrist to set the hook. If I use the same aggressive hook set with a traditional 7½' 6X leader . . . it's almost a guarantee I'll break off the fish. *Note:* I love to tinker and experiment with various leaders but I do so under the assumption that I may miss or break off more fish due to unfamiliarity with the leader, as it relates to setting the hook. If you're new to fly fishing, my suggestion is to stick to a consistent leader length and type, as this will allow for greater consistency in knowing how hard

Using a mono nonslip loop for larger dry flies and terrestrial patterns. Some anglers feel this loop knot allows more movement when large dry flies interact with the surface currents. Some of my guide friends swear by using a mono non-slip loop knot for fishing larger terrestrial patterns.

or fast to set the hook. Once you feel you're consistent with setting the hook with one leader, then I would suggest experimenting with another leader type. Even some of the better dry fly anglers I know, when experimenting with a new leader, may struggle with a short period of time as they dial in their hook set. It's all part of the fun!

Additional Dry Fly Pointers

Late-season dry fly tactics: One of my favorite times to blind cast big dry flies is during the late summer/early fall season, when low-water conditions exist. This is not about getting numbers. Instead, it's about the ability to catch larger fish. Although I believe many of our larger trout become nocturnal during this time of the year, I've found moderate success blind casting large hopper and stimulator patterns in likely feeding locations. Much of the bug activity has slowed down, which creates less subsurface food availability for trout. As a result, I've found trout are far more willing to eat large dry flies off the surface during this time of year. This phenomenon has consistently occurred on my home central Pennsylvania waters during the low-water periods of August and sometimes September. This occurrence isn't

The perfect low-water/late-season targe to blind cast. This sunken log offers protection and depth, and larger trout will hold near these areas during daylight periods. This is great spot to present a large terrestrial or stimulator pattern, even when you see no signs of surface activity.

Although many of the larger brown trout turn toward nocturnal feeding during the late season in central Pennsylvania, it's common to catch them in the daytime. At times, I believe dry fly tactics may be a better option than nymphing in extreme low-water conditions since you're able to present the fly from a greater distance. This Pennsylvania limestone trout at a size 10 stimulator at midday on sultry August day, during extreme low-water conditions. This was not a fluke as I've taken several quality fish in the same spot/same time period during recent summers.

Pairing a larger dry fly with a small midge allows you to keep track of the midge's general location. Set the hook if you see any rise near your larger dry fly. Pictured is Brandon Collette fishing BWO and a midge duo while floating a western river.
PHOTO BY KEVIN LANDREN

nationally widespread but occurs on some of my home water and maybe on the waters you fish as well?

Winter midge fishing: Some of the most intense dry fly activity on my home waters have not occurred during spring season. Instead, it often occurs during the coldest months of the year, for a short period of time. First, I've only witnessed a surface midge feeding frenzy during low-water periods. Second, midge activity often occurs during the warmest part of the day for a short period of time, but when it happens, it's like all the trout in the

Although I focus on nymphing and streamers in the winter, I always carry a small working box full of midge patterns in the event I encounter trout eating adult midges. This small midge box doesn't take up much space and is always available if winter dry fly tactics are available.

I found this beautiful rainbow feeding on midge clusters on a Pennsylvania limestone stream, during an extreme cold snap. I was euro nymphing but cut off the nymph, added a long 3-foot 7X tippet section and tied on a Griffiths Gnat. I landed this fish along with several others in a short period of time. I landed more fish on a midge pattern in 30 minutes than the few I caught nymphing for several hours before the surface activity occurred. Even during the coldest water conditions, you need to be prepared to fish the surface.

The perfect checkpoint—a gentle bubble line pushing alongside a concrete abutment. This has been one of my most productive locations for blind casting dry flies. Even in low water, trout feel comfortable rising for a drifting insect under the cover of a bridge. Find a nice slow-moving bubble line under a bridge, and you'll likely find a great spot to blind-cast a dry fly.

As the saying goes, "foam is home." Whether in stillwaters or moving waters, find the foam and you'll likely find feeding fish. Pictured is a trout positioned near a foam line, but not far from the protection of a large boulder.

stream come out to eat. I've found the bite windows are narrower during the winter months, but when it happens it's a spectacle to take part in.

Prospecting dry flies without signs of surface activity: Blind casting a dry fly can be a productive approach but only when the fly is presented in the right water types. This is why I blind-cast in higher-probability areas including feeding lies or shallower water where trout don't have to travel far for my dry fly. Tailouts, shallow riffles and runs, shallow banks, and flats are all excellent choices for blind casting a dry fly. For my local limestone/spring creek fisheries, I avoid blind casting in water greater than 2 feet in depth. Anything deeper than 2 feet and my ability to bring fish to the surface drastically decreases. In short, target shallow water where trout don't have to move far to eat off the surface. The deeper and faster the water, the less of a chance of a trout rising for your dry.

It's also worth noting some trout species have a proclivity to surface feed. For example, Yellowstone cutthroat is known for its willingness to rise on a dry. I spend a couple days every year chasing these beautiful creatures with a dry fly, and many of the fish I've caught have been through blind casting into the "fishy"-looking areas. PHOTOS BY CHRIS DANIEL

The best of both worlds—a boulder garden collecting bubbles. Note the little cuts and depressions around the rocks. Years of hydraulic scouring created these depressions, but more importantly they serve as trout feeding huts. Never pass up an opportunity to blind-cast a dry fly to similar water types.

Choke points are where multiple currents get pulled into a tight area. Think of rocks or logs that protrude off the bank. Choke points often collect large amounts of foam and act as a magnet to floating objects, including insects. These objects act as a funnel, pulling any floating objects into a narrow feeding lane. This is the ultimate food line, and trout know this and will take up feeding positions in these lanes. Anytime you find exposed structure (e.g., logs, debris jams, boulders) pulling currents to its position, you have a choke point and plan to attack with presenting your dry fly. One of the best artificial chokepoints are the long wooden boat docks I find when floating on many of northern Michigan's trout waters. These vertical wooden structures also serve as an ambush location where trout can pin a food item against the bank. Or it can be any vertical structure along the bank, where a trout can pin down its prey. For example, I've caught several of my best late-summer dry fly fish along several concrete bridge abutments. Using a large terrestrial or stimulator, I've seen several 18-inch-plus trout pin these large dry flies against one concrete wall not far from my home. My friend and local Michigan guide Matt Verlac always looks for wet splash marks around dry docks and partially submerged logs. A splash mark on dry timber is a good indication that a trout has been eating dry flies.

BIG BUGS AND THE MORNING AFTER OR A WEEK AFTER THE HATCH

Despite the crowded waters, along with the frustration of competing with millions of naturals on the water, fishing the eastern green drake hatch (and within the last several years, hitting the Hex hatch on northern Michigan waters) is still a highlight of the season. It's like being part of a National Geographic documentary as millions of these massive insects hatch while the largest trout in the river gorge themselves. As much as I love witnessing Mother Nature at her best, the odds are often against you during these intense periods. Yes, you can catch some damn nice fish, but sometimes the fishing can be maddening as you place your imitation among dozens of naturals. Therefore, I often fish at first light immediately after these intense hatches. Although hatching activity is done, a few spent bugs often remain floating on the water, and trout are still looking up. This is the perfect time to blind-cast the spent spinners of these larger mayflies as trout are still looking for large floating items before greater periods of sunlight begin.

If you take the time to stop casting and pay attention to where trout move on a stillwater, you'll likely recognize consistent pathways or highways a trout regularly takes. Once you locate these highways, it's easier to spot cruising fish as you'll know exactly where to expect to see them traveling. PHOTO BY CHRIS DANIEL

The eastern green drake is a mayfly worthy of tying an extended body, since its ready body often lays flat on the water, instead of curling upward off the water. Remember to use softer materials for the body and tail when making extended bodies. If an extended body is too long and stiff, it may be too difficult for most fish to inhale the entire fly.

The famous salmon fly hatch is known for getting the attention of some of the biggest fish in the river system. While fishing during the hatch is ideal, trout will still be looking up toward the surface several days (maybe up to a week) after the hatch is over. Blind casting salmon fly imitations post-hatch period will still bring good fish to the surface. PHOTO BY CHRIS DANIEL

When "super hatches" occur, sometimes twitching or moving your fly may help separate your pattern from the thousands of naturals on the water. Pictured is Amidea Daniel fishing a spinner fall during an eastern green drake event in Pennsylvania.

Another example is fishing large dry flies up to 10 days after the 17-year periodical hatch. Although the dry fly activity may not be as hot and heavy, fish will still eat a well-presented cicada pattern one week after the hatch is over. The same concept applies to other large hatches, including the western salmon fly hatch.

In closing, I feel there are times when it's best to just sit and wait for a rising fish. Fishing stillwater for cruising trout may be one scenario when it's best to wait for a rise or wait for a cruising fish. I've had too many trout sneak up on me as the result of blind casting my dry fly into the abyss and never noticing the rising trout as it approached me. I think the best dry fly fishers are also some of the most patient anglers on the water. Meaning, you need to be intentional with your dry fly presentations, especially when fishing waters where trout are on high alert. Too many times I've accidentally lined and spooked a fish because I was randomly casting to the water. A random approach may be useful on smaller mountain streams, where trout are aggressive and less prone to spook. However, when working challenging waters like the Delaware River, Henry Fork, South Holston, or any calm western trout lake, I think the best approach is sometimes waiting until you spot a target. It means being less active with your casting but usually proves more successful with your final catch rate.

PART III

Streamers

I love streamer fishing because it's active, visual, and exciting. The purpose of this chapter is to discuss tools and tactics to developing a successful streamer approach. Contrary to popular belief, streamer fishing is more than stripping a Woolly Bugger across current. You need to pick the tools and tactics based on the conditions you face. The purpose of this section is to provide my thoughts on essential streamers and my approach to fishing streamer patterns.

Remember, you don't need large streamers to catch large trout. Pictured is Chris Daniel showing a rainbow taken on a small leech while fishing a remote lake in South America.

When I think streamers, I think wintertime. Although streamers can produce year-round, I've found the colder winter months to be some of the most productive times for targeting larger trout with streamers. There are fewer insects drifting and hatching (except for midges on my home waters) so I feel trout are more willing to hunt and chase down food items, since food isn't readily drifting to them. Pictured is Michigan guide Matt Verlac preparing for a streamer day on his home water.

CHAPTER 9

Streamer Tools

As mentioned in other chapters, please remember the tools I'm discussing below are based on my own personal fishing philosophies and the waters I fish. The gear suggestions below are more of an all-purpose approach where I attempt to carry a small amount of gear to cover a wider range of possibilities. Some of the gear mentioned below is streamer-specific, but many of the tools can easily be used for other tactics. I don't want to downplay the importance of properly pairing gear with tactics, but I feel most anglers (myself included) spend too much time focusing on gear rather than working on developing good techniques. In short, I tend to beef up (i.e., go heavier) when using streamer tactics, but only when I'm fishing larger patterns or targeting large fish, as we'll discuss below.

Rods

Just as with any tactic, there are general tools and specific tools. In large part, these tools are picked based on the size and power of the targeted fish, along with the patterns you intend to fish. As we'll discuss later in this chapter, I fish smaller streamers (e.g., 1 to 3 inches in length), so I don't feel the need to use a heavier 6–8-weight rod for the smaller streamers I cast, plus

You don't need a 7-weight to catch big fish, but having the mass of the 7-weight fly line does help when casting larger streamer patterns. Pictured is Justin Pribanic holding a quality brown trout taken on his trusty seven-weight rod and sink tip line.

Casting and retrieving streamers is one of the most physically demanding fly-fishing techniques. Take the time to ensure your streamer lines match with the rods you intend to fish. PHOTO BY CHRIS DANIEL

the fact that my home waters produce average- to medium-sized fish.

Although not always ideal, I use my longer nymphing rods for most streamer tactics. Nymphing rods possess a softer tip and have more give/flex with using the rod tip to set the hook. This is not an issue when strip setting, as the pull of the line hand is used more to secure the hook, instead of the rod tip. However, it does become an issue when streamer fishing with a euro jig hook as the rod tip is using the rod tip to set the hook. Euro rods have a lot of give in the tip, so I rely heavily on super-sharp competition-style hooks. Although not as durable and strong as traditional streamer hooks, competition-style hooks require less force when setting the hook. This allows me to use one rod for most of my central Pennsylvania trout-fishing conditions. Although I feel a stouter 5- or 6-weight rod would increase my success, I'm at the point in my angling life where simplifying my gear and enjoying my time on the water is more important than worrying about landing every fish.

The one time I'll use heavier rods in the 7- or 8-weight class is when I'm headhunting larger trout with larger flies. This occurs during my travels near and far, when I plan to do nothing but target larger fish with large streamer patterns. I'm not going to tell you to use this model or line weight rod because in truth, just about every rod company is making good products. The most important consideration when choosing fly rods is making sure the lines (floaters, sink tips, full sinkers, and mono rigs) match the rod action, allowing you to cast and present streamers with the least effort. As you read further, I think fly line type and design are the most important considerations with streamer tactics. If you know what lines you plan on using, then make sure to test-cast any rod with those lines before making a purchasing decision. It may be a good idea to cut the hook point off some of your favorite streamer patterns and test-cast them with any future line or rod purchase. Don't look at brand and don't look at price—test-cast any product with an open mind and simply pick (if you can afford it) the best-performing rod.

Lines

Lines fish your streamer more than you know. The line is responsible for both delivering the streamer to the target and fishing your pattern at a desired speed and depth. I've mentioned before, a lighter rod can land larger fish. Some lighter rods and lines lack the power and mass to physically cast larger/wind-resistant patterns. If you're planning to cast larger patterns, then you'll need a

I once heard Larry Dahlberg mention one stage of a fisher's life is using their preferred method to catch fish. Personally, I love working streamers and the aggressive strikes. I know nymphing and other tactics may be more effective, but there are days I would rather catch one decent fish on a streamer than several trout taken on a nymph. This average fish was the only fish I caught all day. And up to the time I finally got lucky, I loved every fishless minute of that day.

heavier line mass to move them, and vice versa. I rarely need a line weight heavier than a 3- or 4-weight for the smaller streamer patterns I fish on my home waters. However, the list of lines I discuss below are the types I currently use (both frequently and not often) and want to provide a few talking points to the merits of each line type. Let the waters you fish influence your line choice.

FLOATING LINE

I would choose a floating line if given only one line choice to fish streamers. Why? The floating line's versatility allows me to fish lightweight or neutral buoyant streamers in shallow water and heavy patterns deep in the water column with a slow retrieve. Again, your environment dictates line choice and is the reason I find myself using a floating line (compared to sinking or sink tip lines) for streamer tactics involving line hand retrieves. As with dry fly tactics, I like the on-the-water mending capabilities of the double taper line. I use mostly weighted streamer patterns with floating lines, so an aggressive tapered line isn't needed as the weight within the fly basically propels itself to the target.

Mending in the air and on the water is a large part of my streamer presentation. If I want to slow down the presentation, I reposition the line to reduce drag. If I want to speed up the presentation, I create a larger bow with the line laying on the water. If I want my streamer to change direction or follow a certain path during the retrieve, I position the line on the water, so the streamer follows the line path. You cannot reposition any full sinking or sink tip fly line that is physically positioned below the surface. The only way you can mend

I enjoy the flexibility of a floating line. I can fish shallow or I can fish deep, and it allows me to reposition (a.k.a. mend) the fly line during any state of the presentation. Pictured is the author working a streamer upstream while fishing a small Yellowstone National Park trout stream. PHOTO BY CHRIS DANIEL

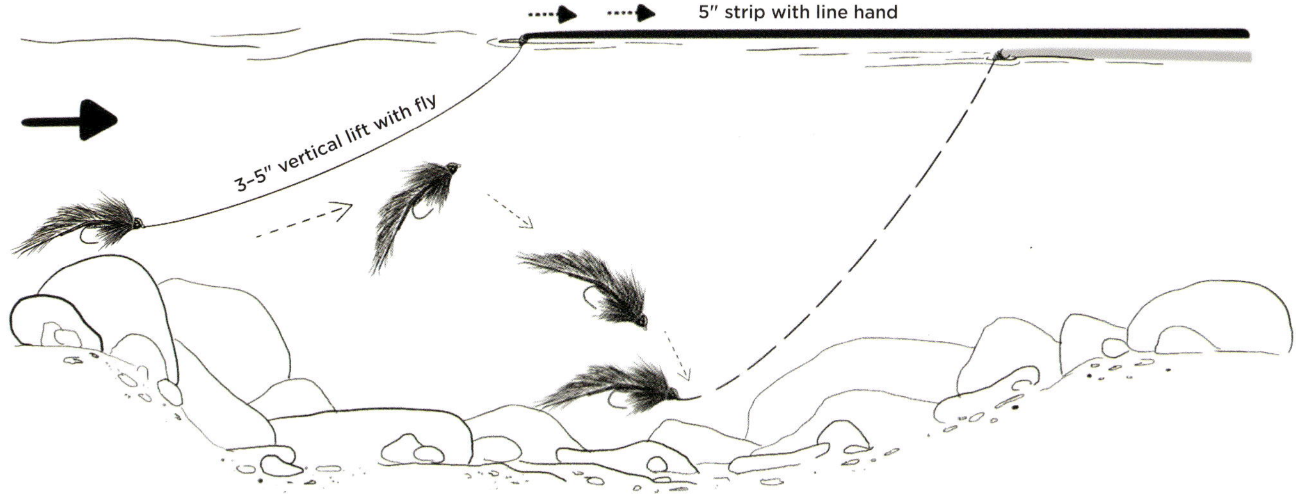

Remember the fly follows the fly line during the retrieve. For example, a floating fly line tip will pull a weighted streamer toward the surface during each retrieve. Hence, use a shorter strip and longer pause if you want to keep your weighted streamer remaining closer to stream bottom during a retrieve. If you strip 6 inches of fly line, the fly may lift 6 inches off stream bottom.

a sunken line is to bring it to the surface (i.e., breaking water tension) before attempting to reposition. A line lying on the surface can be repositioned anytime during the presentation.

I tend to fish my streamers slower than most, and a floating line allows me to fish weighted patterns slow and deep. Remember, the flies follow the path and level of the fly line during the retrieve. If the line is laying on the surface, the streamer will move upward toward the floating line during each retrieve. For example, a weighted fly will stay near the surface with a fast, long, and continuous retrieve. Anytime you want a fast streamer retrieve, remember the fly will essentially swim at the same height of the last 15 to 20 feet of the fly line in the position on the water. For example, a fast retrieve with a floating line will pull the sunken fly upward toward the floating tip. So use a slower and shorter retrieve when striving for a deeper presentation when using a floating line and weighted streamer.

I also want to emphasize the length of the retrieve as it relates to how vertically a fly moves upward during the retrieve. Let's stay with the floating line and weighted fly approach. A sunken streamer and a long 2-to-3-foot strip may lift the weighted streamer 2 feet off the bottom toward the surface (i.e., in the direction of the floating line). So if you're making long strips and pulling the streamer up toward the surface, use a pause to allow the streamer to drop back to the correct level before beginning the next retrieve. Long pulls/retrieves will require a longer pause, and so on. The point is you can fish a weighted fly deep (and keep it deep) with a floating line but use short strips

Sink tips are great options for the wading angler. Only the short tip section sinks while the rest of the line floats on the surface, allowing the angler to strip in line without worry about the retrieve sections sinking and wrapping around their feet. Pictured is an angler working a streamer tight to the bank during a western snowfall event. PHOTO BY CHRIS DANIEL

with long enough pauses between retrieve, allowing the fly to settle back to the correct depth.

Sink Tips

I think the best-looking streamer retrieves involve a sunken line and unweight/neutral buoyant streamers. Most baitfish have air bladders, allowing the fish to create an air pocket and suspend in the water column. Wounded baitfish will drift at any height in the water column kicking and twisting as they struggle to stay alive. A sinking line or sink tip line pulling downward on a buoyant or neutral buoyant streamer nicely imitates a struggling baitfish. The sunken line pulls the streamer downward during the retrieve (when tension is pulled downward), then lifts upward during the pause (when tension is relieved).

I've been using more sink tips recently than full sink fly lines due to the ability to mend the floating line portion of the sink tip throughout the retrieve. Meaning, the sink tip remains below the surface (fishing the streamer) while positioning the floating line section to achieve the ideal retrieve. Just as with nymphing with a suspender, I feel strongly about the need to manage any line floating on the water during the retrieve. I feel I have more control throughout the presentation with a sink tip fishing the fly below the surface, while managing the rear floating line portion on the surface.

Let the stream conditions you face determine the sink rate and length of the sinking head. For example, I would choose a shorter sink tip section when wade fishing since I'm stripping line and allowing it to fall near my feet. If fishing a long sink tip or full sinking line, there's a good chance part of the retrieved line will sink at your feet. Sunken line will wrap around submerged obstacles or your feet. Plus, the sunken line will need to be brought back to the surface before attempting the foreword cast. I may use a longer sink tip when fishing from a boat as the retrieved line will fall on the boat floor and not the water.

Again, think about where and how you fish and make the best choice possible. For example, sink tips are excellent for fishing broken water (i.e., little to no uniformity in surface speed currents. Mending is useful when placing any floating or sinking line on a water's surface where various speed currents exist. Think about the dynamic speed and direction of water flow in pocket water. Now think about attempting to make a straight-line cast across currents with a dry fly or suspension rig without the ability to mend in pocket water. The result would be excessive drag. The same type of drag will occur with streamers if we're unable to mend the line. We often need drag to fish streamer patterns, but I feel many anglers fish streamers too fast as a result of excessive drag. Also, sunken lines will wrap around submerged boulders and obstacles. Having a short sink tip to fish the streamer, while mending the floating line section, allows us to work streamers around (not through) potential snags.

Just as with fly rods, there's never going to be a single sinking line to match all conditions. However, spending time thinking about the waters you plan to streamer-fish, along with talking with other experienced streamer anglers, will streamline future fly line purchases.

FULL SINKING FLY LINES

I use full sinking lines anytime I want to fish a pattern on a continuous retrieve. Swimming patterns like the gamechanger perform best with an almost continuous retrieve. A full sinking line lying deeper in the water column will keep such patterns swimming deep during the retrieve as compared to sink tips or floating lines where the pattern will climb an upward angle. Mending is not possible once a full sinking line begins sinking below the water. Precise line positioning needs to occur before the line sinks. Sinking lines are good choices for stillwaters or larger moving waters possessing even or uniform flows. A stripping basket is needed if fishing a full sinking line while wading, as the retrieved line will sink and catch your feet or any submerged object. Therefore, I fish full sinking lines from a boat rather than when wade fishing.

Reverse jigging with sink tips and sinking lines: Anglers often think of a floating line or euro approach when jigging streamers. That is, lifting the fly upward on the retrieve and allowing a vertical drop during the pause. This up-and-down movement is one of the most

Full sinking lines are excellent choices when you want to fish flies deep with a faster retrieve, but a countdown is needed to allow the line to sink to the correct depth before retrieving the fly.

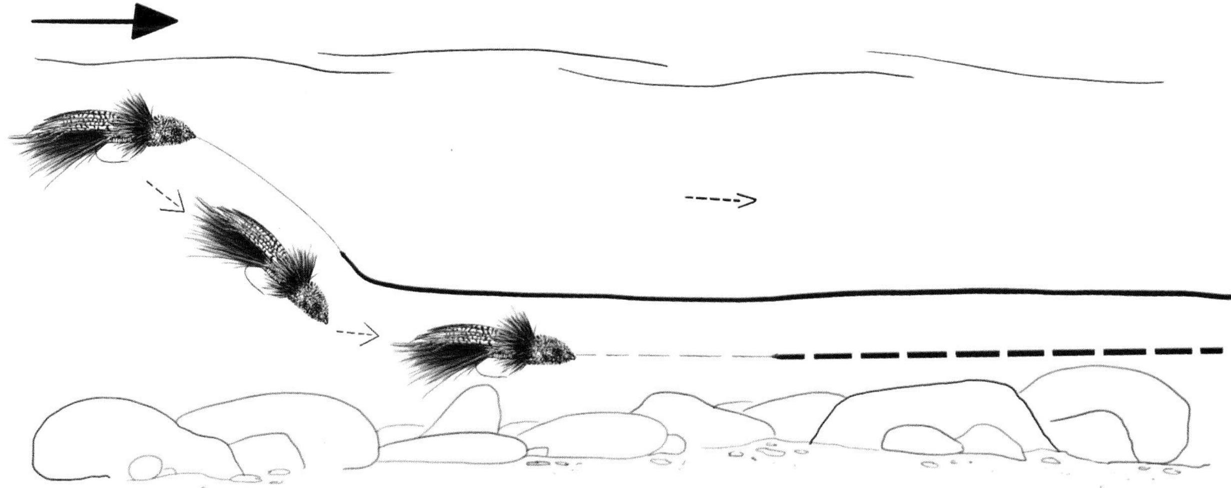

Let the sinking line fish the streamer. This is so true when fishing buoyant streamers like the Zoo Cougar and Drunken Disorderly with a full sinking or sink tip fly line. In other words, you need to create height separation between sinking line and fly. In this case, the fly line needs to be positioned below the streamer height before beginning the retrieve. This results in the line quickly pulling the buoyant streamer downward toward stream bottom. Then a longer pause allows the streamer to float back toward the surface.

You are selling your presentation to the fish when streamer fishing. Don't just lazily strip the fly in at the same speed and length each time—mix it up! Strip fast. Strip short. Strip long. Strip while wiggling the rod tip. Think about a baitfish and how it moves and behaves in the water and replicate those erratic movements during the presentations. Pictured is Justin Pribanic pausing after a strip while Brian Wilt positions the boat.

effective streamer tactics, as this retrieve sends out the dinner-bell signal to predatory fish. However, the same up-and-down movement is possible with a buoyant/neutral buoyant streamer and sinking or sink tip line. The only difference is the process reverses itself with a sinking line or sink tip pulling downward on the buoyant or neutral buoyant fly. That is, the line needs to be positioned below the streamer before the strip. Remember the fly follows the path and level of the fly line. A line positioned below the fly will pull the fly downward during the strip or retrieve. Then a pause occurs when a small amount of slack is placed back into the line, allowing the sinking line to sink downward and the buoyant or neutral buoyant streamer to drift upward.

The key to jigging is creating separation between fly line and streamers. When it comes to sinking line, a long enough pause (immediately after the cast or after each retrieve) should occur, allowing the line to settle well below the streamer. When you hear someone say "let the fly line fish the fly," this is exactly what they mean. A hard downward pull followed by a pause creates a tantalizing movement with the streamer.

Sinking line myth: Heavier-grain fly lines sink faster. The truth is a 150-grain type 6 sinking line (i.e., a line that sinks 6 inches per second) will sink the same rate as a 450-grain type 6 sinking line. Grain weight relates to the rod tip action, not sink rate. For some reason, there's a misconception that a heavier 450-grain-weight sinking line used on a 12-weight rod will sink faster than a 150-grain line used on a 5-weight. In truth, more tungsten coating is needed to sink the 450-grain due to its larger surface area. The point is designated sinking lines and sink tips all sink at the same rate despite the difference in grain or line weight. An increase in grain weight will only provide more mass to aid in casting larger patterns—not increasing the sink rate.

European mono rigs for streamers: I must admit I've used a mono rig for over 50 percent of my streamer fishing within the last several years. One reason is the simplicity of switching between nymphing and streamer tactics. And the other reason is about getting the fly into the strike zone. It's the same concept we discussed with euro rigs when euro nymphing—a thin mono line held off the water allows any weighted pattern (nymph or streamer) to drop fast into the depths. Streamer fishing is no different than nymphing—you should fish your flies slower and deeper if fish are not aggressively feeding. Trust me, there's nothing more exciting than casting a

Using a mono rig to jig streamers is a good idea when you need to fish your streamers slow and deep. Pictured is Brian Wolfkiel jigging a streamer during a Pennsylvania polar vortex.

The mono streamer rig allows you to hold line and leader off the water, reducing drag and allowing you to keep your streamer in the strike zone. It's basically high-stick nymphing with an active retrieve.

I find it difficult to hold onto mono during cold weather. Either the line slips through my fingers during a hook set or I accidentally let go of the mono during a retrieve, so I may switch to a thin euro line during these times. The euro line is easier to hold onto when my hands lose partial function in the cold.

large streamer to bank, retrieving it back at a fast rate, and having a large shadow rise from the depths and crush the pattern. Those aggressive streamer-eating days are almost as limited as good dry fly days, so if you want to consistently catch using streamers, I suggest using a euro rig to dig deep in the water column. Just as my mentor Joe Humphreys discusses with nymph tactics, "a single split shot adjustment can change everything."

Although I prefer mono for its thin diameter and enhanced strike detection, I will use euro fly lines during extreme cold weather. One reason is mono tends to hold more memory during extreme cold temps and is difficult to hold onto with frozen hands. Most euro lines seem to coil less in extreme cold temps, and the fly line finish is easier to grab when setting the hook. Too many times I've had mono slip through my cold finger tips while attempting to set on a streamer-eating fish. I would stick with all mono during the winter if I had better dexterity, but I don't in cold conditions, so I usually switch to a thin euro line.

Although lacking visibility, I prefer stiff Maxima Chameleon material for my mono setup, followed by

I like to keep both line and rod hand extended away from the body while euro jigging streamers. Also, I prefer to use a hand retrieve during the jigging movement. This allows my line hand to remain away from my body, giving me lots of room to strip with the line hand (in combo with rod tip) when a trout takes. PHOTO BY DOMINIC LENTINI

A long leader, floating line, and micro jig streamer were used to capture this rainbow while fishing a south-central Pennsylvania spring creek. When fishing floating lines, I like to use a minimum leader length of 8 feet. On this occasion, my leader was 9 feet and constructed of 5-foot 15-pound Maxima Chameleon and 4-foot or 2X fluorocarbon while using a 3-weight euro rod.
PHOTO BY JAY NICHOLS

Use a shorter leader with sinking lines if you're looking to achieve a deeper drift. Sinking lines tug on your streamer during the retrieve, so keep the leader short (maybe 2 to 4 feet long) if you want to keep the fly deeper during the retrieve. Pictured is a trout taken with a sink tip line using a 2-foot leader during a cold Pennsylvania morning. Just as with nymphing, depth control is important with your streamer game. Shortening up the leader may allow a deeper streamer presentation.

sighter and fluorocarbon tippet. The reason is for less give during the hook set. Since I'm usually euro jigging streamers with a softer-tip action euro rod, I feel I need to use a stiffer (less giving) material to help set the hook. I've used countless hi-vis soft nylon materials for euro jigging but feel there's too much give in both rod tip and leader while attempting to set a streamer hook. This is not an issue when nymphing with smaller-diameter hooks, but I've noticed a decrease in secure hook sets when euro jigging with softer nylons. This concept of "too much give" is not an issue if using softer nylons with a faster-action rod, due to the increased force during the hook set. Experiment yourself and find what works best for you. I usually connect mono to tippet using a two- or three-turn surgeon's knot, but I know others will use a larger tippet ring or snap swivel.

Leader Materials and Leaders

Keep streamer leaders simple. I use a simple two-section leader containing a nylon butt section and a fluorocarbon tippet (50-50 ratio). Rarely do you need a manufactured tapered leader as weighted streamers propel themselves or you're relying on the mass of the fly line to deliver the fly. I prefer using a two-section leader to create a weaker link between the tippet-to-butt section, so I only lose a couple feet of expensive fluorocarbon. Also, I mentioned in another chapter that I prefer to keep the loop of my fly line if possible. Using a larger-diameter nylon loop to connect to the fly line loop reduces the likelihood of cutting through the welded fly line loop. Although I prefer using a single-strand tippet section (rather than a tapered two-section leader), I've cut several welded fly line loops when connecting to level 0X–2X tippet sections using a loop-to-loop connection. Therefore, I use a thicker 15-to-20-pound test maxima butt section to connect to the fly line using a loop-to-loop connection. You can cut off the loop and use a nail knot to attach the leader directly to the line, but I've found my lines last longer when I keep the loop, given the number of times I switch out leaders. I always use fluorocarbon tippet for better knot strength and abrasion resistance.

As a suggestion, I shorten the leader as the line's sink rate increases. I use an 8-to-10-foot leader when fishing floating lines, 6-to-8-foot leader with intermediate lines, 4 to 6 feet with type 3 or 4 sinking lines/sink tips, and 3 to 4 feet when fishing type 5-to-7 lines. There are always going to be exceptions for using a longer or shorter leader, but this scale is a good one to work from.

CHAPTER 10

Streamer Patterns

What is your game plan for today's streamer approach? I ask myself this question not just with streamer tactics but with any fly-fishing approach. Previous streamer fishing mindset was casting and ripping Clouser Minnows and Woolly Buggers. While this simple approach does work, there are multiple approaches to fishing streamers. Casting angles, retrieve depth/speed, and fly action are now common scenarios to think about. Stream conditions and fish behavior should dictate which approach is best. This isn't meant to complicate streamer tactics but instead get you to think about developing a plan that will increase your success. We've already discussed line and leader choices, so let's discuss streamer designs and their applications.

I've reclassified streamers into several types: jigs, swimmers, swingers, and kickers. I no longer carry massive boat boxes full of streamers. I try to recall how many streamers I used and how many I lost after each trip. Today I fish fewer than five or six patterns in total but carry a small variety of pattern types and colors for each trip. Years ago I would carry hundreds of streamer patterns in large suit box–size streamer boxes. These

Justin Pribanic looks through his impressive streamer fly box. Justin is an amazing streamer angler and is great at matching the streamer design/type to the technique being used. First, think about what technique you're planning to use and then pick a matching streamer design.

This is how I currently store all my streamer patterns. Instead of carrying large suitcases of streamers on the boat or in my pack, I spend a few minutes thinking about what patterns I'll need for the day's trip. I'll then grab several types, along with backups, and insert them into an empty box. When I'm done fishing for the day, I'll take the flies out of the box, dry them, and put them back into storage.

large boxes took up so much space and required excessive maintenance if it rained while fishing, which meant pulling every fly off the foam and drying them that night. I found this to be excessive for my personal fishing.

If you're guiding streamer trips, I get it and would also carry more streamers. Streamer fishing is taxing both physically and mentally. When the streamer bite is off, it's off, and it can make a day of streamer fishing feel more like a day of practice casting. Switching streamers is like giving yourself or a client "new hope" with the idea of rebuilding confidence and tightening up your technique. For me, changing patterns seldom rebuilds my confidence, especially if I feel I'm correctly presenting the fly. I feel good technique and presenting the fly at the right time is more important than switching patterns every 25 to 30 minutes. This is not taking a jab at anyone as many of my good fishing friends religiously change flies every 25 to 30 minutes, and I consider them just as good if not better than me.

Again, the point here is creating a streamer selection that fits both the waters you fish and your personality. It's taken me years to develop this minimalist streamer pattern mindset. Depending on conditions, I may only carry two or three streamer types with one or two color variations and have one or two spares for each. So basically, I carry less than one dozen streamers with me at a time. The only time I carry more is when I'm jigging streamers, as I tend to lose more jig styles since I'm fishing these patterns along stream bottom. You shouldn't lose too many streamers, which is why I carry fewer these days.

Jigs

As I mentioned earlier, I'm using jig streamers more often given their effectiveness and how using a euro jigging approach has consolidated the gear I carry. I do want to mention jigs have been and can be fished using any fly line type. For example, the Clouser Minnow is one of the all-time jig streamer greats and has accounted for lots of fish on multiple line types. Today, I usually stick to using a mono rig with jig patterns, but remember, you can fish jig patterns on any fly line. Jig patterns should be simple, in that these are not patterns designed to swim or kick. Instead, jig patterns need a heavily weighted section on the front end. This front end lifts up during the strip (i.e., tension) and drops sharply between strips (i.e., slack) creating a tantalizing up-and-down movement.

Second, I feel jig patterns need to drop faster into the water column. A heavily weighted front end like a conehead or dumbbell helps, but just as important is the pattern's profile and the material used to construct the fly. I look at jig patterns like perdigon-style nymphs—a slim profile that quickly drops through the water column. Using water-phobic materials (natural or synthetic) allows the fly to slide fast into the depths. Also, I like the feel of the water-phobic material gliding through the water without any friction, which is why I no longer use rabbit or wool materials. Patterns made of wool

The kreelex strikes again. The late Chuck Kraft's kreelex pattern has become my favorite jig streamer when dealing with dirty or off-color water. Every time you jig the streamer, the reflective flash looks like a flashbulb is going off.

and rabbit feel like you're pulling a wet sock through the water column. Thin strips are fine with patterns like Barr's Slumpbusters and Mayer's Leech, but using larger/wider strips results in excessive friction during the retrieve. When jigging with a euro approach, the rod tip lifts up and down to lift and drop the streamer. Using a mono system, you can feel a well-designed streamer slide through the water and feel even the softest take. You lose that sensitivity with jigs made from water-absorbing materials. Good jig patterns use materials that glide (rather than drag), while maintaining a slim profile. It's so easy to overbuild streamers—less is more. My jig selection is simple. I carry a variety of sizes, colors, and weights for the following patterns.

KREELEX

Chuck Kraft was a gifted fly fisher and fly designer. His kreelex pattern has become a favorite jig pattern for numerous species. I still use the original version, using a standard streamer hook and dumbbell eyes, when

Kreelex

Hook: #8 euro jig nymph
Thread: 6/0 olive dun uni thread
Bead: 5.0 Mm slotted tungsten
Tail and body: gold over silver Kreelex material

Spark Plug

Hook: #8 euro jig nymph
Thread: 6/0 olive dun uni thread
Bead: 5.0 mm slotted tungsten
Tail: white craft fur
Flash: gold flashabou
Body: medium UV white polar chenille
Wing: copper ice wing

planning to use fly lines and stouter streamer hooks. However, I'll switch to a larger competition jig hook and heavy tungsten bead version when planning to use a mono rig and softer euro rod. The water-phobic flash material and tungsten bead aids in dropping the pattern fast into the depths. The pattern maintains a baitfish profile yet glides through the water with little to no friction. The pattern looks like a flashbulb flashing on and off as it jigs up and down in the water, and it is a favorite pattern when fishing dirty water or low light conditions. It's like a distressed sinking ship sending out a flare in the middle of the night—the kreelex gets the trout's attention. A variety of kreelex material is available so countless color-scheme options are possible, but I prefer gold over silver.

SPARKPLUG JIG

What is better than the original sparkle minnow? How about a sparkle minnow modification tied on a jig hook? I tie the spark plug jig in both gold and copper variations, although color options are endless. Instead of a using a dubbing brush for the body, I tie in either gold or copper flash behind the bead—reverse tie style to create flowing body and baitfish profile. A black permanent marker can be used to add a third color tone to the top. The sparkplug jig imitates two of Pennsylvania's most common cold-water baitfish: blacknose and longnose dace.

SCULP SNACK

My Sculp Snack is just one of thousands of Woolly Bugger variations, but there's something about a thin UV polar chenille body and a rubber leg skirt tied with

The sparkplug jig is my take on the famous sparkle minnow. I feel it does a great job imitating one of Pennsylvania's most popular trout forages, the blacknose dace.

a heavy tungsten bead or conehead. I tie this pattern as small as size #12 jig hook all the way up to a large 1/0 for large trout and bass. Polar chenille maintains a nice baitfish profile without adding bulk and resistance during the retrieve. The color combinations are endless, but I keep it simple and tie this pattern in olive, black, and white variations.

Sculp Snack

Hook: #8 euro nymph jig
Thread: 6/0 olive dun uni thread
Bead: 5.0 mm slotted tungsten
Tail: sculpin olive marabou
Flash: pearl flashabou
Body: large UV olive polar chenille
Legs: barred pumpkin sili legs

The Sculp Snack jig is my favorite bugger variation, and I carry it in a small variety of colors including white, olive, black, and yellow.

Chartreuse and white are a favorite color scheme for fishing dirty water. Pictured is Fred Moy holding a brown taken on a chartreuse-and-white swim-style streamer while fishing a Pennsylvania tailwater.

TROUT FRY

A simple Chickabou Marabou streamer concept I learned from a Michigan guide in 2005. Using banded Chickabou for the tail and collar, this pattern looks like a trout fry or even a smaller perch. It's a natural-looking jig streamer that performs well anytime, but I use it when fishing clear water or anytime I suspect trout or salmon par have hatched.

ADDITIONAL STREAMER TIPS

Where should the hook point be? I like having the hook point dead center of single-hook point streamers. I keep hearing trout and other predatory baitfish always attack headfirst. I disagree. Predator fish will attack from any angle, but they usually eat headfirst. Putting the hook dead center (i.e., halfway between head and tail) still allows for a good hook set if a trout attacks from any angle. I find this concept useful if I plan to present the streamer from a variety of angles. The only time I would intentionally position closer to one side is when presenting the fly from only one angle. For example, I'll tie in a stringer hook in the rear when swinging flies down and across for steelhead. Think about the angles you plan to fish and let that determine where to position the hook point if you plan to use a single-hook point streamer.

Using mono versus wire for articulations: Memory developing within the wire has been a struggle for long-lasting streamer patterns. Within recent years I've progressed leaps and bounds in not losing streamers. My focus while casting has improved, and I have no issues climbing trees or submerging my arm into cold water to retrieve a fly. This has resulted in several patterns lasting one or two seasons before falling apart. What I have found with articulated patterns connected by wire is once the wire develops a kink/memory, there's no way to undo it. Mono also will kink and develop memory, but it takes a lot longer than wire. In short, switching to mono articulations has lengthened the life of my streamer patterns. I've consistently fished mono-linked streamers for over 12 months before the connection started twisting.

I use 25-pound test Maxima Chameleon for both strength and stiffness. Mono has a tendency to slip when being secured on the hook, which can cause the back portion of the fly to also twist. I use several drops of Krazy Glue to lock in the first mono section (either on top or on one side of the hook shank). Once glue and mono is locked onto the hook shank, I'll then take the other mono end and run it through beads (if wanted) and rear hook point and loop it around and secure it on the hook shank. Adjust the loop so there's some play, allowing the rear hook to sway from side to side. But don't allow too much movement as this may cause the rear hook to constantly foul while casting and retrieving the fly. Then lock in the second mono section with several additional drops of Krazy Glue. Using articulated shank products will eliminate this issue, but it's something to think about if planning to articulate hooks with a wire or mono connection.

Jigging tip: You can turn any streamer into a jig pattern by adding a heavy split close to the eye of the fly. Plus, you don't have to tie jig patterns in a variety of weight—make any weight adjustment by adding various-sized split shots near the eye of the fly. While it doesn't

Jig Fry

Hook: #12 euro nymph jig
Thread: 6/0 olive dun uni thread
Bead: 5⁄64" slotted tungsten
Tail and collar: natural yellow chickabou
Body: gold ice dub

Picture of a twisted mono connection, which will result in a twisted rear fly. Always take time to make sure the mono or wire connection is properly set before finishing the front fly.

Using a few drops of super glue will hold the articulated connection mono in place, reducing the likelihood of the rear fly twisting.

I use the euro jigging approach anytime the fish are holding deep and showing little sign of activity. This approach allows you to get the streamer to these deeper-holding/less active fish, with the hopes of creating some response. This system works because it quickly gets the streamer to the trout, which is essential when fishing from a moving boat.

look as sexy and lean as a clean jig pattern, a split shot attached to any pattern still works. My only concern with using split shot is when using smaller-diameter (e.g., 4X–5X) tippet. Adding split shot increases the chances of adding nicks to tippet. While this isn't a big deal with heavier-diameter tippets, I feel this is a bad idea with light tippet, which is already under enough pressure with aggressive strikes. And yes, I do fish 4X–5X tippet with smaller micro jig patterns on my local waters. The smaller-diameter tippet allows the fly to settle deep and fast, and the soft action rod tip absorbs the shock of aggressive strikes. Using smaller diameters like 4X–5X allows me to switch back and forth from euro nymphing to euro streamer fishing. Therefore, I rely on the bead weight to sink the pattern (not split shot) and rarely use split shot when jigging with smaller-diameter tippets. I use 4.0–5.5-mm tungsten beads for most trout jig. I may go heavier (e.g., Spawns Super Tungsten Slotted Bead 6.3 mm) when dealing with extreme conditions.

Swimmers: As the name implies, swimming patterns continuously move during the presentation—acting like a fish casually swimming away or fleeing for safety. The gamechanger style of pattern is without a doubt a great swimming pattern and is the only swimming pattern I carry, but experiment with other swimmers and find what works best o n your waters. I must be honest in saying that I no longer tie my own gamechangers as these patterns take time to tie, along with an attention to detail. Proper taper from head to tail allows these styles of patterns to swim in serpentine fashion. Within the last year, the Flymen company has been producing quality gamechanger patterns at an affordable price. When I calculate the time it takes to properly tie one of these patterns versus buying them, I save when I purchase them from my local fly shop.

GAMECHANGER

I only fish these patterns in the most challenging streamer conditions—slow and clear water where you may need a more realistic presentation. I would fish these patterns more often if I were fishing large tailwaters like the South Holston, Delaware River, and Arkansas's White River. However, given the smaller streams with broken water (e.g., pockets, riffles, runs), I feel jigs and other patterns provide just as good if not better results without the added cost or time of fishing gamechangers. I feel the gamechanger style is a bit of overkill for my trout streams but use these style patterns all the time for local bass and musky fishing, where I feel it makes a significant difference with my catch rate.

This style pattern is an excellent choice where trout can see your pattern from a distance or when dealing with heavily pressured trout—anytime when you need more time to sell your presentation to the trout. When fishing gamechanger-style patterns, I would say the most important tip is mastering the retrieve to swim (not jerk)

Gamechanger

Front hook: short shank/wide gap streamer hook
Shanks: three 20-cm shanks
Thread: 6/0 white uni thread
Tail: pheasant breast
Body: yellow filler flash and pheasant breast feathers

I like using swimmer-style streamers when fishing shallower water and for trout that are in a hunting mode. I enjoy the activity of casting and retrieving these patterns, but I only do so when working shallower waters, when low light or dirty water conditions exist. If I believe trout are not active and resting in the depths, I'll switch to a euro jig approach. Amidea Daniel took this brown while swimming a gamechanger across a shallow riffle on an early May morning.

Although dry fly tactics are my first option when approaching cutthroat, fishing streamers is an excellent searching tactic, especially on large western waters. Pictured is Chris Daniel with a beautiful cutty taken with a swung streamer.

the pattern. Most gamechanger-style patterns are not designed to be jerked with the line hand. Instead, these patterns are usually designed to be pulled in a long or continuous motion, allowing the tapered fly to seductively swim in the current.

Two favorite retrieves for gamechangers are 1) the hand-over-hand (a.k.a. roly-poly) retrieve where the rod is tucked around your armpit, allowing you to use both hands to pull/retrieve the gamechanger back to you in a steady, controlled manner. 2) Long wiggle strip: Instead of short, powerful pulls, this strip involves a *long* and steady line pull while wiggling the rod tip. The rod hand fully extends straight with rod tip facing the fly line. The rod tip touches the water surface to keep the line from jumping during the retrieve, which maintains tension on the line and leader, keeping the gamechanger swimming at a constant speed. The rod hand smoothly wiggles the rod tip from side to side as the line hand makes one long controlled pull. Try to smoothly accelerate the pull (not just pull a single speed), as the gamechanger will speed up to a stop during the pause, causing the streamer to glide sideways. The pause is short while the line hand reaches for the first stripping guide to grab the line before making the next accelerated pull. Again, position both rod and line hand in a manner allowing for a long, smooth, accelerated pull. Make sure the rod tip remains touching the water during the long pull, as this will keep the streamer swimming under continuous tension, allowing the gamechanger to swim in a seductive manner. The retrieve is correct when you see the gamechanger's tail wiggling or swaying from side to side.

Swingers: I look at swinging streamers as similar to fishing wet flies—a great approach for covering water for active fish. I use smaller-sized streamer since casting longer distances is involved with this tactic. For example, I'll swing streamers on larger rivers like the Yellowstone (within Yellowstone Park) for cutthroat. Casts of 40 feet or more are normal on the Yellowstone, and trying to cast this distance with a larger pattern is challenging, so I stay with smaller patterns when distance casting. Just as with wet fly tactics, I may use a second streamer to cover more water. This is the one time I'll fish two streamers as I find it challenging fishing two larger patterns when jigging, swimming, and jerking patterns.

Some of my favorite swing patterns include the smaller trout fry tied on a regular shank hook, micro Sculp Snack buggers, and micro leech patterns like Mayer's Leech. Just as with soft hackles, I'm looking for patterns that move and breathe in the water during the swing. Materials like micro zonker strips, soft hen hackle, and marabou are all excellent choices. Since I use a floating line for swinging patterns, I'll add a smaller bead or conehead (brass or tungsten) to keep the fly below the surface.

Mayer's Strip Leech

Hook: #12 scud hook
Thread: 6/0 olive dun uni thread
Bead: ⅛" brass or tungsten bead
Tail and collar: micro squirell zonker
Body: black tinsel

SWINGING STREAMERS

Mending line on the water is an important skill to have when swinging patterns. We want the streamer to swing but we don't want the patterns to swing too fast. This goes back to the lesson I learned with Davy Wotton while wet fly fishing. That is, I created too large of a belly in my line during the swing, which resulted in the patterns swinging too fast. Give the fish a moving target, but don't make it too fast. The simple act of lifting the rod tip up and repositioning the back end of the fly line (without moving the fly line tip) will slow the swing down, which may improve the day's success.

Let the conditions dictate how fast to swing the presentation. In cold or off-color water, slow down the swing. In clear water and optimum water temps, you may want to speed up your swing. The angle of the line laying on the water and the size of the line belly dictate the degree of tension and speed of the swing. Another tip during the swing is to tap the rod blank with your index finger or using the line hand to stoke the line back and forth. This additional movement may help invoke a strike.

Gliders/jerk strip patterns: I define this category as patterns that require a hard/aggressive pull of the line hand. Depending on the design, these patterns can glide and bend horizontally, dive downward toward stream bottom, and wobble from side to side, along with numerous other movements. Without a doubt, my favorite streamer approach is pulling hard and long on the fly line and watching a larger streamer glide, kick, and bend sideways. In truth, it's fun watching these patterns perform and it's the one thing that keeps my confidence up during slow periods. Here's a short list of the gliders/jerk strip patterns I fish throughout the year.

MATT'S WEDGEHEAD

This pattern is a culmination of numerous streamer designs put together by my friend and favorite Michigan guide, Matt Verlac. The recipe you're currently seeing and reading about has been a work in progress for well over 5 years. I'm sure future tweaks will occur, but this pattern has become one of my confidence jerk strip patterns. This pattern has several features. First, it has *some* neutral buoyancy qualities. Meaning, the pattern isn't going to sink fast but it will slowly sink so you can fish it on a floating line for shallow water presentations or fish it deeper with a sink tip for full sinker. Second, this pattern has three sections, starting with a wide deer-hair head that tapers to a thin/lightweight tail. Going back to the jackknifing concept—good line-pulling technique is essential, but the right pattern design also helps. If you want to talk about a perfect pattern designed to jackknife, look at Matt's Wedgehead. The wide deer-hair head can be pulled fast through the water, but the moment you stop pulling on the line, the surface area of the head forces the pattern to come to a sudden halt. Then the light back end quickly kicks to the side.

Matt often uses a three-section pattern (two articulations) for targeting larger northern Michigan trout, and I'll do the same when fishing larger trout waters. I'll downsize the pattern or use only two shorter sections when fishing for smaller trout near my home waters.

Matt's Wedgehead

Front hook: short shank streamer hook #8
Rear hook: timeco
Thread: 6/0 olive dun uni thread
Head: dumbell eyes
Tail: schlappen fibers
Flash: flashabou
Body:large UV polar chenille and schlappen collar
Legs: barred pumpkin
Wing: barred mallard flank coated with UV
Head:deer body hair (trimmed wedge shape)

The ability to stall and pause your streamer pattern is important when imitating a wounded baitfish. Wounded fish kick, turn, and pause, but rarely is it a continuous movement. Patterns you can stall in shallow water and then violently strip allow you to better imitate a wounded baitfish. Pictured is the author with another beautiful Michigan brown trout taken on a Matt's Wedgehead.

This shallow water is perfect for a neutral buoyant streamer fished on a floating line system. A weighted fly would likely snag stream bottom, but a neutral buoyant pattern would likely hover above the bottom during the presentation.

The olive-yellow and olive-black color schemes, along with the wide deer-hair head, make an excellent sculpin imitation. One word of caution: Don't pack the deer hair too tight when planning to fish this pattern with a floating line. A tight-packed deer-hair head equals greater buoyancy and may not sink enough, even with heavy dumbbell eyes. It will take time but you'll eventually learn how much deer hair you need to work with both floating and sinking lines.

Tips for deer-hair heads: Don't pack the deer hair too tight when trying to achieve some level of neutral buoyancy within your streamer. If the deer hair is tightly packed, the deer-hair head will float like a balloon and not allow the sinking line to pull the line under. The key is creating a wide head profile without excessive buoyancy. Otherwise, your pattern will perform like a surface popper during the retrieve.

PEANUT ENVY

Still one of my favorite patterns created by Russ Madden and modified by Kelly Galloup. Basically, a conehead version of the popular circus peanut, this pattern is easy to tie, easy to fish, and continues to produce. I'll

tie these patterns as short as 3 inches all the way up to 9 inches. I'll use marabou tail for shorter sizes and schallapen for longer patterns. A wing or synthetics (like craft fur) or natural materials like barred marabou or mallard can be added to create a barred look and create a wider baitfish profile. There are countless material and color options allowing for an unlimited number of peanut envy options. For example, I'll use UV Polar Chenille and dubbing brushes for a flashier synthetic look or use schallapen and regular chenille for a toned-down appearance.

Neutral buoyancy advantage: The idea of a fly or lure hanging (rather than rising or dropping) in the water column has been around for years. One situation where I find this style of pattern to work great is when fishing extreme cold water and off-color water conditions. Both scenarios often demand a slower presentation, allowing the pattern to hover during the pause. The idea is to slowly work the fly with frequent pauses. If a fly is too heavily weighted with this type of retrieve, it will drop fast and likely hang on stream bottom. You want the fly to stay and remain in the strike zone for as long as possible. It takes time experimenting, but eventually you'll come up with a few line (floating, sink tip, full sinker) and pattern combinations, keeping your streamer moving horizontally during the retrieve and pause.

When fishing streamers along shallow banks during the cold winter months, my preference is using a neutral buoyant streamer, which allows me to slow down the retrieve without worrying about the fly snagging the bottom.

Peanut Envy

Hooks: #8 3XL streamer hook
Thread: 6/0 olive dun uni thread
Tail: marabou
Flash: flashabou
Body: large UV polar chenille
Collar: marabou
Legs: barred pumpkin sili legs

One of my favorite examples was placing a split shot on a Zoo Cougar's nose while using a floating line setup while fishing shallow dirty water after a rainstorm. The dirty-water trout are feeding in water that may only be 4 to 8 inches deep, and any weighted fly is likely to snag stream bottom. This scenario is perfect for a neutrally buoyant streamer. The split shot would counter the Zoo Cougar's deer-hair head, allowing the pattern to remain halfway between stream bottom and surface during the presentation. You can tie a pattern with neutral buoyancy qualities, or you can modify a buoyant streamer streamside, as I did with the split shot and Zoo Cougar.

CHAPTER 11

Presentations

A quality tied and engineered streamer is important, but the most important part is how you fish it. Presentation is everything, and when you're streamer fishing, you are trying sell the presentation to the fish. Uninspired line pulls or a monotone retrieve are not going to work with these patterns. These categories of patterns should glide, kick, dive, lift, or wobble from side to side. The point is you need to be aggressive with the line hand and/or rod tip to get the most action out of these patterns. If you want that pattern to glide and make a hard turn on the pause, the line hand must pull on the line and accelerate that fly to a hard stop—the same principles as with a basic fly-casting stroke. The goal with any articulated patterns tied in this category is to jackknife. That is, the back-end portion will kick hard to one side during the pause. It's like a tractor trailer speeding on the highway and suddenly slam on the brakes, causing the trailer to "jackknife" off to one side. Jackknifing won't occur unless the semi is moving fast and suddenly stops. If the semi is moving 20 miles an hour down a city road and slams on the brake, little if any jackknifing will occur.

Instead of stripping the moment the buoyant streamer lands on the water, wait a few seconds and allow the sinking or sink-tip line to sink deeper in the water column. Then begin to work the fly, but make sure to pause long enough between each strip to keep distance/separation between line and streamer. Pictured is a Matt Verlac Wedgehead that fooled a southern tailwater brown trout.

Watch your pattern during the strip. If you're making 6-inch strips, then your streamer should move 6 inches fast to a hard stop. Coming to a hard stop is like slamming on the brakes, which will cause the fly to sway or turn hard. If the line casually stops after the strip, it's like a car braking slowly when approaching a stop sign and will result in little movement after the pause. I'll say it again: Pull hard and stop hard with the line hand. Get that fly to turn and kick and you'll make an easy sell to the trout, or any species for that matter. These patterns are not easy to fish—they require work! Your line hand and fingers should be fatigued after a good day of streamer fishing.

Roll casting sinking lines: Not all full sinking line tapers are created equal, and that's why research is needed before a purchase. Few anglers think about roll casting streamers with a full sinking line, but certain stream conditions exist where the roll cast is your only presentation option. For example, tall vegetation and trees encircle long stretches of Michigan's Pere Marquette River (a.k.a. the PM), providing little space for backcasting. Roll casting full sinking lines is a good option if you're planning to use unweighted streamers but you need a line you can roll-cast. This was a lesson learned when fishing with Jac Ford on PM. Basically, I tried casting a level-tapered full sinking line with poor results. Jac watched me flail the sinking line on the water several minutes before suggesting I use his sinking line. Instead of a level taper, this full sinking line had a long aggressive front taper, allowing me to create momentum and easily roll-cast within the PM's tight quarters and begin catching a few fish. I would not have had the same results attempting to roll-cast my line. So the moral of the story is, again, research and pick the right tools for the job.

Timing of the cast and setup is a big difference between roll casting when roll casting sinking lines. A delay normally occurs, after the rod tip slides the line back behind the angler, creating a D loop. The mechanics of roll casting a sinking line are similar except for one thing: There is no pause between setup and forward roll cast. The key to roll casting a sinking line is having the line lying on the surface during the forward roll cast movement. A roll cast isn't easy if the line is partially sunk, as the line must break the surface tension before making the forward movement. Instead of pausing to let the D loop form, the rod tip drifts backward to a stop and immediately accelerates forward to complete the cast—just as if it's a continuous motion with a split-second pause between setup and forward cast. Watch the streamer on the end of your tippet—keep skating on the surface before making the forward casting stroke.

Casting articulated patterns in tight brush: Articulated patterns kick and bend during the retrieve. The articulated link (mono, wire, or shank connection) is meant to bend in the water, but it will also bend during

A northern Michigan trout stream after a recent snowstorm. This is a perfect example of why you need to learn how to roll-cast weighted streamers and sinking fly lines.

The first step to roll casting a weighted streamer or sinking line is to begin sliding the rod tip behind you—just as you would with a regular roll cast. This is a continuous movement where the goal is to slide the weighted fly and/or the sinking line at the surface while you begin to set up for the forward casting stroke. Sometimes I feel it makes more sense for the hand to be fully extended away from the body before you begin this movement. The farther the hand is away from the body, the more distance it has to move back toward you during this sliding movement.

The final stage of roll casting a weighted streamer or sinking line is to immediately begin the forward casting stroke—once the rod tip is positioned behind you with the fly line belly hanging off the rod tip. This hanging line belly off the rod tip forms a D shape, and it's this hanging line that helps load the rod during the forward casting movement. In short, there is no pause between setup of the D loop and the forward casting stroke—it's one continuous movement. If you pause too long after setting up the D loop, the line and/or fly will sink, making it difficult to make the forward casting stroke due to the fly/line having to break the surface tension.

an erratic casting movement. This was a lesson learned while floating a small northern Michigan stream with Matt Verlac. The articulated fly never fouled while casting in large openings, where I didn't feel rushed making the cast. However, the fly would foul (i.e., catch itself) when casting in tight quarters, where I felt rushed and tried pushing the cast. Matt would say the fly was "misbehaving," but after a full day's fishing, I realized my rushed casting was causing the articulated streamer to foul. Let's face it, sometimes you must force or push the cast when there's no backcasting area behind you. When these situations arise, I suggest switching from an articulated pattern to a single hook point to reduce fouling. There's nothing more frustrating than making a great cast as you punch a large articulated streamer under a low-hanging limb, only to notice it's fouled up during the retrieve. This is the reason I switch to single hook point (non-articulated) streamers when fishing tight quarters.

The strip set: There are several advantages to the strip set. First, predatory fish often strike or attach prey several times before going in to inhale the prey. Often called short striking, an angler will feel or see a fish nip or bunt their head against the pattern. Using the rod tip to set the hook usually pulls the fly out of the water and away from the aggressive fish, which may only be short striking your fly. So many times, I've had trout short-strike my streamer several times before going in for the kill. However, if you keep the fly in the water after a short strike, there's a good chance that fish will come back to take another look. There's still hope of a fish coming back a second time, even if you stick them with the hook. I've fished several marginal trout fisheries where the few large trout living in those waters made a living eating panfish, which possess a sharp dorsal fin. So, these trout are accustomed to getting pricked in the mouth when eating baitfish.

The second advantage of strip set is the power created during the set. Little energy is lost when the angler points the rod tip straight at the fly and pulls straight through the guides. Any energy loss would likely occur as the line or leader stretches during the set. Some line companies produce no-stretch lines to increase strike

Trout don't always inhale the fly on the first round of attacks. This trout hit the streamer several times before finally committing to eating the pattern. Several series of strip sets kept the fly in the water after each strike, allowing me to keep the fly in play before the final take.

When swinging streamers down and across a fast current, the streamer and line are already under a high degree of tension. This is when I find simply lifting the rod tip upward may create a better hook set than strip setting. The dampening of the rod tip allows the trout to inhale the streamer when the line is under pressure versus sometimes pulling the streamer out of the trout's mouth when strip setting.

detection and increased power during the set. As I mention below, there's a time and place to use the rod tip to set the hook and there's a time to use the strip set. Compared to dry fly and nymph hooks, streamer hooks are usually thicker wire. As a result, greater power is needed to pull the thicker diameter hook point into a fish's mouth, which is why more power is needed to set a streamer hook than a thin dry fly hook.

Learning to set the hook with your line hand (rather than rod tip) may be one of the most challenging things to learn in fly fishing. Everyone learns differently, but one of the best tips on learning to strip set is changing the language you use while setting the hook. For example, you're more than likely to quickly lift the rod tip anytime you hear the word *set*. So, stop using the word *set* in your streamer vocabulary and instead use the word *strip*. This is what the best saltwater guides will do with their clients, especially those who have little saltwater experience. Instead, the guides will tell their clients to strip slower or strip faster when they see a fish eating their fly. This simple change in my fly-fishing language has helped both myself and my clients achieve a good strip set when needed.

When to Strip Set or Trout Set

One common streamer myth is to always strip set with streamers. While the strip set is important for most streamer scenarios, there are times when you may want to use the rod tip or simply let the fish hook themselves. For example, when swinging streamers or fishing any streamer tactic down and across current, the line, leader, and fly move under a higher degree of tension. Strip setting is a forceful set, and I may avoid using this set when I feel the fly is already under a high degree of tension, like when I'm fishing down and across. I've found I'm usually ripping the fly out of the fish's mouth when strip setting while the streamer is already under a high degree of tension. Therefore, I may use a short forearm lift of the rod hand to set the hook. The rod will flex and absorb energy during the set, allowing the fish to inhale your fly instead of ripping it out of its mouth. It is possible to use too much force during the set. However, I'll use the strip set anytime I'm fishing an upstream angle since the streamer is moving with the current, which is when I need more power when setting the hook. Again, I'll use a strip set when my flies are moving with the current and switch over to a rod tip set when the flies are under a high degree of tension.

Avoid slapping retrieves with spooky fish: There are extreme situations when the line slapping the water during the retrieve will spook fish. I've seen this on saltwater flats where keeping the rod tip off several inches off the water caused the line off the rod tip to slap the water and spook bonefish 50 feet away. While this is something I pay more attention to while fishing saltwater flats, I realize I've spooked countless trout due to slapping the line on the water. Keeping the rod tip planted on the water's surface will eliminate line slap and may reduce the spooking of trout during extreme conditions. Something to think about.

Change of direction! The term "triggering a strike" is a much-discussed topic. There may be qualities we can add to the fly or our presentation that will "trigger" a fish into taking our fly. The one trigger I want to discuss here is changing the direction the streamer takes at the end of the presentation. What I'm doing is a blend of the figure eight used in musky fishing and the Leisenring Lift with trout fishing. While streamer strikes often occur early in the presentation, trout will follow a streamer a long distance while deciding fight or flight. Changing the streamer's travel path may force a trout into making a quick decision to strike. Basically, I'm quickly repositioning the rod tip at the very end of the presentation to change the direction of the streamer on the stream. That is, the forearm will move the rod tip in the opposite direction the streamer is traveling during the presentation. This repositioning changes the pattern's route and then lifts the fly upward. This is done close to the angler, using no more than a rod's length of leader outside the guides, and works while fishing broken or off-color water. A trout can see an angler from a distance in clear water and will likely stop following the fly when it realizes an angler is close by. On the other hand, I've had so many trout eat a streamer at my feet in dirty water, where it couldn't notice me while chasing down the streamer. This simple tactic works and is a movement I make after every streamer presentation (mono, floating line, sink tip, or full sinking line).

Don't develop a mindset of always casting to the bank: As I'll mention again and again, develop situational awareness when making your approach. In this case, we're talking about where to cast. For some reason, anglers have a "casting to the bank" mindset when fishing streamers, especially when fishing from a boat. Often, banks are shallower feeding lies where trout position to feed. These are my favorite spots to fish in low light or when I'm the first angler to hit the water. However, trout may leave these areas with increasing angling pressure or

Shallow banks may hold fish only a small percentage of the time. Get to know where the drop-offs or deeper slots are on the waters you fish, and you'll likely encounter greater success with your streamer approach. PHOTO BY CHRIS DANIEL

When fishing deeper water, I may allow the streamer to sink a few seconds before beginning to strip or work the pattern. Remember to allow the fly to get to the fish's strike zone first, then worry about your presentation.

as the sun lights up the water. For example, I've noticed a dozen drift boats following one another on well-known tailwaters, all peppering the same banks with streamers. It makes sense if the banks are deep and have lots of cover for trout to hold, but it makes no sense if the banks are shallow. Trout feeding in shallow waters know they're exposed and will flock to deeper water when sensing danger. This goes in line with the idea of changing depths before changing fly color. In other words, target drop-offs or deeper water (away from shallow banks) with bright light or increase angling pressure conditions.

Another myth is fishing the banks in high water. Some moving waters have little midstream substrate protecting fish from higher flows, which is when most fish are pushed to the banks. However, most streams have plenty of mid obstructions or depressions, allowing fish to hold and rest during the most extreme flow. Only those that know these spots intimately will recall where to fish during higher water conditions.

One of my favorite examples was watching a live bait guide (fishing live minnows) fish his clients midstream on Arkansas's White River during high water releases, while myself and every other fly angler around was focused on fishing the banks. And yes, the only reason he was able to fish these deeper pockets in high water was the result of using thin mono line instead of the thick fly line. Even the fastest sinking line will not drop fast enough when trying to fish your streamer 6 to 10 feet below raging water—there's too much surface drag. But watching him guide his clients into good fish in those conditions gave me confidence in fishing away from the bank in higher water. I soon began to effectively cover these deeper cushions in high water, when using the jigged streamer approach on a mono rig. While I love the concept of casting fly lines and actively retrieving streamers off the bank, I'll make the switch to a mono rig and fish farther out in deeper water when I feel the bank isn't the place to be. It's a tough habit to break, but one worth learning!

Should I strip immediately or let the fly sink? A popular streamer question deserving of thought is should I strip the fly immediately or let it settle before moving it? My thought is when I'm fishing a shallow section of water, where trout are likely to attack the fly as soon as it lands, I'll immediately begin working the fly. There's no need to wait in shallow water as the fly is already within the strike zone. When fishing deeper water, use a pause to allow the fly to settle before working/stripping in the fly. This is more of an educated guess, but having some situational awareness helps in making an educated guess. For

I find slapping the streamer on the water creates a dinner-bell scenario for the trout, especially when my home waters have this greenish limestone stain look. However, I'm less likely to slap the fly during periods of low and clear water.

example, if you're fishing low light and the larger trout appear to be on the hunt. Or maybe the water is beginning to rise after a rainstorm. These are situations where I may begin working the fly immediately.

On the flip side, maybe the sun is high and larger trout are seeking depths. Or maybe an increase in angling pressure has pushed the fish to greater depths. These are situations where you may want to do a countdown, allowing the fly to drop deeper before beginning the retrieve. Remember to treat streamer fishing the same way you fish nymphs. Change depths when action slows down.

Slapping the streamer: Dirty water after a rainstorm is a favorite time to fish streamers. Trout use their lateral line to sense movement of prey, especially when they can't see in off-colored water. So, it may prove useful to fish streamers that create a larger impact on the water during the initial presentation and retrieve. For example, the wide deer-hair head on Matt's wedge is an excellent choice for creating commotion when presenting and retrieving the fly. Think about how you would position your hand while slapping something or someone: Your fingers would spread out while making contact with your hands positioned in a wide stance. The wider hand position makes a louder sound while encountering its target. Now think about using a karate chop on the same target, where the hand is in a narrow upward position (as opposed to a wider one). The sound of a karate chop is quieter than that of a slap due to less surface area encountering the object. The point I'm trying to make is to use a wider-profile pattern (like Matt's Wedgehead or Galloup's Zoo Cougar) if you want to create a louder impact cast. The combo of a wide-profile streamer and forceful cast will create an impact trout can feel, so they can locate your pattern in low light or dirty water. Also, the larger-profile patterns will push water, creating additional vibrations trout can locate during the retrieve. Sometimes I feel you can't slap the fly hard enough while fishing muddy water. And do the exact opposite if you want the streamer to create less commotion during the presentation.

Let a bad cast play out: You're targeting larger predatory fish when using streamers. Predatory trout hunt for forage and will react to any fly that falls within their strike zone. When fishing broken water or off-color water, the zone may only be several feet. When fishing shallow flats, the strike zone may be 20 feet. The point here is if your cast falls short of its target, let it play out. Don't pick up the presentation and recast! Trout and most fish have innate senses, allowing them to know when any possible food items have fallen or are swimming nearby—it's how they stay alive. Even if your streamer falls 5 feet short of the logjam you wanted to hit, fish it as if you made the perfect presentation. Aggressively feeding trout (not resting trout) will move good distances to investigate an ill-placed presentation. So many times, I've made a bad cast and immediately picked up the line to recast, only to see a large trout swimming toward the streamer that is now traveling in the air and away from the fish. Once a trout moves on a streamer, the chances of success with each succeeding cast drops significantly. As many of you have or will experience in your angling lives, sometimes the best fish of the season is caught on the worst cast. Let a bad streamer cast play out.

Avoiding kickback: Streamer fishing often involves casting heavy flies and/or weighted fly lines. Kickback occurs when some form of resistance sets in while on a fast-moving object. For example, you're shooting line on the forward cast when suddenly there's no more line to shoot. All the slack line shoots out through the guides and tugs on the reel, causing the weighted sinking line and weighted fly to kick back on itself. The result is excessive slack in line and leader. Several long strips of line occur before regaining any control, causing you to miss any strikes happening at the beginning of the presentation, which happens frequently with streamers. The idea is simple: Have slack line to shoot on every streamer cast, avoiding the line to pull on the reel. You're going to see kickback in your presentation if you hear your reel's gears getting pulled out by the line. Remember to have some line to give (a.k.a. shoot) with each cast, allowing the line and leader to fall in a straight and controlled manner.

Heavy jig head–style patterns like this will create excessive kickback if not enough slack is provided when the pattern is traveling to target. Make sure you have plenty of line to shoot while casting heavy streamers like the one shown.

Pinching off line with O ring: As mentioned earlier, using the "O" ring enables you to stay in control with line and fly. The O ring also serves another purpose when shooting line: the ability to quietly drop a streamer without any kickback. Remember, kickback occurs when a fly object stops "dead in its tracks." We can use the O ring to apply slow and steady pressure on the shooting line to slow down the path of fly and fly line. Same as when slowly applying pressure to your vehicle's brakes while driving on a slippery road—the application of power (from foot to brake pedal) is slow and steady. The same process should occur with the fly line between your fingers. The grip between fingers and fly line is soft at first, but tension increases as you pinch off the line. If you apply too much pressure too soon, kickback will immediately occur. Also, this tactic is helpful in any situation when you feel you're overshooting your target and need to stop the fly from traveling any farther. As with many other casting tactics, practice this in the yard or on water before actual fishing occurs.

Retrieving Hung Streamers from Trees

You're not fishing aggressively enough if you're not occasionally hanging streamers in trees. Sometimes we need to figuratively hit the trout on the head with our streamer, getting an aggressive response on our streamer. But when we overshoot the target and hang our fly in a tree, we need to do our best to retrieve the fly. I dislike losing flies, especially expensive streamers, but what I dislike even more is seeing dead birds hanging in the trees. Hanging flies in trees is part of fly fishing, no matter how good of an angler you are. However, it's our responsibility to do our best to retrieve the fly. Below are some suggestions for retrieving a hung fly. Although located in this streamer chapter, these tips apply to all other fly-fishing rigs.

The first rule is not to yank on a hung pattern. If you overshoot the cast and hang the streamer in the tree, *chill out!* Don't do anything at first, except take a deep breath. If you pull immediately on the line, you're likely to bury the hook point into the tree. Also, if you see your fly literally wrap around a limb numerous times, none of the tips below are likely to help. These tips are for streamers hanging over the trees, not fully wrapped around.

Scenario 1: If fishing a sinking line or sink tip, kick enough slack outside the rod tip, allowing a large belly to form between rod tip and streamer, but make sure the belly isn't touching the ground. Now grab onto the rod handle with both hands and start making fast/accelerating up-and-down movements with the rod tip. The idea is to send a shock wave of up-and-down movements of line toward the streamer, creating perpetual momentum with the line and leader to catapult the fly over the limb. The more violent and wider movements made with the rod tip, the better the results. For some hung streamers, it's taken me several minutes to retrieve a single pattern, but it works most often. This tactic will not work if you hang the streamer and immediately pull the line, causing the streamer to bury itself into the stream. Another suggestion is to wiggle the rod tip from side to side during the up-and-down movement to help clear additional limbs or any possible sticking points. Again, this is a good tactic when using a light-to-unweighted streamer and fly line.

Scenario 2: Now let's discuss hanging a medium to heavily weighted streamer in a tree. It's like the first approach, but this time we're making the weighted fly kick back on itself. This fly retrieval works better if hanging several inches below the limb it's hung on. If the fly is positioned close to the tree branch (i.e., the fly is actually touching the branch you're trying to retrieve the fly from), give the line some slack in the hopes of dropping the fly several inches below the tree. The next step is to create a slingshot effect, where the angler will use the line hand to quickly feed slack into the line (dropping the fly fast) and immediately begin pulling the fly upward. This causes a bounce and often catapults the weighted streamer over the limb. This will only work if the fly is hanging over the tree, not wrapped around it. Don't pull if the fly wraps several times around the tree. Instead, point the rod tip at the hung fly, grab the line with your line hand, and try to spring it (short but fast pull with line hand). This springing action relaxes the noose, allowing you to slowly unroll the hang-up. This is a tip I learned from my mentor Joe Humphreys, and it has retrieved countless flies for me over the years. Just as with casting, this is a great tactic to practice at home or anywhere you can find tree limbs to hang your fly in.

Casting angles: I feel the casting angle is just as important as the streamer and fly line type you use. The casting angle determines the streamer's speed, angle, and retrieval direction. I've already written about this extensively in the nymphing chapter, but let's chat about casting anglers as it relates to streamer fishing. Remember to let the stream conditions and trout behavior dictate your presentation angle.

An upstream presentation places less tension on the line and leader (or mono rig), allowing the streamer to drift slower and deeper. I began thinking about an upstream approach (compared to the traditional

Reach casts are not just for dry fly presentations. The reach is also important with streamer tactics as the angler can determine the path the fly takes during the retrieve. Remember the fly follows the fly line during the retrieve, so position the line on the water the way you want the streamer to move during the retrieve. Pictured is legendary Michigan angler Jac Ford demonstrating a perfect reach cast while working a streamer.

down-'n-across I learned) while fishing with my future father-in-law, Walt Dickey, a live-minnow angler. It's worth noting we were fishing a deep/slow pool on a cold January day. Casting his minnow rig upstream and allowing it to sink, Walt kept a high rod tip and occasionally jigged the tip to add some movement as the minnow drifted downstream. I noticed how deep and slow he worked his minnow, compared to my fast and furious (down-'n-across) streamer approach. Despite the fact he was fishing a live minnow, his results were far better than my own. I started adapting this upstream approach to my streamer game, catching more fish during the colder winter months.

The upstream angle allows a slower and deeper presentation, a good approach for fishing deeper water and during periods of low trout activity. If I were to sum up streamer casting angles, it would be as such: Cast upstream when trout are holding deeper in the water or showing signs of less activity. Cast across current when fishing shallower water or during aggressive feeding periods. So this means I'll cast and retrieve streamers with speed when fishing shallow water. Larger trout holding in shallow water are usually hunting and willing to chase down food. This simple concept is all about adjusting the speed and depth the streamer travels during the presentation. Experiment with various pattern designs and colors, but I believe experimenting with casting angles is more productive. Success is usually the result of picking the right tools and technique, not about fly color.

Euro Jigging

I like nothing more than casting larger articulated streamers on a sinking line and watching them swim back to me during the retrieve. This active and visual approach to working streamers is maybe the reason it's my favorite fly-fishing tactic. With that said, I find this shallow and active presentation works well during certain times of the season, especially when fish are aggressively feeding (willing to move great distances to chase down food) or when fishing closer to banks, where water levels are normally lower. But when fish are not shallow and aggressively feeding, I think we need to shift gears and get the streamer working deeper and slower in the water column. As I've mentioned before, I look at streamer tactics similar to that of nymphing, where presentation depth may be the most important variable to the day's success.

I believe a good number of streamer takes occur more out of aggression or territoriality than actual hunger. No matter how amazing your articulated streamer looks in the water, strikes are not likely to occur if your streamer presentation is several feet away from a trout that isn't hungry. However, if you can sink that fly deeper in the water column and fish it closer to a less aggressive fish, then your chances of creating some sort of positive response (i.e., attack from a trout) greatly increase.

One of the best ways to increase sink rate is to decrease surface tension, and what better way to do this than using a European nymphing rig (a.k.a. traditional tightline) and heavily weighted streamer? This combination of keeping most line off the water with a smaller/heavier-weighted jig streamer creates an opportunity for your pattern to quickly achieve a slower and deeper presentation. In other words, you are bringing the fight directly to the fish when using a euro streamer jigging approach.

Basically, you're using a mono nymphing rig with heavier tippet and possibly heavier mono line. The leader still contains a long section or mono, a sighter, and tippet. The rod tip remains at a higher height/angle to keep most mono off the water to reduce drag and allows the weighted streamer to drop and remain near stream bottom. Either the rod tip or a combination of rod tip and line hand places movement into the fly during the retrieve. The process of holding thin monofilament line off the water with a higher rod tip reduces drag, keeping the streamer riding slow and deep throughout the presentation.

One major difference is the rod tip moves to set the hook instead of the line hand pulling to create a strip set. Lifting rod tip to set hook may be the only option given the rod tip position is high during the jigging presentation. If you want, you can cast a weighted jig streamer to a target with a mono rig, lower the rod tip, and use the line hand to retrieve the fly as with any streamer approach. You don't need to use a jig when fishing a mono system, but if you are stripping the fly, you may find it easier to use a thicker mono or a thin euro line that allows you to get a grip and set the hook more efficiently.

However, I feel the advantage of the euro streamer approach is your ability to keep the pattern riding slower and deeper in the water column. No matter how fast a full sinking line or sink tip is, you're still placing a larger surface (i.e., fat fly line versus mono) area on or within the water, so expect greater drag. This slow and deep concept is so important when trout are holding deeper and less active. And since lifting the rod tip sets the hook, I rely on thin-diameter hook points (e.g., competition-style jig hooks) that require less force to penetrate a trout's mouth.

To make this presentation, cast at an upstream angle, allowing the streamer to drop (if needed) while keeping as much leader off the water. Use the sighter as a depth gauge. Instead of immediately moving the rod tip to jig the fly, point your rod tip toward the jig streamer and use the line hand to strip or hand-retrieve several feet of line at first. This movement reduces the distance between

The euro jig approach is a must if you fish streamers in between massive log jams. Pictured is the author dropping a jig pattern in between fallen logs, which is almost impossible to fish if using a traditional floating or sinking line.

rod tip and fly. This helps you keep the rod tip closer to the water during the jig streamer retrieve, giving you better control, creating less fatigue on your shoulder, and, more importantly, providing a better rod tip/rod hand position for setting the hook. The worst thing that can happen is having too high of a rod tip angle when the fish strikes, where the rod tip has less area to travel when setting the hook. My favorite position is the rod tip held parallel off the water or no greater than 45 degrees. Any angle greater than that makes setting streamer hooks challenging with the rod tip. I like the upstream approach as it allows the streamer to drop faster, but you can present jig streamers from any angle.

The beauty of this approach is you drift the jig with no additional movement, use the rod tip to place movement into the fly, or use short little strips—just enough to animate the fly during the presentation. It doesn't take much movement (i.e., short strip of line hand or short lift of rod tip) to get a "jiggy" action from the fly. When using the rod tip to jig the fly, try to use more of a short, powerful forearm lift instead of jerky/wristy movement. I believe using the forearm (rather than the wrist) helps in at least two ways. First, this repetitive forearm movement isn't just jigging your streamer, but it also serves as a hook set when a trout takes. A wristy movement uses more of the softer rod tip section, while the forearm uses both tip and the powerful and stouter midsection of the rod, providing more power during the hook set. Because of the weight of the fly used with this approach, you will feel most strikes.

I feel a good jig approach is when the jig is under tension during both the lift and drop, because trout (and other fish species) often eat the fly during the fall. Using the forearm also provides greater control. Using short wristy movements usually places a lot of slack into the leader and sighter, creating a loss of contact for several moments before tension is regained. The forearm lifts and drops the streamer under a controlled manner. One way to know if you have control is watching the sighter as you lift and drop the rod tip. If the sighter goes limp, then you have slack and are likely using too much wrist. If the sighter remains tight during the up-and-down jigging action, then you have control and will detect any strikes occurring during the drop.

We need enough weight within the rig or fly to maintain tension during this up-and-down lifting motion. Simple- and thin-profile jig streamers tied with tungsten beads, tungsten conehead, or any heavy jig head allows you to maintain contact with both rod tip and fly. You're likely not fishing a heavy enough streamer if you're making control lifts with the forearm and the sighter is showing signs of slack. Rarely do I use less than 4 mm tungsten bead with my jigs.

Even though you are fishing a heavy fly, with this method you can have depth and line control from the very beginning of the cast, just as you do with euro nymphing. Allow the sighter to drop closer to the surface when fishing deeper water and hold it higher in deeper water. If you're hanging up too often, hold the sighter higher during the next presentation, and vice versa. Think about a shallow flat near a bank with a steep drop-off. After the cast is made, the sighter may be held higher off the water to prevent the fly from hanging up. Then you may need to lower the sighter, allowing the jig streamer to drop deeper as the fly approaches the drop-off.

If you want to fish your patterns more actively, then lead with the rod tip more as you jig the streamers. If you want to slow down the presentation, let the sighter go vertical while using short movements to jig the patterns up and down. The best way to see how your pattern behaves and moves is using a bright-colored fly during the presentation. Use a chartreuse jig and experiment with various hand strips or forearm lifts, noticing how each movement affects the path, speed, and direction of the jig. Then you'll have confidence when fishing drab-colored jigs in deeper or off-colored water, since you'll know exactly what the pattern is doing with each movement you make with rod tip and/or line hand.

The reason we miss strikes or lose trout during the fight is often the result of not paying attention to your hook point. For example, I lost three good fish in a row before looking at the hook point of the fly position in the lower left corner of this picture. I immediately replaced the jig and went on to land several good fish. Also, given the cost of large tungsten beads these days, I use a wire cutter to cut the bead off the hook and reuse it.

EXTREME CONDITIONS

I believe euro jigging streamers really shines in extreme conditions: winter, high water, and low water. Although challenging to handle with freezing air temps, it takes a longer time for your guides to completely freeze over when using mono rigs. Thicker fly lines transport more water as they pass through the guides, speeding up ice buildup within your guides. Even using a thin euro line will decrease ice buildup during extreme cold conditions. Unless you plan to cast dry flies, a mono or thin euro line may be a better choice for winter conditions.

When fishing broken water or heavy pocket water, your target is a small cushion of water surrounded by raging currents. Placing any sink-tip or full sinking line in the raging currents will cause immediate drag, ripping your fly out of the strike zone. The ability to drop a heavily weighted fly into a small pocket while holding all leader off the water allows you to keep your fly with that pocket for an extended period.

This is also a great approach during high water/flooding events where raging water surrounds your target or hydraulic cushion. For example, a downstream euro jigging approach helped me win my last US National Championship during a major flooding event.

A rainstorm transformed our streams into a raging torrent of chocolate milk—making it nearly impossible

Keep your jig patterns simple. These patterns are not designed to swim or kick. Instead, their main function is achieving depth, so keep jigs thin and use material that cuts through the water. Pictured is the author holding a white version of his Sculp Snack pattern. PHOTO BY DOMONIC LENTINI

to fish, let along fly fish. The only areas slow enough to fish were seams along the banks, and these holding areas were narrow (about 1 foot wide) at best. Visibility was several inches at best so I felt the best approach was to stall my streamer (i.e., hold it in one location) until a trout located it in the mud. Using a euro jig setup with a straight downstream approach, the heavy fly landed within the pocket while holding all line and leader off the water. The slower downstream current kept constant tension on the jig while I positioned myself upstream holding line and leader off the water. I would occasionally drop the rod tip, allowing the jig streamer to drop, then slowly lift the fly upward. The key was holding the jig streamer in a narrow seam or pocket for up to several minutes, while giving it a little action in hopes of a trout locating it. It was boring as heck, but it brought several fish to the net within a 3-hour period. The only way I was able to stall the jig patterns in the small pockets was using a euro jig approach. I would have blanked if attempting to use any traditional streamer line in those conditions due to excessive drag.

The euro jig approach is also useful during low-water conditions, where trout may spook once any fly line lands on the water. For example, I faced some of the spookiest trout while fishing Big Spring Access on Tennessee's South Holston River during low flows. As soon as any fly line landed on the water (even a well-presented 3-weight double taper), fish spooked 30 to 40 feet away. The only rig that didn't scare every fish in that area was casting a micro jig streamer on a thin 4-pound mono rig. Trout spooked even with only the micro jig (#12 with 4 mm tungsten bead) landing on water, while a higher rod tip lifted the mono off the water. However, it was the only streamer presentation I could make without alarming the entire pool. I only landed three fish that one morning, but I know I would have had zero if attempting to place any fly line on that water.

Casting Jig Streamers

Casting jig streamers on a mono rig is like casting a heavy lure on a spin rod. First, rarely are you making a traditional back-and-forth cast. The basic cast goes like this: Allow the heavy jig to hang no more than several feet below the rod tip. The cast (actually a lob) occurs as the rod hand pulls the rod tip toward the target while the wrist smoothly flips the jig over the rod tip. Usually a wider movement with the wrist allows the jig to ride higher over the rod tip, rather than through the rod tip or

The euro jig approach allows you to literally hold or hang a jig streamer in place for an extended period, a great approach when visibility is limited. Pictured is the author holding a jig streamer in a pocket during a flooding event.

Freshly hatched brown and brook trout hatch in the spring. Patterns like the jig fry match this newly available protein source, and it has been a favorite jig pattern over the years. This quality Pennsylvania brown trout was taken on a 2-inch jig fry.
PHOTO BY AMIDEA DANIEL

The jig streamer is held under the reel during the underhand flip while the rod hand forearm drifts away from the body and the wrist flicks upward at the end of the movement. This movement is the same as spin anglers use when pitching lures in tight brush.

across the back of your head. Either the thumb or finger on top works with this traditional lob.

To prevent the fly from dropping too fast in the water, hanging up too quickly in shallower water, I use an underhand flip, like you would see when a spin angler is pitching a lure under an obstruction. The line hangs under the rod tip and your casting elbow is positioned close to the body. The rod hand is positioned off to the side with the palm facing the target and the thumb facing an upward angle. Let the fly hang several feet under the rod tip. Keep the palm facing the target as the hand drifts level to the target. This drifting of the hand toward the target begins loading the rod. Continue to drift until the rod is fully loaded (the amount of weight you use determines how fast the rod loads). The movement is shorter with heavy jig and longer with lighter rigs. When ready to pitch the jig, the bottom of the hand flips upward (so your palm is facing the sky). This movement kicks the fly under the rod tip and sets the jig upward. This upward trajectory is good for at least two reasons. First, it allows you to cast deep into overhanging obstacles. Second, the speed of the heavy jig begins to slow as it travels upward, then it falls back toward the water with less energy. This allows a gentler presentation as the jig falls slower toward the water rather than rocketing toward the water.

When fishing super-heavy jigs that have tungsten beads of 5.0 mm or larger, I will use a heavier rod. The lighter tip actions on euro rods are excellent for casting most medium to lightweight rigs. However, these rods will fold in half when placed under extreme tension by heavy rigs. You'll know if your rod is underpowered if the rod begins to wobble on the forward cast. This wobble (i.e., rod tip not tracking straight) creates an uncontrolled and inaccurate cast. You'll need to use a shorter/stiffer rod if you're noticing excessive wobble while jigging streamers with your euro rod.

INDEX

E

F

G

H

I

J

K

L

M